MW00648340

Japanization

Since 1996, Bloomberg Press has published books for financial professionals, as well as books of general interest in investing, economics, current affairs, and policy affecting investors and business people. Titles are written by well-known practitioners, BLOOMBERG NEWS® reporters and columnists, and other leading authorities and journalists. Bloomberg Press books have been translated into more than 20 languages.

For a list of available titles, please visit our Web site at www.wiley.com/go/bloombergpress.

Japanization

What the World Can Learn from Japan's Lost Decades

William Pesek

BLOOMBERG PRESS

An Imprint of

WILEY

Published by John Wiley & Sons Singapore Pte. Ltd.
1 Fusionopolis Walk, #07-01, Solaris South Tower, Singapore 138628

Other Wiley Editorial Offices

John Wiley & Sons, 111 River Street, Hoboken, NJ 07030, USA

John Wiley & Sons, The Atrium, Southern Gate, Chichester, West Sussex, P019 8SQ,
    United Kingdom

John Wiley& Sons (Canada) Ltd., 5353 Dundas Street West, Suite 400, Toronto, Ontario,
    M9B 6HB, Canada

John Wiley& Sons Australia Ltd., 42 McDougall Street, Milton, Queensland 4064, Australia

Wiley-VCH, Boschstrasse 12, D-69469 Weinheim, Germany

Library of Congress Cataloging-in-Publication Data

ISBN 978-1-118-78069-5 (Hardcover)
ISBN 978-1-118-78070-1 (ePDF)
ISBN 978-1-118-78072-5 (ePub)
Typeset in 11.5/14pt, Bembo Std by MPS Chennai Limited

10 9 8 7 6 5 4 3 2 1

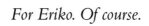

For Eriko. Of course.

Contents

Preface

F ew words strike greater fear in the hearts of economists and politicians than *Japanization*. That specter of chronic malaise, deflation, crushing debt, and political paralysis drove central bankers
from Ben Bernanke in the United States to Mario Draghi in Europe to
flood markets with liquidity as never before in an all-out effort to avert
their own lost decades.

Decades ago, the fear was of Japanese dominance. Ezra Vogel's 1979
bestseller, *Japan as Number One*, was emblematic of passions across the
Pacific. The Harvard University social sciences professor sketched out
a scenario of a tiny island nation with no natural resources dominat-
ing the economic world that seemed as plausible as frightening to the
American and Europe business elites.

Subsequent years would see entire generations of editors rushing
Japanese-are-coming scare pieces into print. *Time* magazine's March
30, 1981, Japan cover, "The World's Toughest Competitor," was illustra-
tive of the hysteria, as was the timing. Amid oil shocks, stagflation, fiscal

crises, and the Iran hostage crisis, Japan's meteoric rise was an existential blow to an America whose main business was doing business better than anyone.

Over the next decade, Japan was just as exciting and feared in world economic terms as China is today. Its companies and banks dominated top-10 lists, while once-proud U.S. automakers were eating Japan's exhaust. If you wanted to see some of your favorite Van Gogh, Picasso, or Warhol paintings, you had to visit Tokyo or Osaka. As jewels like Rockefeller Center, Universal Studios, Pebble Beach golf course, and myriad skyscrapers fell into Japanese hands, commentators screamed about the commercial equivalent of Pearl Harbor. Japan-bashing was sweeping Capitol Hill, too. In 1990, Congresswoman Helen Bentley said the United States "is rapidly becoming a colony of Japan."

By 1992, when Michael Crichton's jingoistic novel, *Rising Sun*, about economic imperialism, hit bookshelves, it was already over. By the time the film version of *Rising Sun*, starring Sean Connery and Wesley Snipes, began in theaters in 1993, the Nikkei was plunging and Japan's fabled banks were in need of government bailouts. The Nikkei 225 stock average—which peaked at 38,957—was in freefall and taking Japan's once-limitless confidence down with it.

Since then, Japan has ricocheted from one hapless government to the next (it's had 16 prime ministers since 1990 to America's four presidents), rolled out trillions of dollars of stimulus packages, cut interest rates to zero and below, and done battle with currency markets to weaken the yen countless times, and still deflation has deepened and growth has remained negligible. This noxious mix of trifling growth, high debt, falling consumer prices, waning confidence, and political dysfunction has come to be known as *Japanization*.

It should worry China, then, that experts on this dreaded scenario are turning their attention to Beijing. Take Brian Reading, whose quest to understand what the world can learn from Tokyo's mess dates back to his 1992 book, *Japan: The Coming Collapse*. In July 2013, he wrote a 40-page report with Lombard Street Research Ltd. colleague Diana Choyleva, titled "China's Chance to Avoid Japan's Mistakes."

Over in Hong Hong, investor inquiries on the similarities between China and Japan also drove JPMorgan Chase & Co. economist Grace

Ng to revisit the topic. Her warnings that China today and Japan in the 1980s share an uncannily similar build-up in broad measures of credit to almost double the economy's size brought furrows to many a brow in Beijing.

So, just how susceptible is China to Japanization? How vulnerable, for that matter, are the much larger economies of the United States and the European Union? The answer, at least to varying degrees, is quite a bit. The same could be said for India, Indonesia, Thailand, and other developing economies if national leaders aren't careful.

In February 2009, none other than U.S. President Barack Obama cited Japan's "lost decade" as something his presidency would seek to avoid. In July 2010, James Bullard, president of the Federal Reserve Bank of St. Louis, warned that America could be "enmeshed in a Japanese-style deflationary outcome within the next several years."

When economist Lawrence Summers warned of a "secular stagnation," an economic rout that has more or less become permanent, on November 8, 2013, he was indeed hinting at such an outcome. As the world emerges from the wreckage of Wall Street's 2008 crash and Europe's own crisis deepens, few lessons are more timely or critical than those offered by Japan, a once-vibrant model for developing economies that joined the world's richest nations, lost its way, and has been struggling to relocate it ever since. Its deflation, tepid growth, waning consumer spending, and monumental debt buildup were met with timidity at the government's highest levels, compounding Japan's pain. Conventional tools like fiscal spending and lower borrowing costs did little to revitalize growth and have lost potency.

Why? Tokyo's biggest sin, aside from being slow to act, was hiding myriad structural problems with macroeconomic largess. Beginning in the early 1990s, Japan avoided a wholesale cleansing of the excesses from the 1980s by engaging in endless rounds of Keynesian-style fiscal inducements and ultraloose central bank policy. Instead of breaking ties between the government, banks, and companies, deregulating industries, and letting any of the forces of creative destruction championed by economist Joseph Schumpeter play out, officials maintained the status quo. Rather than encourage entire industries to modernize or rekindle the entrepreneurial spirit needed to raise the nation's game, the government doubled down on the export-led models of the past.

In place of innovative changes to the tax, education, and social-welfare systems, the government poured untold trillions of dollars into public works projects to avoid changes to the micro-economy, leaving Japan with the world's biggest public debt and a credit rating on par with Bermuda, the Czech Republic, Estonia—and China.

In this book I explore what the world can learn from a Japanese economic funk that began more than 20 years ago and has never really ended. That means exploring where Japan went wrong, how it sank under the weight of hubris and political atrophy, and missed opportunity after opportunity to scrap an insular model based on overinvestment, export-led growth, and excessive debt.

This argument will seem decidedly at odds with what we read in the international media in 2013. The story has been one of Japanese revival, of reformist Prime Minister Shinzo Abe taking on the political and corporate establishments, of a newly confident nation reclaiming the mantle of innovative powerhouse and diplomatic authority, of an economic power that is, to use Abe's own description, "back." I will counter this conventional wisdom and detail how *Abenomics* is largely the same old mix of fiscal and monetary excess that left Japan with a public debt it may never be able to pay off, zero interest rates indefinitely, and little to show for it—jazzed up as something new and different. Abenomics is a brilliant marketing campaign in search of a product.

This book will explore the forces stunting Japan's evolution into a more vibrant, creative, and competitive economic species and what the world can learn from each of them. They include: how Japan papers over economic cracks with monetary and fiscal policy; when the bond market becomes a monster; how institutionalized sexism kills growth; how the rampant cronyism the created the Fukushima nuclear crisis holds Japan back; how isolation, known as the *Galapagos effect*, stunts Japan's evolution; how amateurish diplomacy undermines Japan's global soft power; and whether Abenomics can save the world, as no less an authority than Nobel laureate Paul Krugman argues.

Acknowledgments

T hanks to my parents for their unwavering love and teaching me to be always and everywhere curious. To my sisters and brothers for being my loyal companions in this adventure called life. To Ochiais near and far for their encouragement and support. And to the following people for their advice, inspiration, and assistance: Shamim Adam, Jake Adelstein, Marco Babic, Terrence Barrett, Kler Batino, Stuart Biggs, Kevin Carroll, Chrisanne Chin, Kyung Bok Cho, John Connor, Michael Forsythe, Brian Fowler, Phil Gibb, James Greiff, Nisid Hajari, Patrick Harrington, Nick Hayward, Peter Himmelman, Barry Horowitz, Momoe Ikeda, Netty Ismail, Aki Ito, Tony Jordan, Adrian Kennedy, Simon Kennedy, Jeff Kingston, Walter Krumholz, Miho Kurosaki, Peter Langan, Yoolim Lee, Roger Lewis, Adam Majendie, Kanoko Matsuyama, Jim McDonald, Damian Milverton, Joe Mysak, Elio Orsara, Tomoko Sato, David Shipley, Rocky Swift, Chian-Wei Teo, Tomoko Tsuchiya, Peter Vercoe, Matthew Winkler, and, of course, Nick Wallwork and the terrific folks at Wiley for taking on this project. Finally, a shout-out to my old friend, the late Daniel Pearl: It was the last time I saw you, 13 years ago, in that smoky bar in Mumbai, when you encouraged me to write a book about Japan. Well, sir, here you go.

Chapter 1

How Japan Papers Over Economic Cracks with Monetary and Fiscal Policy

O n November 24, 1997, Lawrence Summers was having an unusually busy Monday morning on a trip to Vancouver, and things were about to get steadily worse. The Asian financial crisis was ricocheting around the globe, and at that very moment claiming its biggest victim yet. South Korea, then the world's eleventh-largest economy, was days away from receiving a $57 billion international bailout. But on that day, the deputy U.S. Treasury secretary had a far bigger problem on his hands, not in Seoul but in Tokyo: the collapse of 100-year-old Yamaichi Securities Co., an event that sent the Dow Jones Industrial

1

Average down 113 points nearly one month to the day after Asia-crisis worries drove the index down 554 points in a single day, the largest drop ever.

I was among a handful of journalists traveling with Summers to British Columbia for a two-day Asia-Pacific Economic Cooperation summit of 18 world leaders. It started out innocuously enough for the star economist. On the schedule for the twenty-fourth were a bunch of bilateral meetings with finance peers from around the Pacific Rim and the occasional debriefing rendezvous with his boss, President Bill Clinton. At a dinner with his traveling press the night before, Summers seemed to relish a few days away from the madness of Washington and the mounting number of demands ending up on his desk as he prepared to replace Robert Rubin as Treasury secretary two years later. Summers gazed out onto Vancouver Harbor, breathed easily, and enjoyed the calm before the proverbial storm.

Yamaichi's breathtaking implosion the next day represented the largest business failure in Japanese postwar history, and it raised the specter of the then-second-biggest economy joining Indonesia, Malaysia, South Korea, and Thailand in turmoil. For Summers, November 24 was a marathon of frantic face-to-face meetings with Japanese officials, including then–Prime Minister Ryutaro Hashimoto, and International Monetary Fund staffers. By day's end, the most optimistic assessment Summers could offer was that Japan probably wouldn't require a bailout from the International Monetary Fund (IMF). This was a good thing, considering an economy Japan's size might not be too big to fail, but too big to save.

The next day, Hashimoto sought to buttress the point by making a pledge that seemed insignificant at the time. He said Japan is considering a variety of measures to support its shaky financial system, including using public money to bail out the nation's debt-strapped banks. "Japanese citizens, parliament, and the ruling Liberal Democratic Party are all conducting serious debate on this matter, and I'm watching it with real interest," Hashimoto said in Vancouver on November 25. "I'm looking at all possible options and considering further policy steps."

The "options" and "steps" to follow would play a big role in why Japan's first lost decade, the 1990s, would give way to a second and perhaps even a third. Pinpointing the exact moment when modern-day Japan became Japan is fraught with risk and subjectivity. But the downfall of Japan's oldest securities house in 1997 offers a variety of fascinating bookends. Between 1997 and 1998, for example, a year of historic upheaval and big layoffs, Japan's suicide rate jumped 35 percent and has remained around 30,000 per year ever since.

■ ■ ■

Yamaichi was founded in 1897, at the height of the Meiji Restoration, a period of enormous political, economic, and social change that marked Japan's emergence as a modern power. In the years following U.S. Commodore Matthew Perry's arrival in Tokyo Harbor in 1853 and the end of the Tokugawa Shogunate in 1868, Japan sought to leave its feudal past behind and build a market economy. As the nineteenth century wore on, the seeds of Japan's industrialization and economic rise were planted. It was during this era that family business conglomerates, or *zaibatsu*, bearing still-familiar names like Sumitomo, Mitsui, Mitsubishi, and Yasuda, began to dominate. These fabled giants would later make their way into Japanese pop culture, as well as Tom Clancy novels and Western video games like *Grand Theft Auto*. These early corporate formations eventually gave way to Japan's better-known *keiretsu* system of large, state-protected conglomerates that dominated the economy in the twentieth century. Elements of the *keiretsu's* corporate ways persist even today. The most obvious is the practice of strong parts of an organization carrying weaker ones. Another is the custom of cross-shareholdings, whereby companies friendly with each other loan shares of their companies to avoid hostile takeovers.

As the 1800s were drawing to a close, Yamaichi opened its doors and persevered, decade after decade. It survived World War II and helped provide financing for the nation's impressive rise from the rubble and its ambitions for global domination. From the economic launching point that was the 1964 Tokyo Olympics to the heady bubble days of the 1980s, Japan's star rose and rose and its companies couldn't lose. That was until an impossible thing happened as 1989 gave way to the 1990s—at least from the vantage point of top executives in Tokyo. The real estate prices Japanese conventional wisdom said could never fall did just that. The stock market that even many skeptics felt would never stop rising did as well. The proverbial music was stopping and Yamaichi President Shohei Nozawa was left without a chair.

Few Japanese can forget Nozawa's tearful news conference following Yamaichi's 1997 bankruptcy filing where, between sobs, he begged for mercy from the nation. As corporate theater goes, it was unbeatable. Television footage of the bawling Nozawa made the rounds again in February 2010, when Toyota Motor Corp. President Akio Toyoda wept openly at a Washington meeting with car dealers amid a series of safety lapses. Yet Toyoda was no match for Nozawa in the hanky department.

That November week started with one of the masters of Japan's financial universe apologizing and Hashimoto saying he was "ashamed" the Finance Ministry didn't spot the 265 billion yen ($2.6 billion) in hidden losses that brought the brokerage house down. And it seemed like an epochal turning point for Japanese bureaucrats. It's often said, quite correctly, that prime ministers don't run Japan, the bureaucracy does. These largely nameless, faceless policy makers had long decided which companies would live and die—which would get financing to grow and spread their tentacles abroad and which would stay modestly sized backwaters. Yet Yamaichi was a tantalizing example of markets deciding, Lehman Brothers–style. It was skeptical traders who ferreted out Yamaichi's concealed losses and creative accounting. A week later, those same market sleuths were already on to a new target: Yasuda Trust & Banking Co., one of Japan's biggest banks. Moody's Investors Service had said it might knock its debt rating down to junk status. As Yasuda's stock plunged, depositors lined up to withdraw their money, a scene all but unthinkable in wealthy, cosmopolitan, and finance-savvy Japan. Fear was in the Tokyo air. Yamaichi marked the first time Japan allowed a bank to fail in the five decades since World War II, and no one knew who would be next. Who else, a nation of 127 million wondered, might be hiding devastating losses on their balance sheets?

The same week Yamaichi failed, Daiwa Securities, Japan's second-largest brokerage, held an emergency press conference to deny that it, too, was harboring massive losses. That November week is significant because it's arguably the point when global markets began to understand the true depths of Japan's bad-loan crisis and the breadth of the culture of concealment that enabled the problems to fester for many years and at the highest levels of government. It also, with the benefit of hindsight, could have been a major turning point for Japan's approach to dealing with its bad-loan crisis.

That Tokyo let Yamaichi, the oldest of the big four securities houses, fail was seen as heralding a wave of Schumpeter-esque reform. (Joseph Schumpeter was the Austrian economist who championed "creative destruction" and free markets to make nations more competitive.) Financial systems, after all, need to be seen as punishing their weakest links, especially if they lack the transparency global banking norms demand. Yet it would be five years before Japan began getting serious about forcing debt-laden banks to write off the 52.4 trillion yen ($500 billion) of bad loans the government admitted to the industry harboring. For example, in 2002, Standard & Poor's put the number at three times that. That came under then–Prime Minister Junichiro Koizumi (2001–2006), whose economy minister, Heizo Takenaka, clamped down on the banks.

In October 1998, Japan saw its next traumatic banking experience when Long-Term Credit Bank of Japan Ltd. (LTCB) crashed, this time under Hashimoto's successor, Keizo Obuchi (1998–2000). Rather than allow one of the three main banks Japan used to fund its economic miracle to fail, Prime Minister Obuchi's government took control as it launched what at the time was the world's biggest banking industry rescue. The government moved to take over insolvent banks and recapitalize weak ones with a 60-trillion-yen fund. The bailouts continued under Obuchi's successor, Yoshiro Mori (2000–2001), until Koizumi's government said "enough."

Yet the five-plus years between Yamaichi's crash and eventual Koizimi-era reckoning is a period Japan will never get back. It was a window of opportunity to rein in financial excesses, restructure the banking industry, and keep Hong Kong and Singapore from encroaching on Tokyo's place as Asia's premier financial center. How did Japan manage to delay painful and destabilizing change? By employing the so-called *Bubble Fix*, a term popularized by former Morgan Stanley economist Stephen Roach, whereby central bankers and government officials soothe markets with monetary and fiscal stimulants in the short run in ways that create financial imbalances in the long run, essentially curing bubbles with new ones.

It was during the turmoil of Yamaichi failure and LTCB's nationalization that the Bank of Japan first cut interest rates to zero. That honor

will always be Masaru Hayami's. His unsteady run as Bank of Japan
(BOJ) governor between March 1998 and March 2003 set the stage
for the monetary policy regimes later adopted, to varying degrees, by
Ben Bernanke at the Fed, Mario Draghi at the European Central Bank,
and current BOJ leader Haruhiko Kuroda. The problem with this
monetary largess is that it reduces the need for structural change and
artificially pumps up asset prices. By creating the illusion of vibrancy in
stocks and real estate, and in turn, entire economies, all this free money
does more harm than good.

Marc Faber, Hong Kong–based publisher of the *Gloom, Boom, &
Doom* report, likens the last 15 years in markets to a relapsing alcoholic,
and central banks to irresponsible bartenders. To dole out more booze,
as monetary officials have been doing, is the wrong medicine. The
problem, particularly in Japan's case, is the lack of an exit strategy. Even
when the world's third-largest economy is churning out growth of,
say, 3 percent, it's more artificial than organic. Free money sapped the
urgency from Japan Inc. at the very worst moment, just as it needed
to keep up with a cast of growth stars in Asia, China included. All the
liquidity the BOJ has been pumping into the economy since the 1990s
was meant to support so-called zombie companies and industries that
employ millions. In reality, it led to a zombification of the broader
economy, complicating Prime Minister Abe's revival efforts. Japan is
still reluctant to abandon the strategies that propelled it into the orbit
of Group of Seven nations.

One problem was that even when Japan tweaked its regulatory system, its underlying core remained very much intact. In the 1980s, for
example, Japan's "convoy system," whereby stronger banks protected
weaker ones, survived, as did the moral hazard policy of not letting
banks, large or small, fail. In the first half of the 1990s, even as banks
began approaching failure, bankers still felt certain Tokyo wouldn't let
a major one fail. While Yamaichi's collapse a few years later altered that
view somewhat, Japan spent much of the decade of the 2000s bailing
out financial institutions. It can be argued that Japan's entire economy
operates in a convoy-system capacity. Because Japan lacks an expan-
sive national safety net, banks inadvertently became one. The government would bail out banks so that they could keep even the dodgiest
of companies afloat—and unemployment low.

This arrangement deadened the urgency for banks to write down the bad loans of the past, but so did regulatory structure. In an October 2001 paper, Bank for International Settlements economist Hiroshi Nakaso explored the two main structural problems behind Japan's foot-dragging both on recognizing the depth of its nonperforming-loan crisis and addressing it: insufficient provisioning for debts that go bad and totally inadequate transparency.

"Public disclosure on NPLs was virtually non-existent before 1992," Nakaso wrote.

The initial disclosure requirement introduced that year was based on tax law standards and covered a limited range of loans to legally bankrupt borrowers and loans past due 180 days or more. Moreover, borrowers' creditworthiness was not necessarily reflected. For example, if a borrower close to bankruptcy had two loans of which one was performing and the other was past due more than 180 days, the disclosure standard required only the latter to be included in the disclosed figures. Consequently, a substantial portion of NPLs remained outside the scope of public disclosure.

Also in 1992, Lombard economist Brian Reading published his prescient *Japan: The Coming Collapse*, tracing the nation's economic miracle, one that formed the core of a development model pursued from South Korea to China to Thailand. The former *Economist* editor has described Japan as "communism with beauty spots, not capitalism with warts." Hyperbole aside, Reading's point is that the mechanics of Japan Inc. have long been rigged in labyrinthine ways to thwart the forces of capitalism.

The core of this system is often referred to as Japan's "iron triangle" of politicians, bureaucrats, and big business, each occupying a corner. Each facilitates the others in achieving their goals and aspirations—rising status for politicians, power for bureaucrats, and riches for corporate chieftains.

"Each side involved exchanges of favors for money," Reading said.

Under the single-vote multimember electoral constituencies, factional party politicians needed money to buy votes and

career advancement. They delegated executive power, and to a
large extent policy formulation, to bureaucrats. The bureaucrats
used their power to do big business favors and were rewarded
with sinecures on retirement. In return for preferential treatment, big business supplied politicians with money. Corruption
was endemic.

In Reading's view, one could also call this a "plywood triangle," with
layers of polygons stuck together. "Each involved an incestuous relationship between individual industries or services, the ministerial or
divisional bureaucrats that regulated them, and the politicians who spe-
cialized on representing its interests," Reading said.

Industrialists, bureaucrats and politicians bonded with their tri-
angular partners, colluding to protect their own patch against
all others including divisions with ministries, notably in the
Ministry of Finance. Each triangle was an independent fiefdom.
There was no overall authority to impose change from above.
Cabinets rubber-stamped compromise agreements. There is no
room here to explain how the system evolved. Suffice it to say
there was no central planning. Power was dispersed between
segregated boxes.

This arrangement worked wonders for decades, with gross domestic
product (GDP) growth averaging nearly 9 percent from the early 1950s
into the early 1970s. But then Japan ran into what Reading calls its
"three-strikes-and-you're-out" problem. It first began to emerge in the
mid-1960s when the nation's obsession with a high savings rate sowed the
seeds of deflation. Strike two was the breakdown of the Bretton Woods
exchange-rate system, which made it harder to maintain an undervalued
currency. The international oil crisis of the early 1970s was strike three,
dealing a sizable blow to the nation's capital-intensive industrialization.

Japan's remedy was its first crack at the Bubble Fix. In the 1960s
and 1970s, structural changes were needed to reinvigorate growth. But
that would mean upsetting the carefully calibrated ways of Japan Inc. It
also would have required considerable political will. Instead, three temporary fixes were agreed upon: engineering a current-account surplus,
large budget deficits, and extremely easy credit to boost asset markets.

The rationale, Reading said, was that

excess savings could be lent to foreigners to buy Japan's excess products. A foreigners' financial deficit, also a Japanese current account surplus, would then absorb the private sector's financial surplus. This was the solution to strike one in the late 1960s. But strike two, Bretton Woods collapse, ruled this out as a permanent one. Foreigners are only willing and able to run deficits and debts for a certain period. When they cease to do so, the exchange rate appreciates. Strike three, the oil price explosions, temporarily eliminated current account surpluses and absorbed excess savings by adversely affecting Japan's terms of trade and thereby reducing real income.

U.S. policies during President Ronald Reagan's days from 1981 to 1989, primarily loose fiscal and tight monetary policies, gave Japan a break as the dollar surged. But then the dollar plunged and the yen skyrocketed, thanks to the so-called Plaza Accord in 1985 that Japan agreed to and later regretted. When economists call it one of the greatest policy mistakes Japan ever made, that's saying a lot. Japan, after all, amassed the world's largest public debt, cut interest rates to zero, and scuttled myriad recoveries with bad policies. Some observers think all may pale in comparison to Japan's agreement to let the yen strengthen from 260 yen per dollar to around 125 yen per dollar.

"The currency realignment was too sharp and too large," said Stephen Jen, cofounder of SLJ Macro Partners LLP in London. "Such a sharp appreciation in the currency led to an easy monetary stance that nurtured the financial bubbles (equities and properties), mainly because the BOJ observed that the consumer price index was low, and therefore [it was] safe to run easy monetary policies." He added that "in conjunction with a naïve and short-sighted BOJ, it helped create such large bubbles that helped put Japan out of contention for a generation."

That left Japan turning to massive budget deficits and ultralow interest rates. It's sobering that amid all the talk in 2013 about the Fed finding an exit strategy from quantitative easing, Japan has yet to find its own. Never mind the monetary exploits of the last few years; Japan still needs to find an exit from the 1990s. It hasn't learned how to live without zero interest rates and the world's biggest public debt and it might not for decades to come.

If anything, *Abenomics* is nudging Japan further—and faster—down this uncharted and dangerous path. The BOJ's unprecedented stimulus, including a doubling of the monetary base, is enlivening asset markets as rarely seen before and drumming up fresh optimism that Japan's economy is back. Meanwhile, Abe's first act after becoming prime minister for the second time in December 2012 was unleashing a 10.3 trillion yen fiscal-spending package—that, in a nation in which public debt is roughly 250 percent of gross domestic product.

Monetary and fiscal stimulus is a good start, but what really matters is Abe's program to deregulate an overmanaged economy as a means of increasing Japan's competiveness and boosting job creation. That means sweeping tax reform, deregulation, joining free-trade agreements such as the Trans-Pacific Partnership, empowering women, supporting entrepreneurs, and increasing productivity. Japanese have heard lots of talk of economic upgrades over the last decade but have seen almost zero action. Until Abe implements these supply-side changes, his stimulus amounts to little more than papering over economic cracks with easy money. All low rates and capital injections from central banks offer markets is breathing room. They treat symptoms of the problem, not the underlying disease, and may just be inflating another giant asset bubble. In April 2013, a report by Merrill Lynch economists in Tokyo asked this tantalizing question: "Shouldn't *Abe* stand for *Asset Bubble Economics?*" Remember that Japan's interest rates have been at zero, or well below it, for more than a dozen years and it still has deflation. Japan's economy has yet to return to normal.

Then again, *normal* is a relative word. It can be argued that Japan's entire postwar economy is a bubble of sorts—of GDP, not just assets. The bubble years of the 1980s sent Japan's cost of living soaring with asset prices, putting Tokyo and Osaka at the very top of most-expensive-city tables. It meant that the value of all goods and services produced in a given year was being skewed higher. And while real estate and stock prices fell sharply during the 1990s and 2000s, consumer prices didn't. Japan's deflation has always had a glacial, almost hydraulic quality. Costs ratcheted down steadily, but genteelly enough that the falling-price trend didn't destabilize the nation as economists like, say, Nobel laureate Milton Friedman had warned. What Friedman called the "scourge of deflation," households from Yokohama to Fukuoka merely came to accept—and in some ways, even enjoy.

In general, deflation is a dreadful phenomenon. It slams financial assets, boosts debt-servicing costs, and undermines corporate profits. It erodes business confidence, lowers tax revenue, and is a "third-rail" issue to many foreign investors, who often avoid economies grappling with it. For consumers, though, deflation offers a kind of stealth tax cut as households regain some purchasing power. It has helped make a wildly expensive country a bit less wildly expensive.

Even after China spooked Japan into restructuring, a distribution system based on multiple layers of intermediaries and regulations that favor giant, established companies with bloated staffs over newer ones keeps prices artificially high. Defenses against foreign competition also contribute to everything costing too much. Institutionalized inefficiencies and a dearth of competition force consumers to pay dearly for things like rice, electronics, vegetables, fruit, and clothing that could be flown more cheaply from China than driven in from 10 miles away.

Yet deflation has helped root out some of these inefficiencies. It prodded bloated companies to downsize and made corporate Japan think twice about the feasibility of uncompetitive industries. Deflation also nudged banks to reduce bad loans. A dozen years of waiting for growth to bail out Japan came to naught. It's no coincidence that bad-debt writedowns accelerated once it became clear that deflation wasn't a passing fad. So what passes as normal in Japan might not anywhere else.

Will the United States do better? "Since the financial crisis, the U.S. economic situation has taken on many of the characteristics of Japan," said Barry Bosworth, an economist at the Brookings Institution in Washington. As Bosworth sees it, monetary policy has been exhausted, quantitative easing largely ineffectual, huge fiscal stimulus insufficient to boost demand left America with record deficits that can't be sustained, and the political system is as dysfunctional as it's ever been.

Yet many believe the United States will indeed fare better, including none other than former Federal Reserve Chairman Ben Bernanke. At a press conference on April 25, 2012, Akio Fujii, a Washington-based reporter for the *Nikkei* newspaper, asked Bernanke if the United States can escape Japanization. Here is Bernanke's response:

> I would draw two distinctions between the U.S. and Japan, or the Japanese experience. The first, as I mentioned earlier—and I think this is very important—is that we acted aggressively and pre-emptively to avoid deflation. Now of course Japan had a much bigger bubble and a much bigger shock when the bubble collapsed, and so these differences may be certainly understandable. But again, we did avoid deflation. The other thing which I think we have done reasonably well here in the United States was that we moved fairly quickly to make sure that our banks were recapitalized and were recognizing their bad assets. And I think the stress tests that we conducted last month are good evidence that the U.S. banking system is considerably stronger and, indeed, much more resilient than it was a couple of years ago. So those two things are positives and would tend to suggest that we will avoid some of the problems that Japan has faced. That being said, I think it's always better to be humble and just avoid being too confident. And we need to continue to maintain strong monetary policy support to make sure that the economy continues on a recovery path and returns to a more normal situation.

All this remains to be seen. Many economists would argue that the period following 2008, after the crash of Lehman Brothers and many of Wall Street's biggest players, ushered in the start of at least a semi–lost decade for the United States. While GDP growth returned, the Standard & Poor's 500 roared, and house prices stabilized, unemployment remains stubbornly near 7 percent. What's more, a weak global economy means U.S. stimulus efforts lack the traction President Barack Obama expected. Political paralysis also should be a concern. On the question of whether the United States will go the way of Japan, the jury is very much out.

Yet there are two reasons to worry: denial and easy money. Yes, U.S. authorities, as Bernanke argues, acted faster than their Japanese peers. American banks also came clean quickly about the magnitude of the toxic assets on their books and disposed of them expeditiously, certainly compared with Japan's bank executives. U.S. accounting rules make it harder to hide losses, and America eschewed the practice of cross-holdings of equities, whereby friendly companies buy each other's shares to avoid outside pressure, that can wreak havoc on Japanese balance sheets.

The big problem facing the United States, though, is about banking structure—just as it was with Japan. Even after the debacle of 2008, U.S. regulators and investors are hawking the appealing tale of a chastened but sophisticated and efficient financial system that can manage risk once again. Yet the United States has merely treated the symptoms of its underlying illness. Increasing capital adequacy ratios and imposing greater transparency on Wall Street is a good start. What's needed is an end to the too-big-to-fail era that still persists today. If another global crisis were to flare up—say, Europe unraveling or China crashing—U.S. financial companies might prove to be too big to save. To me, giant investment banks are America's *chaebol*, just as they were Japan's in the 1990s. The reference here is to the huge, family-run conglomerates that tower over the Korean economy and suck up much of the economic and political oxygen. When the economy is good, they roll in profits, influence, and hubris. When the economy goes bad, these giants can pull everything else down with them.

Bernanke's quantitative-easing experiment is another question mark. Over time, the Fed will find that politicians, bankers, investors, and businesspeople alike get addicted to free money all too easily and clamor for more. Once central banks start embracing assets such as corporate debt, commercial paper, mortgage-backed securities, exchange-traded funds, real estate trusts, and the like, they tend to get stuck. That's especially so in nations carrying large, and growing, debt burdens. That's the thing about the global banking system going Islamic—it's hard to come back. *Sharia* law bars the receiving or paying interest on loans or deposits and a huge market infrastructure has been built to facilitate clients that include wildly rich Persian Gulf oil tycoons. Yet hasn't this industry in a sense been pirated by the BOJ, Fed and other central banks offering interest-free loans? As U.S. President Richard Nixon, echoing Milton Friedman, famously quipped in 1971: "We are all Keynesians now." By 2009, we had all become Islamic bankers.

In April 2013, IMF Managing Director Christine Lagarde asked her staff to examine what might happen to the global economy when major central banks raise interest rates again. She's wasting their time. For if Japan can teach the world anything, it's that slashing rates to zero and beyond is a lot easier than restoring them to normalcy. Japan is on its sixth central-bank governor since its bubble burst in 1990, and Kuroda is doubling down on quantitative easing in ways his predecessors never dared.

What the IMF really should be studying is how the economics textbooks written by Friedman, John Maynard Keynes, and Adam Smith are losing relevance in this world of zero. Japan, of course, is Exhibit A. The nation has been living with zero rates for so many years that they seem, well, rational. Yet under the surface, credit spreads have come to mean little, not when the underlying assets on which they are based are drugged up on monetary stimulants. Bank balance sheets are muddied, as are the government's books as it becomes harder to pinpoint where a central bank's holdings begin and end. Corporate shenanigans are easier to disguise, too. Why bother with creative accounting when liquidity is plentiful with compliments of the central bank.

In reality, ultralow rates have done more to undermine Japan than revive it. It has concentrated capital in nonproductive sectors such as construction, telecommunications, and power, and it starves others—like startup companies—that could fuel job growth. At the same time, it has reduced the urgency for policy makers to make industries, from electronics to steel, more competitive and innovative. Zero rates also deadened Japan's resolve at the worst possible moment—just as an ascendant China was grabbing the number two economy spot in 2010.

Finally, a subzero monetary environment could be setting Japan up for a reckoning of a magnitude the world has never seen. Someday, bond traders will decide that a fast-aging nation carrying debt load far in excess of its $6 trillion worth of output is ripe for a huge correction—that 10-year bond yields below 1 percent for a nation with that debt profile make no sense. For now, though, all's well in Bondland, where Japan's IOUs are a safe haven in a world of shaky investments.

The United States must execute its exit from quantitative easing (QE) as soon as financial conditions allow, to avoid Japan's plight. Bernanke began the process in earnest on December 18, 2013, by moving to trim the Fed's monthly bond purchases to $75 billion from $85 billion. But it won't be easy politically to accelerate the so-called tapering process. It doesn't take a vivid imagination to picture the congressional inquisition that would greet the Fed's moves toward monetary normalcy. Markets won't much like it either; the Fed going further to scrap QE would signal that a $3 trillion trade is about to be unwound. And the economic fallout could be considerable. The Fed's massive portfolio of mortgage-backed securities is a case in point. In an economy as housing-centric as America's, selling those off could devastate a sector closely tied to consumer confidence.

Yet an exit must be found to avoid the scenario Jeremy Grantham, cofounder of global investment management fund GMO LLC, fears: that pretty much every asset class, everywhere in the world, is in the midst of a bubble of some kind and that each imbalance reinforces another. "Sustained strong fundamentals and sustained easy credit go one better: They allow for continued reinforcement," the Boston-based Grantham argued. "The more leverage you take, the better you do. The better you do, the more leverage you take."

It's fascinating to look back at how little of this dynamic was appreciated even two months before Lehman Brothers collapsed and slammed world markets. That's when the leaders of the Group of Eight (G-8) nations met on the northern Japanese island of Hokkaido. The July 7–9, 2008, summit saw then–Prime Minister Yasuo Fukuda angling to get former U.S. President George W. Bush, Chancellor Angela Merkel, and others to commit to carbon emissions–reduction targets. An important goal for sure, but a focus at odds with the monumental meltdown brewing 7,000 miles away. The G-8's statement on the world economy was surreally perfunctory given the gravity of global risks:

> We are mindful of the interrelated nature of the issues surrounding the world economy. We remain committed to promoting a smooth adjustment of global imbalances through sound macroeconomic management and structural policies.

In retrospect, the setting of the Hokkaido confab, where leaders mused about "sound" economic management, oozed with irony. Japan chose the Windsor Hotel Toya, a resort that opened in 1993 under the name Hotel Apex Toya. Its start was as inauspicious as it gets. The hotel's main creditor, Hokkaido Takushoku Bank, went bust in November 1997, around the same time Yamaichi's bankruptcy was panicking markets. Hotel Apex Toya suspended operations in early 1998, and then reopened as the Windsor Hotel Toya in 2002. As fate would have it, that was the same year Prime Minister Koizumi and his economy minister attacked Japan's bad-loan crisis.

And so, as seven visiting world leaders converged in a building that's as good a symbol of 10 years of squandered growth as any, they had a prime opportunity to debate what lessons Japan held for the G-8 and beyond. At the same time that meeting was convening, a Hong Kong real estate mogul speaking on the other side of Japan, in the western city of Fukuoka, made one of the most prescient predictions of the last five years.

"What if the lost decade in Japan becomes the global norm?" Ronnie Chan, chairman of Hang Lung Properties Ltd., said at the Asia Innovation Initiative conference on July 8, 2008. "Can you imagine that? Perhaps we should. Perhaps people should get used to slower growth, or no growth."

It's not that Chan, who runs one of the largest real estate development companies in Hong Kong, is a pessimist. Property developers don't often relish 10 years of lost growth here and 10 years of declining asset values there. Chan saw a rare confluence of economic and demographic trends that bode poorly for a global rebound.

No one should be surprised by the rapid pace of economic expansion after World War II. It began from a low base, following the devastation of economies in Europe and parts of Asia. Next came rapid population growth and a boom in innovation. Then there were new social and institutional paradigms as democracy spread and organizations such as the United Nations and the World Bank offered support.

But in 2008, just two months before Lehman's collapse, the picture was looking vastly different to anyone perceptive enough to notice. As everyone tried to stabilize growth, things then were hardly at a low base. Population growth was fueling demand for commodities, driving up inflation, and increasing poverty rates. But at the same time, innovation globally was beginning to slow as investment dried up. And institutions such as the IMF hardly seemed up to the ever-increasing challenges of the day.

In the case of Asia, one of these emerging challenges was cracks in the region's embrace of democracy. It simply wasn't proving to be the panacea that leaders in the United States and Europe promised. Poverty rates remained stubbornly high in many Asian democracies like Indonesia, the Philippines, and Thailand, and so did corruption. And more and more, the former was a result of the latter. It certainly wasn't that democracy is bad. Yet there's something to be said about what Chan calls "premature democratization" in Asia. Elections matter only when nations build strong institutions such as independent courts, ministries, a free press, credible central banks, and ample systems of checks and balances. Their absence means many governments don't operate as transparently or successfully as expected. The immaturity of Asia's democracies, at least structurally, did indeed complicate the region's attempts to avoid the worst of the credit-market crisis. Chan wondered if the type of prosperity during the decade before the 1997 Asian crisis will be more unusual in the future. "Those ten golden years of rapid growth and high returns may well have been an aberration," Chan said.

The combination of surging energy and food prices challenged economies with political rifts, such as Thailand and Malaysia. Nor does it bode well for high-poverty ones such as Indonesia and the Philippines, or those trying to compete amid China's boom—Korea, Singapore, and Taiwan, for example. But the core of the problem was that policy makers were merely putting off the inevitable and treating the symptoms of what ails the global economy. If they weren't careful, Japan's experience during the 1990s would become a familiar one. "It's not a scenario many expect for the West or for Asia," Chan said. "But I'm not sure it can be ruled out."

How right Chan was became apparent on November 8, 2013, when Summers made his secular-stagnation speech to a group of researchers at IMF headquarters in Washington. There, he silenced a packed room containing some of the world's best and brightest theorists by stating he wondered if "a set of older ideas that went under the phrase *secular stagnation* are not profoundly important in understanding Japan's experience and may not be without relevance to America's experience."

The pessimism inherent in these comments surprised the other economists sharing the stage with Summers, including Bernanke, former Bank of Israel Governor Stanley Fischer, Kenneth Rogoff of

Harvard University, and Olivier Blanchard, the IMF's research director. It also generated huge buzz among leading economists, particularly those on the liberal end of the policy-making spectrum, catalyzing
immediate and intense debate among Paul Krugman, Jared Bernstein
of the Center on Budget and Policy Priorities, and Miles Kimball of
the University of Michigan.

"Conventional macroeconomic thinking leaves us in a very serious
problem," Summers said. "The underlying problem may be there forever." He added: "We may well need in the years ahead to think about
how to manage an economy where the zero nominal interest rate is a
chronic and systemic inhibitor of economic activity, holding our economies back below their potential."

Summers, of course, was Obama's original candidate to run the
Fed before the president went with Janet Yellen. He had also served
as World Bank chief economist, President Bill Clinton's Treasury
chief, Obama's National Economic Council director, and president of
Harvard, the latter job immortalized by a highly memorable scene in
David Fincher's 2010 film, *The Social Network*. This wasn't some fringe
figure effectively suggesting that the entire global financial system was
turning Japanese.

The crux of Summers's argument was this: The global crisis that
nearly bankrupted Wall Street in 2008 was a highly odd one, and not
just because of its size and brutality. At the time, many believed monetary policy dating back to the days of the Greenspan Fed had been too
lax; there was loads of imprudent lending going on; and households
began to feel richer than they really were. Bottom line, the conventional wisdom was that there was too much liquidity, too much credit
being extended, and too much paper wealth being created. Yet even
with all these imbalances, U.S. economic growth didn't boom, factories weren't under any great strain, unemployment didn't plummet, and
inflation was tame. So, oddly, a great financial bubble didn't create huge
excesses in aggregate demand across the economy.

■ ■ ■

Fast forward to, say, 2010, when the direct effects of the crisis were
waning. In a more classical recession environment, economists would

expect a great deal of catch-up as the economy's engines begin humming again and inventories get rebuilt. "So you'd actually kind of expect that once things normalized, you'd get more GDP than you otherwise would have had, not that four years later you'd still be having substantially less than you had before," Summers said. "So there's something odd about financial normalization, if that was the whole problem, and then continued slow growth. So what's an explanation that would fit both of these observations?"

> Suppose that the short-term real interest rate that was consistent with full employment had fallen to negative 2 or negative 3 percent sometime in the middle of the last decade. Then what would happen? That even with artificial stimulus to demand coming from all this financial imprudence, you wouldn't see any excess demand, and even with a relative resumption of credit—normal credit conditions, you'd have a lot of difficulty getting back to full employment. Yes, it has been demonstrated absolutely conclusively, that panics are terrible and that monetary policy can contain them when the interest rate is zero. It has been demonstrated less conclusively but presumptively that when short-term interest rates are zero, monetary policy can affect a constellation of other asset prices in ways that support demand even when the short-term interest rate can't be lowered. Just how large that impact is on demand is less clear, but it is there. But imagine a situation where natural and equilibrium interest rates have fallen significantly below zero.

The problem, in Summers's view is that most of what would be done under the auspices of preventing another crisis could actually be counterproductive. After five years of dealing with the fallout from 2008 with few indications that things are returning to normal, it's high time to think about the remedies policy makers are applying. That includes thinking that easier monetary and fiscal policies are always and everywhere the answer and looking to other levers to manage lending, borrowing, and the level of asset prices.

"So, my lesson from this crisis—and my overarching lesson, which I have to say, I think the world has underinternalized—is that it is not over until it is over, and that is surely not right now and cannot be judged relative to the extent of financial panic, and that we may well need in the years ahead to think about how we manage an economy in which the zero nominal interest rate is a chronic and systemic inhibitor of economic activities, holding our economies back below their potential," Summers said.

Financial Times columnist Martin Wolf (November 19, 2013) summed it up like this:

> Merely restoring a degree of health to the financial system or reducing the overhang of excessive pre-crisis debt is, then, unlikely to deliver a full recovery. The reason is that the crisis followed financial excesses, which themselves masked or, as I have argued, were even a response to pre-existing structural weaknesses.

Here, as Summers ponders how disorienting the world of economic policy making has become in recent years, he could just as easily be talking about Japan as the United States. Japan has been living with zero rates for so long that they seem par for the course. Under the surface, interest rate relationships mean little, not when the underlying assets on which they are based are gussied up on monetary stimulants. Bank, corporate, and government balance sheets get murkier and it gets hard to pinpoint where a central bank's holdings begin and end. Corporate malfeasance is easier to disguise.

Prominent economists like Yale University's Robert Shiller also warn that the United States risks a prolonged, Japan-style slump if it doesn't get more creative about its crisis response. As the debris of the global crisis was still settling in 2009, Shiller cowrote a timely book with George Akerlof, a Nobel Prize–winning economist, titled *Animal Spirits*, a phrase borrowed from Keynes's 1936 work. Their central thesis was that confidence and human behavior play an underappreciated role in driving the American economy and global capital markets. Yet, as Shiller notes, in a world of zero and skewed measures of risk, how can one tell if such confidence is real or delusional, or manufactured from on high, for that matter? There are ways in which the 1980s success of Japan Inc. was more fantasy than reality. Here again, Yamaichi serves as a microcosm for how and why things went so wrong, so quickly.

By the mid-1980s, overconfidence fused with the BOJ's easy-money policies and raised stock and real-estate speculation to not only an art form but a genuine mania as assets surged in value to unimaginable levels. The Nikkei alone tripled in value between 1985 and 1989. But even more than optimism about Japan's economic outlook, the boom was fueled by the underlying idiosyncrasies and mechanics of Japan Inc. One was the nation's *keiretsu*, or networks of huge businesses involving a web of cross-shareholdings. The practice boosted share prices throughout the 1980s, and contributed to the ballooning wealth of corporations and the overseas perception that Japan Inc. had found a financial Holy Grail of sorts.

At the root of this excess was a practice known as *zaitech*, or financial engineering. Word derivations can offer crucial clues about the sustainability of any business strategy, and *zaitech* was no exception. It literally blends the Japanese word for corporate dealings, *zaimu*, with *technology* and its effect was no less damaging than the financial innovation that would get Wall Street in so much trouble 20 years later. Powered by ultralow borrowing costs and labyrinthine accounting norms, firms would speculate in asset prices across sectors, in all corners of Japan. Those investments paid off as the underlying assets rose, boosting corporate profits and giving executives even more incentive to further leverage balance sheets. This dynamic would come back to haunt Japan as recently as 2011, when Olympus Corp. blew up. Among the regulatory weaknesses it exposed was a corporate governance system still geared toward hiding losses. Olympus was a prime example of untold billions of yen poured into speculative *zaitech* trades of the 1980s and 1990s, which are still turning sour.

The same went for the practice of *tobashi*, another way to hide investments going bad. Outlawed in 2000, these schemes provide an indirect link between Yamaichi's drama in 1997 and Olympus's 14 years later. Loosely translated, *tobashi* means "flying." In its most common form, a client's losses are shifted from account to account. A customer or business partner might be asked to buy the stocks, bonds, or assets on which another customer had taken a loss, at above-market price. Next, the brokerage or company would promise to buy back those securities or assets from the new owner at a profit after they had appreciated in price. At that point, the flying investment would have flown from client to client—everyone left happy and no one the wiser.

Yet it's a bull-market strategy. It worked brilliantly in the 1980s, when stocks and asset values surged to the point where the grounds surrounding Tokyo's Imperial Palace—all of 1.32 square miles—were believed to be worth more than the entire state of California. But in the 1990s, as markets crashed, Japan Inc. had to eat its losses. As those losses became harder to disguise and manage, executives, including those at Yamaichi, had no choice but to file for bankruptcy.

Still, as the Olympus saga proved, the legacy of those days remains. Japan has been medicating its economy for so long with so many different stimulus treatments that it's unrecognizable from the late 1970s, just as the bubble years were beginning. It's given Japan a distinctive *Alice in Wonderland* quality. Rather than getting bogged down in the inconvenient realities of supply, demand, and globalization, Tokyo preferred to live in a "through-the-looking-glass" world of fantasy and illusion sustained by financial socialism. After tumbling down the rabbit hole, investors are on their own to make heads or tails of Tokyo's policies. It's economics in its most surreal form.

Of course, America has gotten plenty creative with its finances, with scandals from Enron Corp. to WorldCom Inc. to Ponzi-schemer Bernard Madoff. It is true of Europe, too, from the book-cookers at Parmalat SpA to Greek government officials who masked the extent of the nation's budget deficit with the help of Goldman Sachs. Yet at the root of it all, at the core of each and every example of corporate and public-debt malfeasance over the last decade has been Japan-like monetary excesses.

Take the "Greenspan put" that fundamentally altered the relationship between the Fed, hedge funds, and, in many ways, the global financial system. On December 5, 1996, then-Chairman Alan Greenspan (1987–2006) tiptoed up to a delicate question, and used Japan's bubbles as a lens through which to view it: "How do we know when irrational exuberance has unduly escalated asset values, which then become subject to unexpected and prolonged contractions as they have in Japan over the past decade?" His meaning was unmistakable, as the question was raised amidst America's dot-com bubble of the 1990s and speculation that the so-called New Economy had made business cycles and recessions extinct.

Stocks nosedived and lawmakers cried foul, saying that the Fed's job was to maintain price stability, not talk down markets. On December 12,

Greenspan was summoned to Capitol Hill for a 50-minute dressing-down by then–Senate Majority Leader Trent Lott. After that, Greenspan uttered nary a public word about froth in U.S. shares as investors clamored to pour millions into any company that slapped a ".com" on the end of its name and the Nasdaq Composite Index headed to an irrational 5132-point level.

A "put option" insures an investor against a market falling below a certain level, and Greenspan personified it. He pumped liquidity into markets when Mexico fell into crisis in 1994 and Asia followed in 1997 and again in 1998 when the ironically named Greenwich, Connecticut–based hedge fund Long-Term Capital Management imploded. Greenspan showered markets with liquidity ahead of possible "Y2K" computer disruptions as 1999 ticked into 2000 and after the 9/11 terrorist attacks on New York and Washington in September 2001. Yet it was in the mid-2000s, just before Bernanke took over in 2006, that the Fed's largess really began distorting markets. All that liquidity fueled the leverage that almost toppled Wall Street.

This period accelerated the internationalization of the Fed. The U.S. central bank has 12 districts across the United States and conducts its policies based on supply and demand strains around the nation. But the last 15 years have seen the creation of de facto spheres of Fed influence around the globe. It isn't far-fetched to think of Latin America as the thirteenth district, Southeast Asia the fourteenth, Russia the fifteenth, China the sixteenth, and so on. From Seoul to Santiago, investors often care more about what happens in Washington than they do about actions taken by local monetary authorities, hence global concern over a clumsy exit from the Fed's quantitative easing experiment.

Blame it on the ghosts of the mid-1990s. Before markets heard of the "Greenspan put" there was Greenspan's "Great Bond Market Massacre of 1994." Under his leadership, the Fed helped precipitate Asia's 1997 crisis when it doubled benchmark lending rates over 12 months, causing, according to *Fortune*, more than $600 billion in losses on U.S. Treasuries. By the time Greenspan was done, chaos in credit markets drove Orange County, California, into bankruptcy; sank Kidder Peabody & Co.; pushed Mexico into crisis; and strained Asia's currency pegs as the dollar began a powerful rally that forced the region to devalue a few years later.

As the Bernanke Fed mulls how to unwind its unprecedented $3.3 trillion balance sheet, Asians worry anew about dollar exposure. There are three big risks as Bernanke & Co. withdraw liquidity: higher borrowing costs, huge swings in financial markets, and lower economic growth. And that's if the Fed restores normalcy to rates in a gradual, orderly, and transparent way. If it's handled clumsily, as it was in 1994, then 2014 could be a disastrous year for the world's most dynamic region.

The stakes of any Fed misstep are now appreciably higher. Sovereign-debt levels have more than quadrupled, to more than $23 trillion since 1994. A scenario in which too much debt chases too few buyers or decent investments would amplify market turmoil. Also, 20 years ago the world economy was arguably a much healthier place. Back then, the wobbly euro didn't exist, China's economy hardly mattered, and the high-frequency trading now dominating the world's bourses was found more in science fiction novels than Wall Street's reality. Asia now holds trillions of dollars of currency reserves, many in U.S. currency.

Yet when it comes to financial socialism, to manipulating asset markets to mask economic problems, the Fed and U.S. Treasury have nothing on the BOJ and Ministry of Finance. Remember that from 1955 until now, Japan has for the most part been a one-party state. At its center is the symbiotic relationship between government, the bureaucracy, and big business—dubbed Japan's *iron triangle*. Under this system, the bureaucracy had great sway over policy priorities, legislation, budgets, and, ultimately, national interests. Cabinet members would then merely rubber-stamp the ideas and initiatives of unelected bureaucrats of unknown agency and scant accountability.

"This triumvirate of interest has not always agreed on policy issues, but has found enough common ground to maintain a level of cooperation that ensured extended political hegemony," Temple University's Jeff Kingston pointed out in his 2011 book, *Contemporary Japan*. "Political scientists attribute Japan's persistent structural corruption to this triangle of interests and the means they have adopted to sustain their power."

■ ■ ■

Japan's enduring triumvirate, of course, has nothing on China's Communist Party, which doesn't stand for elections. Yet as China employs a development model that in many ways mirrors Japan's, Beijing should heed lessons from Tokyo. From New York to Singapore, the overwhelming view is that China can grow 7 percent to 8 percent indefinitely, its potential is boundless, and it's run by omnipotent geniuses who can't lose. China is today's New Economy and anyone who disagrees just doesn't get it. For that to be true, though, China would have to beat the system, so to speak. No emerging nation has avoided a crisis that sent growth reeling and markets plunging—not one.

Can China avoid Japanization? For Beijing, the answer is bold and creative action on the part of President Xi Jinping and Premier Li Keqiang, of the kind Japanese officialdom has seldom displayed. Think of their 10-year term that began in March 2013 as China's make-or-break period to dodge a major debt crisis.

But if imitation really is the greatest form of flattery, Abe should be thrilled the Chinese are copying his Abenomics strategy to excite investors. The rest of the world shouldn't be. China isn't cribbing the Japanese prime minister's actual blueprint, but his formula of spin and hype that has convinced the world that something that doesn't yet exist is real. The key to a great ad campaign is attracting customers and keeping them, something Abe has done with a brilliance that could teach the Edelman public-relations firm a thing or two.

Abe's campaign has gone as follows. Introduce a three-part revival plan. Then, roll out the first two segments, the easy ones, right away with great fanfare and to spectacular effect. Abe's huge monetary and fiscal stimulus did just that, driving equities higher and foreign investors wild. Finally, use that euphoria as a smoke screen to delay the third part, the really hard one that involves controversial steps to deregulate the economy and take on a bewildering number of vested interests.

Eyeing the Nikkei 225 stock average's 57 percent surge in 2013, it's easy to forget that Abe hasn't implemented a single structural change. Has he lowered any trade barriers? No. Loosened labor markets? Nope. Increased female labor participation? Hardly. Has he encouraged private investment, improved corporate governance, liberalized energy markets, or tweaked taxes to empower entrepreneurship? Sadly not. Yet investment banks and the news media treat Abenomics as if it's already generating the self-reinforcing recovery that's eluded Japan for decades. Li, the Chinese premier, is facing the most daunting economic reform challenge since the days of Deng Xiaoping. Li must reduce the role of state-owned enterprises, modernize the financial and fiscal systems, overhaul land and household registration rules, reduce the economy's reliance on exports, and cap pollution so that China's 1.3 billion people don't choke on their economic success. Getting any of these reforms past corrupt Communist Party bigwigs profiting from the status quo requires a level of political will that neither Li nor President Xi has so far displayed.

And so, Li and Xi are pulling an Abe. Both talk about their "comprehensive reforms" ad nauseam, so much so that economists and investors have come to believe something is actually going on. Just like Abenomics, China's new leaders bamboozled the masses with a pair of grand gestures—neither of which worked as intended—to deflect attention from the third. The first was a credit clampdown in June; the second was the proclamation that a brake was being applied to growth in the name of preventing the economy from overheating.

Closing the credit spigot traumatized markets so much that officials backed off. There's loads of credit being extended around the nation today that will go bad when China experiences trouble, as every industrializing nation invariably does. The broadest measure of money supply, or M2, has exceeded the official goal of 13 percent every month this year, rising at a 14.2 percent rate in September—some clampdown. China's growth, meanwhile, isn't slowing to 7 percent from the average 10.5 percent average pace of the last 10 years by design. The economic model that once worked so brilliantly has run out of steam. China isn't promoting slower growth—it's stuck with it.

Yet China has managed to conflate these two dynamics with the economic upgrades that are key to the nation's stability. Worse, Li and Xi are still maddeningly vague about what they have planned for their economy. Consider this comment by Xi in October, carried by the official Xinhua News Agency: "We must properly handle the relations between reform, development, and stability, and with greater political courage and wisdom, further open our minds, unleash and develop social productivity, and enhance the creative forces of the society."

What does that even mean? It almost seems as if Xi was playing his own game of Buzzword Bingo, ticking off code-words that tested well with some focus group to provide the illusion that bold and smart changes are afoot. Buzzwords and phrases such as *reform* and *stability* and *develop social productivity* sound good to hopeful executives and investors, but seem meant to avoid specificity.

Pardon me if I don't get excited about Politburo member Yu Zhengsheng pledging that "unprecedented" change will emerge from China's current leadership. Forgive me if I don't buy into what's increasingly being called "Likonomics," which is more of a marketing slogan than a credible plan. Game-changing reforms take years to implement in any economy, never mind one as large and imbalanced as China's. Yet Li and Xi, just like Abe, are spending almost all their time talking when they need to be engineering major changes. No industrializing economy has ever avoided a crash of some kind, and neither will China. The more Beijing puts empty sloganeering ahead of retooling its economy, the more it tries to delay its day of reckoning, the bigger it will be. And all the spin in the world can't save China from that reality.

China is not impossibly indebted, considering it has $3.7 trillion in currency reserves. JPMorgan reckons its debt-to-gross-domestic-product ratio rose to 187 percent in 2012 from 105 percent in 2000, compared with Japan's increase to 176 percent in 1990 from 127 percent in 1980. Japan's has exploded since then and could approach two-and-a-half times annual output. That would mark a jump of 10 percent from 2012 alone in a fast-aging nation that's losing global competitiveness.

But China, also aging, couldn't withstand a similar jump; it must rein things in now. Japan became rich before its society became old. It had decades to build a social contract between the public and private sectors, nurture a stable of innovative companies, and open the financial system. That legwork enabled Japan to muddle along for two decades without a huge debt meltdown or social unrest.

Japan's is a tale of hubris and missed opportunities. Rather than quickly scrapping a model based on overinvestment, exports, and excessive debt, Tokyo delayed change at all costs by relying on current-account surpluses, huge budget deficits, and asset bubbles. In many ways, it still does. Does this sound familiar?

"China has so far followed in the footsteps of Japan," Reading and Choyleva argue.

> But its economy is not yet over-indebted. So there is time for China to avoid Japan's mistakes if it changes course. The lesson from Japan's experience in the 1970s and 1980s is that change drives change and liberalization becomes unavoidable. But unless policy is aimed at fundamental structural reform, the temporary solutions of running current account surpluses, budget deficits, and spawning bubbles will eventually run out of steam and cause growth to stall. But China is far from having twenty more years to be blowing up bubbles.

There are troubling signs that Beijing thinks it has plenty of time to deal with the problem. For every pledge to cut excess production capacity, audit government borrowings, and tolerate sub-8-percent growth, there are two others assuring markets that growth won't be allowed to slow too much.

One problem is that of politics over economics. Around China, dozens of local leaders are vying to put their cities on the global map and become the toast of the Communist Party. That means more than delivering rapid GDP. It also means building huge skyscrapers, international airports, six-lane highways, five-star hotel chains, sports stadiums, universities, giant cultural centers, and swanky shopping arcades punctuated with Prada and Hermes shops—all financed with fresh debt. If several of these metropolises go bust, Detroit's $18 billion bankruptcy will look like small change by comparison.

A continued infrastructure boom promises ever-greater riches for vested interests both locally and in Beijing. There are ways Xi and Li could defuse the debt time bomb: greater oversight, expanding the municipal bond market, letting localities refinance with direct bond sales, and increased transparency. China could borrow a page from the 1980s U.S. savings-and-loan crisis and set up Resolution Trust Corp.–like entities to dispose of bad debts.

But to do any of this, Chinese leaders must be willing to spend political capital at levels that are at least commensurate with the epic flow of ill-gotten gains heading back to the nation's capital. It will take some serious mettle to avoid a Japan-like funk, and it's unclear if Xi and Li have it. That means closely studying what Japan got wrong, as well as where officials in Tokyo got it right.

The Bubble Fix takes on many different forms in Asia. Among the most common might be termed the "Cult of GDP." In Asia, *GDP* often seems to stand less for "gross domestic product" than "gross domestic problem." Leaders can be quite crafty at masking challenges with big-headline growth rates. They are just as much about advertising as they are a diversion. Racy data distract investors from the cracks undermining economies and give politicians room to step before the cameras and say we're moving forward. What matters is that growth reaches those who most need it. It's not just a matter of growing faster, but the quality of that growth. By focusing on growth alone without democratizing its benefits, governments risk Arab Spring–like backlashes.

The Philippines is particularly prone to this phenomenon. Gloria Macapagal Arroyo, president from 2001 to 2010, hid behind 6 percent to 7 percent growth rates as her government did little to attack the corruption concentrating wealth among a small, politically connected elite. In 2012, she was arrested on graft charges, as her immediate predecessor, Joseph Estrada, also had been. Benigno Aquino changed that dynamic when he took office in June 2010. The son of former President Corazon Aquino put Arroyo in jail, faced down the business lobby to pass revenue-raising taxes on cigarettes and liquor, and challenged the powerful Catholic Church by providing free contraceptives to slow population growth. His payoff: investment-grade credit scores for the first time, the support of almost three-quarters of the electorate, and even a place on *Time*'s 2013 list of 100 most influential people.

By mid-2013, three years into Aquino's six-year term, the Philippines was growing faster than China. Yet even reformers are susceptible to resting on their laurels. Aquino's impressive track record is tarnished by the economy's failure to create enough good-paying jobs to eradicate poverty and lower an unemployment rate that is among the highest in Southeast Asia. The government's unsteady rescue efforts following the devastating Typhoon Haiyan in November 2013 also raised some alarm flags. In other words, the hype surrounding 7-percent-plus growth is eclipsing the realities on the ground for the nation's 106 million people. At a time when the Philippines needs to redouble efforts to attract more foreign direct investment, improve infrastructure, and increase access to education and training, officials in Manila are basking in the headlines and easing up on reform.

The reason the Philippines can't be happy with big GDP numbers is that Aquino can't run again, meaning all he's accomplished could easily be undone by a successor more interested in self-enrichment than good governance. He not only needs to push forward with his reforms now, while he has a popular tailwind, but also must make sure that his foes can't easily roll them back once he's gone. The Philippines is but one example of a nation that used to be among Asia's most troubled that confronts an end-of-tenure drama. Take Indonesia and Myanmar, where former generals have presided over unlikely transitions to democracy and capitalism. In both geopolitically vital nations, the future remains fragile and uncertain. Today's huge gain could easily be reversed by corrupt or simply ineffective successors.

In Indonesia, President Susilo Bambang Yudhoyono has righted a nation that many feared would collapse into post-Soviet-style chaos after the fall of former dictator Suharto. Taking over in 2004 after a string of ineffectual post-crisis leaders, Yudhoyono surrounded himself with competent deputies, modernized the economy, reduced terrorism, rolled back the military's role in society, and attacked epic levels of corruption. Yet Yudhoyono, who must step down in 2014, has only just introduced a plan to spend $125 billion on infrastructure by 2025. The opportunities for corruption are immense—almost an invitation for a successor to return to the days of crony capitalism.

The challenge in Myanmar is somewhat different, but just like other Southeast Asian nations it's using asset bubbles to hide underlying economic cracks. Former general Thein Sein has presided over a stunning transformation in just the last two years, opening up a country that was once almost as closed as North Korea. Now, Ford Motor Co. is establishing showrooms in Yangon and companies are angling for a piece of Myanmar's 64-million-person consumer market. The Davos set gathered in the capital, Naypyidaw, in June 2013 for a summit heralding Myanmar's reentry into the global economy.

Yet Thein Sein has said he won't run in presidential elections scheduled for 2015. Instead, the charismatic Aung San Suu Kyi, whom the former general freed from her long house arrest, may seek the presidency. She's almost certain to win if she does. No one knows how the Nobel laureate will do as a national leader. There's broad recognition that Myanmar's military must work for the country, not the other way around. Will the generals take marching orders from their onetime political prisoner? Moves to further liberalize basic freedoms—not to mention to open up the economy—could well provoke stiffer resistance if they come from Suu Kyi than from one of their own.

All of these Asian leaders face the same problem: how to ensure that reforms outlive their tenure and create stable economic models. One way is to leverage their popularity, as Aquino has done. If voters are sold on the benefits to be had from a more efficient economy, they will police the government at the ballot box. Just as important is forging a consensus among business leaders in favor of economic and political progress and creating independent judiciaries and other institutions.

At the same time, focusing too much on individual personalities has traditionally been part of the problem in Asia. Leaders must groom a crop of potential successors who share their ideals and integrity. That means remaking political parties, too, so that they're not personal vehicles but truly meritocratic organizations. The allies Aquino helped elect to the Philippines Senate in 2013, for example, are considered serious, reformist lawmakers, not yes-men. They'll be judged less on their personal loyalty to Aquino than their ability to sustain progressive policies.

These are, in one sense, enviable problems to face. In the past, Asian voters had to worry far more about how to get rid of wayward leaders, whether dictators like Suharto in Indonesia, entrenched and overly dominant parties like the Liberal Democratic Party in Japan, or allegedly corrupt executives like Aquino's predecessor Arroyo. The fact that many countries are now fretting about losing good leaders is a sign of maturity. The next step is to detach these issues from the Bubble Fix and individuals and to cement the constituency for change across the population. That's the campaign these lame ducks need to wage next.

■ ■ ■

Thailand is another case in point. In her two-plus years leading Thailand's 67 million people, Yingluck Shinawatra has managed to tamp down the virtual civil war that led to the ouster of her prime minister brother in 2006. Yet the thrust of Yingluck's economic policies is a Japan-like emphasis on scoring political points today at the expense of tomorrow. Her government has subsidized rice prices, provided handouts to car buyers, and favored megaprojects that will enrich the politically connected more than the masses. That comes at the expense of long-term competitiveness and prosperity. Thailand should instead be investing in its future, especially education, if it wants to break out of the "middle-income trap" that befalls many developing nations.

Moody's Investors Service warns that too many lavish and near-sighted subsidies will damage Thailand's credit rating. Yingluck's priorities bear troubling similarities to those her exiled brother, Thaksin Shinawatra, championed from 2001 to 2006. His overhyped "Thaksinomics" never amounted to more than a Tammany Hall–like doling out of cash in return for rural votes.

In January 2013, Yingluck unveiled a plan to lift Thai living standards. She proposed spending about $72 billion over 10 years on transportation, energy, and telecommunications projects. Yingluck's government is pushing an $8.6 billion port-and-industrial-zone project in neighboring Myanmar. In June in Turkey, she called for a "New Silk Road" rail project to link Europe and Asia. Forgotten in this ambitious building boom, though, is any investment in social infrastructure. It's even more important to invest billions of dollars in education and in training to improve the quality of the labor force and raise productivity so that Thailand can keep up in the world's most dynamic region. The country lags not just at the tertiary level, but also at the primary and secondary phases of the education process. Like several other countries in the region, Thailand's focus on rote learning gives short shrift to creative and critical thinking and English proficiency.

"There is little sign that inadequate investment in human capital and the need for reform of the education system is recognized by the current government," said economist Peter Warr at the Australian National University in Canberra. He's done extensive research on Thailand's economic growing pains.

Thailand matters because it's often seen as a role model in the region. As Myanmar exits decades of isolation and tries to build a healthy economy, it's looking to Thailand for direction and financing.

The same goes for Cambodia, Laos, and Vietnam. How Thailand evolves will reverberate around the neighborhood.

At the moment, Thailand is walking in place even if its headline growth rates outpace Japan, the United States, and Europe. To Bank of Thailand economist Piti Disyatat, per-capita gross domestic product tells the story: It has been hovering around 15 to 20 percent of U.S. levels for more than 10 years. This is a precarious moment for Thailand to be stuck at a per-capita GDP of about $5,000. Global growth is tepid, China is slowing, and Indonesia, the Philippines, and Vietnam are winning jobs that Thailand once took for granted. As Thai wages rise, so do production costs. It must move faster up the value chain to build more technologically advanced products in the electronics and automobile sectors—preferably bearing Thai names, not just Japanese ones.

Building a more entrepreneurial workforce requires doing better than Japan Inc. has. It requires innovative policies, big investments, and political will, all of which are in short supply. Corruption, among other things, skews incentives. Massive road, bridge, and power-grid projects are dripping with opportunities for politicians and businesspeople to line their pockets. "There are few if any kickbacks available from investment in education," Warr said. "Physical infrastructure is another matter."

Thaksin's policy of cash handouts to rural areas was the economic equivalent of a sugar high, not unlike Abenomics. It did nothing to strengthen government institutions, build a credible legal system, or invest in human capital. The five prime ministers who led Thailand between Thaksin's ouster and his sister's victory in July 2011 spent all their time avoiding another coup. Thailand must invest in the future. Pouring more money into people rather than rice farms and construction companies, Japan-style, would be a good start.

Our search for potential lost decades also must bring us to India. With its sub-5-percent economic growth, young population, and vast potential, the world's biggest democracy may not seem to be on the verge of a crisis. Look closer, though, at the political chaos in India and things come into focus: The odds of a lost decade are growing, with implications that would be ruinous. India's growth in 2013 has been the weakest in 10 years. That can't be blamed just on Europe's debt crisis, faltering U.S. growth, or China's slowdown. No; this slackening is the fault of Prime Minister Manmohan Singh and the inability of India's leadership to bring about the needed reforms to an economy hamstrung by bureaucracy and entrenched interests.

Singh must get some credit for at least trying. He has backed efforts to allow foreign investment in supermarkets, airlines, and other industries, and to reduce $8 billion of subsidies that contribute to the widest budget deficit among major emerging economies. These efforts have stalled, thanks mostly to his self-serving critics. And these days, that means Mamata Banerjee, who has rallied opposition to Singh's plans. Among her more unhelpful achievements, she has made it harder for companies to buy land, setting back expansion plans by Tata Motors Ltd. and Infosys Ltd.

Banerjee personifies why India relies on half-measures and easy credit to prop up growth when what's really needed is massive restructuring. Really, if economist Joseph Schumpeter had an alter ego, one bent on halting the creative destruction that shucks off old stagnant industries to make way for the new, the chief minister of the West Bengal state would be it. She has emerged as the most strident opponent of the coalition government of which she's a part. Not surprisingly, investors aren't sticking around, sending Indian stocks down.

Yet as wrong as Banerjee is on the economics, as retrograde as her ideas are in the age of globalization, she's only a symptom of the real problem, which is India's political system, and Singh's failure to regain some semblance of control over it risks surrendering a decade of economic progress.

When will India's leaders realize that growth alone isn't enough? China's authoritarian government can get away with ignoring structural flaws with impressive gross domestic product figures. The interesting thing about the scandal surrounding Bo Xilai, a former senior figure in the Communist Party now occupying a jail cell, is that investors were so nonplussed. The odyssey of rights activist Chen Guangcheng caused nary a ripple in markets. For all China's troubles, many investors have faith that policy makers are tending to the economy. India doesn't have that luxury.

Asia's third-biggest economy needs to constantly remind and convince investors that market liberalization is moving forward, even if progress is gradual and unsteady. Right now, India is failing miserably.

With each passing day, Singh's inability to marshal a consensus confirms the perception that officials in New Delhi are weak, distracted, indecisive, and overwhelmed by divergent interests.

A broad economic overhaul that didn't rely on bubble fixes seemed plausible back in mid-2009, when Singh won reelection with a solid mandate. Many bright-eyed observers, including me, thought the former central bank governor who masterminded a set of market changes in the 1990s that propelled India's rapid growth would shake up the economy. Four-plus years later, India is behind schedule on reforms, imperiling the longer-term possibility that it might catch up to, or even trump, China someday. A reasonable argument can be made that based on demographics alone, youthful India with 1.2 billion people could surpass the growth rates of aging China a decade from now, but not if India's dysfunction continues to sabotage its potential.

India needs some serious creative destruction, far beyond what Schumpeter had in mind when he championed market forces exacting the change that only unfettered competition can bring. None of it is occurring. India even risks losing its investment-grade status, the first of the BRIC nations—Brazil, Russia, India, and China—to suffer the indignity. Standard & Poor's consistently warns that India's politics is "unfavorable."

If India were more focused on broad reforms, Banerjee's antics would be a sideshow. Singh needs to make sure that India has coherent policies and the political support to see them implemented. There's no question that capitalism can be a harsh taskmaster, and that checks and balances are needed in a nation where two-thirds of the population lives in extreme poverty. Yet, without taking some risks that might lead India to a higher-growth path, the economy will lose altitude, poverty will increase, and, far from shining, much will be lost.

Asian policy makers must be mindful that economic reforms that increase efficiency and spread the benefits of growth will always pay greater dividends than the Bubble Fix. Excess stimulus and massive capital inflows have a way of boosting growth and offering a false sense recovery is afoot. In reality, they just create new bubbles. Asia did an impressive job of weathering the 2008 global financial crisis. But since then, the lack of economic change has restrained its potential.

Japanese, too, wonder where it all went so wrong. The search for an answer has even inspired the entertainment industry. Take the 2007 film, *Bubble Fiction*, a comedy timed to commemorate the tenth anniversary of Yamaichi's demise. It was the tale of precocious 20-year-old woman sent back in time on an important mission for the Finance Ministry: to warn Japan that a crash was afoot and to stop it. What the movie lacked in cinematic excellence, it made up for in quirkiness. Think *Doctor Who* meets *Wall Street* with a dash of *Bridget Jones* tossed in. Shortly after seeing it, I chatted about the movie with Kuroda, who then was president of the Asian Development Bank. He agreed that the idea of returning to Tokyo, circa 1990, to right any number of wrongs was oddly thought-provoking. What if policy makers could go back and fix their biggest screwups?

Certainly, Summers might like to revisit 1999 to stop the repeal of Glass-Steagall firewalls that enabled the financial industry to dwarf the entire economy. Greenspan might like to return to December 1996 and do more than just make ambiguous warnings about "irrational exuberance." Hans Tietmeyer might fancy a return to his days as German Bundesbank president to speak out even more forcefully against the financial engineering that turned investment products into pure alchemy. Thai officials might want to go back to the Bangkok of July 1997 and handle the baht devaluation differently.

George Soros could return to 1992, bet even bigger against the Bank of England, and double his $2 billion profit. Nick Leeson, the trader who brought down Barings PLC, could return to 1995 and bet on Japanese stocks plunging, rather than rallying. John Meriwether of Long-Term Capital Management could travel back to 1998 and make money from Russia's bond default, instead of being ruined by it. New York Fed Bank President William McDonough could go back and argue against the bail-out he cobbled together for Meriwether.

In Japan's case, the first effort at revisionism might be the Plaza Accord of 1985, which sharply weakened the dollar versus the yen. It did little to improve the U.S. balance of payments, but contributed to asset bubbles that led to Japan's lost decade in the 1990s. The second stop: then–BOJ Governor Yasushi Mieno, to keep him from hiking short-term interest rates so rapidly, wiping out $15 trillion in wealth and triggering an economic malaise that still drags on. It would also be wise to travel back in time and meet with Governor Hayami and talk him out of cutting rates to zero, ground zero for the Bubble Fix still afflicting the economy. It took the onus off timid politicians who should've been reforming the economy's structure.

Tokyo lawmakers also might want to return to Washington on October 10, 2010, when then–Bank of Japan Governor Masaaki Shirakawa told the world what it should have learned from his nation's lost decades: "Structural reform is indispensable." The first significant step Abe took after returning to the prime minister's office in December 2012 was engineering Shirakawa's ouster from a job few thought he had performed competently. But contained in his speech two years earlier was the real Holy Grail for which international policy makers should be searching:

> If foreign countries mistakenly draw the most crucial lesson from Japan's experience as the necessity of short-term stimulative policy measures, they will face a risk of writing the wrong policy prescription. I do not go into the details of economic policy in each country, but I think that it is crucial to maintain the flexibility of the economic structure to smoothly reallocate labor and capital from the lower productivity sector to the higher productivity sector. That is, however, not necessarily easy, given the social climate after the burst of the bubble.

Rather than "smoothly reallocate" the forces that propelled Japan into the orbit of the Group of Seven nations and created breathtaking success and wealth, rather than veer in a different policy direction, rather than thinking out of the proverbial box, officials in Tokyo doubled down again and again on ultralow rates, bubbles, and economic inertia. If there is any mistake Japanese policy makers might love to travel back in time to fix, it's this one.

Chapter 2

The Female Problem

How Institutionalized Sexism Kills Growth

In October 2000, I found myself sitting next to Sheryl Sandberg in Tokyo, long before she joined Facebook Inc. and wrote her best-selling book on female empowerment. We were listening to her boss at the time, U.S. Treasury Secretary Summers, speak about the need for structural reforms to the Japanese economy, in a giant auditorium devoid of women. It was one of several male-dominated events that day where the only women around were serving us tea, not participating in discussions about Japan's economy and politics. The author of *Lean In* leaned over and asked me half-seriously: "There *are* women in this country, right?"

Thirteen-plus years on, Japan's leaders are only now realizing that the two problems are intertwined: The lack of women in the workforce poses one of the biggest structural impediments to faster growth. Japan's institutionalized sexism deepens deflation, hurts competitiveness, and exacerbates the demographic trends that make Japan's debt load so dangerous. It's a reminder to policy makers everywhere, be they running huge economies or small ones, that sexism is dismal economics.

Yet, in July 2013, when Sandberg visited Tokyo to promote her book, I would have liked to relay good news about gender progress in Japan. I would have loved to bring her up to date about how Japan had made great strides since October 2000 in helping women reach high places in business and politics. It would have been great to detail how Abe was putting forth bold and innovative strategies to better utilize half of the nation's population. It would have been grand to tell her that Japan had anything good to teach the world about gender dynamics. Unfortunately, Asia's most developed nation has a decidedly developing-nation view of its women. In fact, a number of far less developed nations in Asia—Malaysia and the Philippines included— are markedly more enlightened about how underutilizing half of your population is retrograde economics. If anyone needs a lean-in movement, it's the women of Japan.

■ ■ ■

Japan ranks a dismal 105th in gender equality—behind Cambodia, Burkina Faso, Malaysia, and far behind China—out of 136 countries analyzed by the World Economic Forum. Not a single Nikkei 225 company is run by a woman, while female participation in politics is negligible. Only 30 companies on the Nikkei, and 130 out of the 1,600-plus companies listed on the Tokyo Stock Price Index, have a female board member. And Japan's male–female wage gap is double the average in Organization for Economic Cooperation and Development (OECD) countries.

"Women could actually save Japan," IMF's managing director, Christine Lagarde, said in Tokyo in October 2012. "Today you have five out of 10 Japanese women out of the job market, as opposed to two out of 10 men."

One single number explains why Japan must pull more women into the job market and help them achieve leadership roles: 15 percent. That's how much of a boost GDP would receive if female employment matched men's (about 80%), according to Goldman Sachs. "Japan is lagging because it's running a marathon with one leg," said Kathy Matsui, the chief Goldman Sachs Japan equity strategist, who has been churning out "Womenomics" reports regularly since 1999. "It must start tapping its most underutilized resource."

This most self-inflicted of Japanese wounds is dawning in Japan's government, too. "If these women rise up," Abe said at a September 2013 speech at the United Nations, "I believe Japan can achieve strong growth." Also that month, Abe wrote in a *Wall Street Journal* op-ed that "unleashing the potential of Womenomics is an absolute must if Japan's growth is to continue."

Abe's stated goal is this: a 2 percent increase in productivity over the mid- to long term will produce, in 10 years, an average of 2 percent of inflation-adjusted GDP growth. Getting there requires capitalizing on the power of women. That means boosting their workforce participation from about 63 percent to 73 percent by 2020 and bridging the wage–equality gap. Women in Japan, by official government estimates, earn on average 30.2 percent less than men, versus 20.1 percent in the United States. "The target year 2020 will coincide with the return of the Olympics to Tokyo," Abe wrote. "I am determined that by that time Japan's boardrooms will be enhanced by a greatly increased number of female directors. I will do all that I can to facilitate this change."

Abe has indeed stepped up with a three-pronged effort to address the problem. It's troubling, though, that his proposals hardly match his rhetoric. So far, he's focused on extending child-care leave, expanding day-care facilities, and asking companies to hire female board members. Yet Abe's government is barely scratching the surface and is reinforcing stereotypes about the role of women in society. Abe is asking his government, for example, to circulate "Women's Notebooks" to warn of the evils of postponing marriage and motherhood. Yes, the subtext seems to suggest, career-oriented women are selfish. What's more, when Abe calls on companies to provide three years of maternity leave, he uses a Japanese expression that a child should be held by its mother until the age of 3. Yes, kids are women's work. Won't knowing that a three-year absence could derail their careers only encourage women to further delay childbirth? Abenomics's brush with Womenomics already lacks creativity and urgency.

The first step Abe should take is to actually enforce the 1986 Equal Employment Opportunity Law, one that has never been fully understood or enforced. Next, Japan should promote diversity and offer tax incentives to companies that do, as well. More-flexible work hours would draw women into the workforce. So would offering subsidized or free day care so more families can afford it. Quotas for female executives also are worth considering. A 2012 McKinsey & Co. report titled "Women Matter" bemoaned the low percentage of female Japanese managers and found companies that champion diversity are more profitable and innovative. Women are good for business, not charity cases.

Part of the problem is Abe's motivation. He is acting from fiscal necessity, not from a sense of social justice or economic logic. As Standard & Poor's and Moody's Investors Service warn, Japan's workforce is shrinking as the population ages and the birthrate declines. That might be manageable if not for a public debt more than twice the size of the economy and the forces of deflation that only necessitate ever more borrowing down the road.

Politically, too, increasing the number of women workers is an easier sell than opening up Japan to immigrant labor. It's far less controversial than lifting barriers to immigration and easier than tightening corporate governance, tweaking taxes to support startup companies, crafting new energy policies that create jobs, cut prices, and phase out nuclear reactors in seismically active Japan, introducing more flexibility into labor markets, ending protections enjoyed by farmers, medical services, or fisheries, or retooling the education system. Manipulating exchange rates is simply easier than upending Japan's postwar model. So is focusing on the economics of gender.

Better utilizing the female workforce is the lowest-hanging of economic fruits for Abe. So why tackle the issue in such a timid and dispassionate way? After all, institutionalized sexism exacerbates many of the biggest challenges facing Japan today. For example, it worsens the nation's demographics. For many women, delaying childbirth is a form of rebellion against societal expectations to have children and become housewives. While things are improving, having children remains a career-ending decision for millions of well-educated and ambitious women.

An intriguing question is how much Abe learned from his first stint as prime minister from 2006 to 2007. Then, too, he talked of empowering women, but it was just that—talk. Many women still seethe over January 2007 comments by Abe's then–health minister, Hakuo Yanagisawa, describing them as mere "baby-making machines." Abe refused to fire Yanagisawa, assuring the nation that "I reprimanded him severely." Even when Yanagisawa apologized he further displayed the cluelessness of Abe's Liberal Democratic Party (LDP) by saying women were "people whose role it is to give birth." What's more, Abe's 2006–2007 government defined "baby-making machines" as women between the ages of 15 and 50. That led many to wonder whether Japan was encouraging teenage girls to help increase Japan's birthrate.

Sexist comments have long bedeviled Abe's party. Take the July 2003 comments from former Prime Minister Yoshiro Mori that women who delay childbirth are selfish and shouldn't be allowed to claim pensions. "Welfare is supposed to take care of and reward those women who have lots of children," Mori said. "It is truly strange to say we have to use tax money to take care of women who don't even give birth once, who grow old living their lives selfishly and singing the praises of freedom." What of women who can't conceive? And doesn't living in a democracy mean having the right to choose whether to have kids?

Around the same time, another member of Abe's party, Seiichi Ota, was asked during a panel discussion about a recent gang rape of a young woman by students from some of Japan's most prestigious universities. "Well, boys will be boys. At least gang rapists are still vigorous," Ota said. "Isn't that at least a little closer to normal?" The media maelstrom that followed brought condemnation from no less than then–Prime Minister Junichiro Koizumi. He said: "Rape is an unforgivable, contemptible act. Being vigorous is a completely separate issue. Why would he make such a comment?"

A few days later, Yasuo Fukuda, a future prime minister who then was Koizumi's minister of charge of gender equality, shocked the nation further. *Shukan Bunshun*, a weekly magazine, reported that Fukuda said to reporters in an off-the-record briefing, "The problem is that there are lots of women dressed provocatively," in comments shared with the magazine by those in attendance.

Such comments make for more than embarrassing international news headlines. They also provide a window into the sexist mores of a party that's run Japan almost without interruption since 1955. Did Mori, who is still a party kingpin, learn any lessons from his women-are-selfish rant? That's doubtful when you consider his 2009 race against Mieko Tanaka, then a 33-year-old former secretary. Rather than speak to her proposed policies and criticisms of his representation of the people of Ishikawa Prefecture, Mori quipped, "She was picked only because she is young and has a nice body." He implored voters not to be fooled by Tanaka's "sexiness."

Ironically, the few years preceding Mori's ugly campaign against Tanaka, one he won by just a few thousand votes, were thought to be promising ones for Japanese women. That year, Tomoyo Nonaka was named chairwoman of Sanyo Electric Co. and Fumiko Hayashi became chief executive officer of retailer Daiei Inc. They were the first women to run major Japanese companies.

But Nonaka lasted only 21 months; Hayashi was knocked back to vice chairwoman after two years in the top job.

In 2005, for example, Koizumi's landslide election victory was largely thanks to 43 seats secured by women. Yet the victory for gender equality was a somewhat Pyrrhic one. Koizumi had taken a page from Italy's Silvio Berlusconi and recruited a handpicked bunch of fresh-faced and photogenic women—including a former beauty queen, a television anchor, and a celebrity chef—to dazzle voters. The media dubbed the candidates chosen for Koizumi's cynical style-over-substance stunt everything from "Koizumi assassins" to "female ninjas" to the "babe brigade."

Making it all the more cringe-worthy was Koizumi's own history of sexist comments. One of the more publicized was that he expressed in January 2002 after Makiko Tanaka, Japan's first female foreign minister, was sacked for reasons that struck many in the media as petty. When asked about tears Tanaka shed at the time, a patronizing Koizumi complained: "Tears are women's greatest weapons. When women cry, men cannot compete with them." After a public outcry, Koizumi doubled down on the parliament floor: "Everyone, not only me, has been saying it, even in novels. I myself am easily moved to tears."

■ ■ ■

In 2009, the Democratic Party of Japan (DPJ) briefly wrested power away from the LDP with a similar strategy. Its own bevy of nubile fresh faces was dubbed the "Princess Corps." Some in the media preferred to give credit to the architect of the DPJ's beauty contest, party leader Ichiro Ozawa, and referred to them as "Ozawa Girls." And it worked: A record 54 women won parliamentary seats in the August 30, 2009, election, a milestone for female representation in an economy notorious for little. The hope at the time was that the DPJ's new prime minister, Yukio Hatoyama, would view women in less ornamental terms than the LDP's leaders had. Sadly, that didn't happen.

With the LDP back in power, the question is whether the latest pledges to empower women are real or mere lip service. It's time for a national dialogue and decisive action. Women should take a page from Sandberg and demand equality. Japanese men must lean in, too. In a top-down society, the real push to end sexism must come from political and business leaders.

"To change things in society, you do need to put change agents in leadership positions," Matsui said. "Women need to fight harder, too, but this problem is so ingrained in Japanese culture, corporate etiquette and what the broader society expects from women and how women themselves have internalized those norms. As much as women need to demand change, men also need to fight on their end."

Matsui crams this laugh-line into every speech she gives about Womenomics: "There is no such thing as a glass ceiling; it's just a thick layer of men." All joking aside, Japan has some of the most-impervious barriers for women in the developed world. Abe boosters, including many women, like to think he is preparing to break through that barrier once and for all. The trouble is, while women in American and Europe face a glass ceiling, their Japanese counterparts face one closer to concrete.

"Japan has some very, very smart, international and thoughtful women," said John Wood, founder of Room to Read, a nonprofit literacy organization. "Why it doesn't use that resource better is astounding to me."

The world can learn from Japan's warped gender policies. Matsui's research dovetails with the findings of the World Bank, IMF, Organization for Economic Cooperation and Development, and the

World Economic Forum: Educating women is good for the economy and for business. "The plusses for societies and economies have become obvious," Matsui said. "Educated women contribute to the quality, size, and productivity of workforces. They can get better paying jobs, allowing them to provide daily necessities, health care, and education to support the family. Our research shows that investments in female education can yield a 'growth premium' in GDP trends and that narrowing the gender gap boosts per capita income."

To Matsui, it's a no-brainer. At a time in history fraught with war, inequality, poverty, hunger, and disease, education is one of the clear "silver bullets" that can appreciably raise living standards broadly and consistently. Why, then, must so many girls and women across societies still fight to gain access to secondary and tertiary education? Why is the gender gap, both in terms of access to learning and the workplace, still so wide?

Since 2005, Matsui has had a front-row seat to this stubborn phenomenon as co-chair of the Asian University for Women's Support Group in Japan. "These hurdles can be rooted in culture, history, or legacy, as well as poverty," she said. "They are unique to each society and community. The only way to get people to change their mores and customs is by getting them to see the benefits."

■ ■ ■

Japan's experience is instructive. Nearly 70 percent of working women in Japan quit after having their first child. This tendency, rooted as much in economics as tradition, is a major cause of Japan's running-a-marathon-with-one-leg problem. But similar handicaps hurt developing economies in Asia, where women and girls can face great hardship gaining access to education and, therefore, are relegated to unskilled, low-paying jobs. "In addition to reducing their chances for a better life, their lack of education costs their country in terms of lost economic growth," Matsui said.

For the BRIC nations (Brazil, Russia, India, and China) and the so-called Next-11 countries (Bangladesh, Egypt, Indonesia, Iran, Korea, Mexico, Nigeria, Pakistan, Philippines, Turkey, and Vietnam), increased investment in female education and training would raise

GDP growth by about 0.2 percent per year, Goldman Sachs estimates. What's more, a narrower gender gap could add 20 percent to income per capita by 2030. If only governments the world over championed the issue.

"Despite the business case for recruiting and developing more women, 70 percent of the executives we surveyed in Asia said greater gender diversity was not a strategic priority for their companies—that is, it was not among their top ten priorities," wrote McKinsey analysts Claudia Suessmuth Dyckerhoff, Jin Wang, and Josephine Chen. "In Europe, the figure was 47 percent. In addition, only a minority of Asian executives—some 40 percent—expected that their companies would step up efforts to improve gender diversity in the next five years."

"South Korean executives were a notable exception: Two-thirds foresaw the rapid introduction of more gender diversity initiatives," they wrote.

> These findings suggest that the status quo is not about to alter greatly. A minority of executives see the need for change and are trying hard to get more women on their teams, but the majority are still not giving the issue much attention. Moreover, given how few women have reached the top, the question arises of whether change is afoot even in those markets and companies where there appears to be wider awareness of the importance of gender diversity.

Japan's modern history is replete with flashes of feminist energy, but few have caught on in a cohesive, sustained, and formidable way. A little Gloria Steinem–style agitation, or even taking a page from *Lysistrata*, would go a long way in a nation badly in need of an economic shakeup. After all, those in power don't tend to yield it easily, least of all Japan's old-boys club. Here, it's worth pausing to consider the person most responsible for the rights women in Japan do enjoy. Ironically, it's a *gaijin* named Beate Sirota Gordon.

Beate Sirota was born in Vienna on October 25, 1923, to Russian-Jewish parents and later married American Joseph Gordon. Her father, Leo Sirota, was a celebrated pianist who in 1929 took an offer to teach in Tokyo. There, Gordon saw firsthand how few rights women had—they were merely property. A decade later, in 1939, she migrated to Oakland, California, to attend Mills College, where she received a degree in modern languages and eventually became a naturalized U.S. citizen before returning to Tokyo in 1945, just months after Japan's surrender.

Gordon—fluent in Japanese, English, French, German, and Russian—was hired by General Douglas MacArthur's occupation army as a translator. MacArthur's team was just beginning to craft Japan's postwar constitution. As its lone female member, Gordon was given an opportunity for which Japan's female masses owe her considerable gratitude: Draft its women's-rights section. It was a highly unlikely job for a 22-year-old who was neither a constitutional scholar nor lawyer. But there was a certain random genius to entrusting the task to a feisty, observant, and independent woman. She saw to it that her all-important Article 14 made it into the final document. It stated, in terms that in 1946 Japan were nothing short of revolutionary: "All of the people are equal under the law and there shall be no discrimination in political, economic or social relations because of race, creed, sex, social status or family origin."

For generations, Gordon stayed out of the limelight. She feared, for example, that the conservative men running postwar Japan would exploit her youth and inexperience to revise the constitution. Many of the Japanese negotiators who worked with MacArthur, after all, hated Article 14 more than all the others. In the 1950s, she joined the Asia Society in New York, where she had an illustrious career focusing on the performing arts. In the decades that followed, Gordon became more vocal about her days in MacArthur's Tokyo. In the mid-1990s, she took to the international speaking circuit to promote her memoir, *The Only Woman in the Room*.

Sadly, few Japanese women knew much about Gordon. She died on December 30, 2013, at age 89, in New York. That's a shame, considering how much they owe her for the freedoms they enjoy. It's time for Japanese to take up the flame of a woman some consider their answer to Gloria Steinem. Nearly 70 years after Japan's constitution was written, sexism remains rampant. Such inequality holds back Japan's economy by reducing the quality of its labor force. Women must demand their due. One problem is a dearth of role models. In fact, that's one of lawmaker Kuniko Inoguchi's biggest complaints about where modern Japan finds itself. "In this country, we have never had a real radical feminist movement like many countries have," she said. "Lacking that, I think we have not been able to make a dramatic change in mind-set."

■ ■ ■

I will never forget the first time I met Inoguchi. It was in October 2007 at Tokyo's swanky Prince Hotel, where Inoguchi was speaking at the Symposium on Women in Financial Services sponsored by the American Chamber of Commerce in Japan. As I arrived, dozens of conservatively dressed businesswomen were chatting in the lobby about the need to raise the profile of women in corporate Japan. Things took a surreal turn as a parade of tall, scantily clad beauty queens suddenly made their way past toward their own gathering: tryouts for the Miss International pageant. The hotel's planners seemed to miss the irony of placing the two events—one celebrating women's brains, the other their sex appeal and tan lines—side by side.

It was as apt a metaphor for what many women experience in Japan, where the desire to be taken seriously collides with those in the executive suite who still see women as ornaments to a business culture ruled by men in gray suits. Along with rolling her eyes at the state of affairs in Japan Inc., Inoguchi is among those in power rolling up their sleeves to remove one of the most-enduring obstacles to faster growth.

She served as Koizumi's gender affairs minister in 2005 and 2006 until Abe took over as prime minister the first time around and promptly ignored the issue. The persistence of Japan's seniority-based management system and what Inoguchi calls its "paternalistic nature" means that for every woman who rises into management, there are scores with little prospect of doing so. But Inoguchi worries, too, that women lack role models. It pains her that, just as in 2007, *Forbes* magazine's 2013 ranking of the world's 100 most powerful women doesn't list a single Japanese. Among Asians, the rankings include Burmese, Chinese, Hong Kongers, Indians, Indonesians, Singaporeans, South Koreans, and Taiwanese, but no Japanese.

In 2007, I asked Inoguchi about one female role model, named Riyo Mori, who had just won the Miss Universe contest. She was suddenly the most famous woman in Japan and hit the speaking circuit to encourage young Japanese women to follow in her footsteps, arguing,

incongruously, that beauty contests were about female empowerment, not skimpy swimsuits. Inoguchi was among those wincing at
the spectacle and arguing that the economy would benefit far more
from young women striving to be Japan's answer to Germany's Angela
Merkel, America's Hillary Clinton, or India's Sonia Gandhi. Great talent exists among Japan's female masses. The nation just needs to give
women the chance to display it.

Here, Caroline Kennedy could be an intriguing wild card. The
daughter of former President John F. Kennedy is the first woman to
represent the United States in Japan, and she arrived in Tokyo at a most
propitious moment: just as Abe is pledging to empower women and
elevate more of them into leadership roles. Kennedy isn't the ideal
feminist role model. For one thing, her knowledge of Japan, is, at best,
superficial. For another, as the scion of America's most-enduring political dynasty, it isn't as if she struggled to get where she is. Yet having a
woman (and a mother of three) play such a high-profile role in Japan
will turn heads not only in the halls of Parliament but also the shopping byways of Ginza.

That isn't the storyline you hear from some foreign-policy aficionados. Many see the White House choosing to reward a big fundraiser
and early backer of Obama's presidential campaign as a misguided and
cynical move. Kennedy, many say, is a debutante without diplomatic
experience. She doesn't know Tokyo. And she's no Edwin Reischauer,
ambassador under her father in the 1960s. Yes, there are challenges facing
U.S.–Japan relations—including American bases in Okinawa, and risks
such as Japan's territorial disputes with China. But in the age of instanta-
neous communication, 24/7 news cycles, and encryption technology, it's
not as if ambassadors make big decisions anymore. And for all the hype
in the media, Abe and Obama have few major policy disagreements.

Many Japanese couldn't be happier that a trusted Obama con-
fidante is coming their way—even better, a famous one. While
Kennedy's predecessor, John Roos, did a fine job, he's not exactly a
household name. Camelot meeting the Chrysanthemum Throne is big
news in a nation that's been feeling a bit unappreciated by the West as
China hogs the spotlight. Kennedy would be wise to understand the
import of her arrival at what could be a crucial moment in gender
dynamics. Kennedy should take every opportunity she gets—and even

create a few—to inspire women to break through that thick layer of Japanese men.

Among Japanese women trying to do just that is Rina Bovrisse. The 40-year-old has become a minor celebrity for her widely publicized discrimination lawsuit against Prada and being the first Japanese of her gender to bring her case before the United Nations. I first met the single mom in September 2010, several months after she shocked the famed fashion house with a sexual harassment suit and a blizzard of embarrassing headlines. After all, Bovrisse contended Prada fired her for being "ugly."

When we met in Shibuya, Mecca for the nation's fashionable youth, to go over her story, Bovrisse presented me with a business card identifying her as a "Fashionista Feminista." Fashion, of course, is an industry that prides itself on empowering women. And when you think about fashion brands committed to doing just that, Prada probably earns a spot near the top of most lists. It was a dream come true in April 2009 when Bovrisse was hired as a senior retail manager.

The dream faded into nightmare territory: Bovrisse claims she was harassed by Prada Japan's top executive for her appearance, age, and weight and unfairly dismissed, claims Prada denies. Rather than slink away, Bovrisse, a 20-year fashion-industry veteran, sued Prada and turned to the local and international media. Her case might garner modest attention in Milan, New York, or Paris, where sexual-harassment battles are commonplace. Coming in Japan, where women's rights are often a novel idea, it was a shocking spectacle. Japanese women are supposed to maintain a stiff upper lip when being mistreated in the workplace: That's how it is. Deal with it. Bovrisse was having none of that, and good for her. In her frustration, she's doing her part to highlight a major cause of Japan's malaise: a chronic disregard for the female workforce. It hinders growth, adds to public debt, reduces competitiveness, and feeds other challenges like the nation's falling birthrate. "So many smart, driven, talented Japanese women are tired of not being treated equally," Bovrisse said. "I am speaking out for them. We must have the courage to demand to be treated fairly."

After studying at Parsons School of Design, Bovrisse (the name comes from her marriage to a Frenchman) had worked in New York, London, Paris, and Hawaii and for household names like Prada USA and Chanel SA. Presumably, it was that résumé that prompted Prada Japan to hire Bovrisse to oversee 500 employees in 40 shops. And then, she said, the trouble began. First, she was told to get rid of 15 managers and assistant managers for being "old, fat, ugly, disgusting, or not having the Prada look." Later in her six-month stint there, she claims to have been told to lose weight and change her hairstyle. Bovrisse says she complained to company headquarters in Milan and was fired soon after. In August 2012, representatives from the UN Committee on the Elimination of Discrimination Against Women met with Bovrisse, sharing the Organization for Economic Cooperation and Development's worries about the level of female empowerment in Japan.

Not surprisingly for Japan, Bovrisse's case was dismissed. But what was surprising was the sexist statement accompanying the October 26, 2012, Tokyo District Court decision, and by a female judge: "Sexual harassment and discrimination is confirmed, but legal for the fashion industry," Judge Reiko Morioka wrote, adding that "if a female employee's salary is high, the emotional distress of sexual harassment should be endured." In other words, grow a backbone, Bovrisse-san, will you?

If Prada Japan thought that countersuing Bovrisse for $780,000 (less than what she was seeking in damages) would shut her up, the company was gravely mistaken. Since then, she's spoken all over Japan and the globe about gender inequality in Japan, been feted as a crusading heroine in *Elle* magazine and *British Vogue* and named "Female Icon of the Year" alongside Michelle Obama and Carla Bruni by Portuguese newspaper *Correio da Manhã*. Bovrisse also basked in the glow of Internet activists flooding social media spaces, including Prada's Facebook page, with statements of support and calls to arms. Her case has even warranted its own Wikipedia page. Bovrisse has addressed Hong Kong's Legislative Council and been tapped by the American Chamber of Commerce in Japan in 2013 to become a spokesperson for its global gender initiatives.

But in May 2013 came her biggest coup: the UN's blessing. The LDP greybeards who run Japan couldn't have been happy to read this from the world body's Office of the High Commissioner for Human Rights:

> The Committee urges the State party to introduce in its leg-
> islation an offence of sexual harassment, in particular in the

workplace, which carries sanctions proportionate to the severity of the offence. The Committee also recommends that the State party ensure that victims can lodge complaints without fear of retaliation. The Committee recommends that the State party continue to raise the public awareness against sexual harassment.

Japan's per-capita-income rankings tend to be a mirror image of those reflecting women's participation in politics and corporate management. Women also have fared poorly since the Lehman shock of late 2008, being hit disproportionately by Wall Street's meltdown. Because many are hired on part-time contracts, they are easiest to cut when corporate profits evaporate. Japan's seniority-based and male-dominated model has built bridges, dams, and roads to nowhere and cut interest rates to zero in a bid to raise living standards. It's dragged its feet on better harnessing the talents of its female masses.

"It pains me to think women haven't come further than this," Bovrisse said. Japan needs more Bovrisses to step forward and, in the Sandbergian sense, lean in. If Japanese women are waiting for their male leaders to champion their cause, they're mistaken. They need to demand a bigger say in Japan's business and political systems if they want true change. It's a key to Japan becoming a meritocracy. Societal norms are a powerful dynamic and they're sometimes summed up with a proverb: The nail that sticks up gets hammered down. Cases of sexism often don't get reported for fear of making waves or being at the center of a potential scandal. Yet women should make waves, and big ones. Gender discrimination in Japan often seems like one of those unfixable issues. When you talk about it, people nod knowingly and shrug.

Job applicants in Japan find nothing odd about attaching a photo to their résumés, or including their date of birth. There's little outcry when the response of Tokyo subway operators to complaints about groping on trains is segregation: women-only cars. Just like the economy, it's a matter of treating the symptoms of the problem, not the underlying illness.

The literary and cinematic worlds tell us *The Devil Wears Prada*. In Bovrisse's story, you could say Prada wears the devil. Yet, as even our heroine will admit, this tale is much bigger than the experience of one

woman. It's about the future of the third-biggest economy. And grudgingly, Bovrisse is sensing her Gloria Steinem–like role in Japan's economic drama.

■ ■ ■

As other nations in Asia develop and spread their wings, they would
be wise to heed Japan's cautionary tale. Of course, the Asia region is
a paradoxical one when it comes to the role of women. Take Korea, a
promising economy that does even worse than Japan in gender-equality
measures. Even so, Korea already has what America, never mind Japan,
doesn't: a female leader.

The reason is that Asia is known more for patriarchal succes-
sion than gender equality. Asia leads the world in the number of years
women have ruled. For all the excitement about Hillary Clinton perhaps running for U.S. president in 2016, female leaders are old-hat
in Bangladesh, India, Indonesia, Pakistan, the Philippines, Sri Lanka,
Thailand, and, now, Korea with President Park Geun-hye. Soong
Ching Ling led China briefly on more than one occasion and,
while she never took office, Aung San Suu Kyi was elected leader of
Myanmar in 1990.

It is supremely puzzling, then, that Asia also is way up there
among the world leaders in gender discrimination, all at the price of
growth. The United Nations reckons that limiting female employment
costs Asia $89 billion a year in lost output. A region struggling to raise
many of its three billion people out of poverty squanders roughly the
annual gross domestic product of Slovakia because it favors men. How
silly is that?

"Economic development correlates positively with gender equality," says Astrid Tuminez, vice dean of the Lee Kuan Yew School of
Public Policy at the National University of Singapore.

Korea's President Park should immediately work to narrow a male–
female pay gap that is the worst among OECD members—39 percent in 2010, more than double the OECD average of 15 percent. The
World Economic Forum ranks South Korea 111th in gender equality,
trailing Suriname, United Arab Emirates, and Albania. In China and
India, of course, the challenge for women is being born at all. A cultural

preference for boys and scientific advances increasing the number of sex-selection abortions are causing dangerous demographic imbalances.

Why the disconnect between female leaders and social and economic advancement? In an April 2012 report titled "Rising to the Top?" Tuminez points to Asia's dynastic traditions. Women often attain power on account of who their fathers, husbands, or family are. Here, think Sonia Gandhi in India, Megawati Soekarnoputri in Indonesia, Benazir Bhutto in Pakistan, Corazon Aquino and Gloria Macapagal Arroyo in the Philippines, Yingluck Shinawatra in Thailand, and Park in Geun-hye Korea. Park is the daughter of the dictator Park Chun-hee.

Just as in Japan, the unmarried and childless Park has had to suffer her fair share of gender-related indignities. During the late 2012 election, Park Kwang-on, a spokesman for Park's political rival Moon Jae-in, said: "Candidate Park has no femininity. She has never lived a life agonizing over childbirth, childcare, education, and grocery prices." Others said a woman might not be able to stand up to North Korea.

Korea's failure to address its own gender problems openly and urgently reduces the odds of producing the next Samsung Electronics Co. or Hyundai Motor Co. Only half of the country's women aged 15 years or older were working in 2012 and enrollment of females in higher education is the lowest among 34 OECD members. That must change if Korea is to thrive, and who better to engineer the shift than Madam President? It isn't enough that Park challenges stereotypes in a nation ruled by men in dark suits. She must help women balance the dual demands of work and family. More plentiful and affordable childcare is an important first step. Quotas for female executives and senior government-ministry jobs should be considered. This no longer is just an issue of fairness or human rights. Growth and prosperity hang on gender equality. Put it that way and even the aging, gray-haired men who cling to power in Asia might get it.

Consider an October 2010 study by U.S. and Korean researchers including Harvard Business School's Jordan Siegel that found multinational companies were profiting from Korean competitors. Its conclusion: If you operate in a sexist country full of educated, talented women, it makes good business sense to tap them for management roles.

"There is often a strong economic case to be made for increasing female participation at all levels of the labor force," McKinsey says.

"In Japan—which has one of the lowest female labor participation rates among OECD countries—the labor force is predicted to shrink by 15 percent between 2010 and 2030, threatening GDP growth. Women could help to fill this gap." In Malaysia, McKinsey estimates that raising the participation rates of women to match those of Korea or Singapore could boost GDP by between 6 billion and 9 billion ringgit.

The business case for opening more senior positions to women is painfully clear. As McKinsey puts it: "Unless they do so, companies are surrendering two important sources of competitive advantage: having the best talent in an age of talent scarcity, and capitalizing on the particular performance benefits that women in leadership positions bring to an organization."

It's surprising how governments don't realize that failing to harness half of the population holds back growth. Airplanes that need two engines to fly don't take off when one isn't working, so why do nations think they can thrive in our madly competitive world with one engine? Korea is a case in point. It must close its male–female divide to keep up with Asia's upstart economies as its population ages and shrinks. Drafting more women for senior and middle management may be just what Korea Inc. needs. The same goes for encouraging more women to run for political office.

One of the paradoxes of Korea is education. Its institutions of higher education are meritocratic and produce legions of bright, qualified workers of both sexes. Even so, Korean women are chronically underemployed by OECD standards. Siegel and his team of researchers from the Massachusetts Institute of Technology and Hanshin University looked at hundreds of medium-sized and large companies operating in Korea. In the last decade, they found, a 10 percent increase in female managers was good for a 1 percent jump in profits generated by assets. Samsung Electronics Co. demonstrates the point. In the early 2000s, it had no women executives; by 2010, female employees made up 40 percent of the total workforce of 187,800 and 10 percent of managers. In 2010, perhaps unsurprisingly, Samsung, the world's largest television maker, really began to eclipse Japan's Sony Corp.

Womenomics can be linked to many of Korea's biggest challenges. Rigid mind-sets, for example, make it difficult for women to have both a fulfilling career and a family. Many end up putting off childbirth or having fewer kids, the result of which is one of the lowest birthrates anywhere. Gender will grow in importance as developing Asia thrives. From China to Malaysia, many business cultures are less apt to let gender decide who gets big promotions. It's something Park should be contemplating as China rises and Asian upstarts like the Philippines and Indonesia gain on her population.

Korea's export-led model worked spectacularly. Yet Korea's growth strategy has outlived its usefulness. The next phase must be about ideas and innovation, not factories. Korea will need all the collective brainpower it can muster—male and female. If Korea doesn't begin making the most out of its women, multinationals will.

■ ■ ■

Managing gender dynamics better than Japan will help China, too. Women hold up half the sky, as Mao Zedong famously declared. Decades later, they don't hold up much of anything in the halls of Chinese power. In late 2012, Liu Yang proved the inverse of Mao's point. Then 34, she became the first Chinese woman to orbit the Earth. Yet her milestone highlighted a less heavenly reality remarked on widely at the time: It's easier for a Chinese woman to circle our planet in outer space than to reach the highest rungs of male-dominated Beijing politics.

As self-described reform President Xi prepared to take the reins, there was great hope that a woman would be included in the Politburo Standing Committee, China's most powerful body. While one did make it to the orbit of the broader 25-member Politburo, the outcome had China watchers lamenting how the Communist Party remains an old-boys club. Women will just have to cool their heels for another 10 years.

Of course, China did fare better on the latest *Forbes* list of powerful women than Japan. It included Margaret Chan, head of the World Health Organization; Wu Yajun of Longfor Properties; Zhang Xin of Soho China; Liyuan Peng, China's first lady; Sun Yafang of Huawei Technologies; Jennifer Li of Baidu; and Lan Yang of Sun Media Group. In general, though, women are barely represented in the top echelons of China's government and the biggest state-owned companies.

Boosting their role would invigorate industry and buttress the legitimacy of the Communist Party.

Gender discrimination isn't a big issue among investors. The phenomenon doesn't feed easily into stock valuations, bond yields, or gross domestic product figures. So the negative implications are underappreciated, especially when you consider how readily it can be fixed. Development economists from Lawrence Summers to William Easterly to Jeffrey Sachs have long linked female empowerment to faster economic growth, higher returns on investment, increased productivity, improved agricultural yields, and more favorable demographics. For an industrializing nation to neglect women is akin to fighting with one limb tied behind its back. That's unwise as China faces a widening rich–poor divide that could fan social upheaval and anti-regime sentiment.

The world doesn't tend to see China's gender problems. It sees China's 7-percent-plus growth; a central government with remarkable discipline; trillions of dollars of currency reserves; crane-bristling megacities; armies of bankers and executives working with single-minded purpose; scientists who develop supercomputers that rank among the world's fastest; and legions of engineers capable of rerouting giant rivers like the Yangtze. We rarely consider the structural flaws.

Bureaucratic traditions in business and government aren't flexible enough to accommodate women who want to take time off to have a family. A job in Chinese government can mean a life of liquor-fueled official banquets where professional relationships are forged. Only 2 women have been appointed governor of any of China's 31 provinces and 4 biggest municipalities since the founding of the People's Republic in 1949; none are now serving. In the United States, by contrast, 32 women were elected governors of the 50 states in that time.

The lack of female progress in the public sector belies successes in the private realm. Chinese women may not hold up half the sky, but they account for half of the world's self-made female billionaires, according to the Hurun Report. It found that 14 of the 28 female innovators with riches of more than $1 billion were mainlanders. Matching that record in the public sector would serve China's economy well as the country tries to transform itself from the world's factory floor into a leader in services and technology. By failing to harness the full potential of half of the talent pool, China surely is limiting its growth possibilities.

China needs to act far more urgently than Japan has to close its gender gaps. Among the biggest is a girl shortage. By 2020, as many as 40 million more men than women will reach adulthood and enter the world's most competitive mating market. That estimate, which may actually prove to be conservative, will become a stark economic reality on Xi Jinping's watch. China's president has barely broached this population mismatch in speeches, never mind suggested solutions.

Economics partly explains China's cultural preference for sons. Parents can hope to live with their sons in old age, offering them a clear retirement plan of sorts, whereas daughters tend to enter other family systems. The resulting testosterone glut is the most unintended and dangerous side effect of the one-child policy. Tens of millions—or hundreds of millions in the decades ahead—of young ambitious men unable to find girlfriends or wives can't be good for any economy, never mind one poised to surpass the United States. Will the economics of sexual frustration lead to families auctioning off their daughters? Anyone who has watched the popular Chinese game show *One Out of 100*, where attractive young women pick from a herd of lonely guys, has to wonder about how Chinese mating dynamics will lead to state-sanctioned polyandry someday, whereby women marry multiple men? Neither George Orwell nor Isaac Asimov ever dreamed up a science fiction tale as complicated as China's future. In a 2012 study, "The Competition for Brides in East Asia," researcher Soohyung Lee did just that. Will North Korea's main export soon be marriage-aged women?

"It's critical for China to do everything in its power to redress the deteriorating sex ratio among China's birth population, even if this means moving toward a two-child policy," says Valerie Hudson, a coauthor of *Sex and World Peace*.

Internal, regional, and even international security is compromised by the fact that approximately 15 percent of its young adult males will not be able to form conventional households. China need only look to its own imperial history to see the destabilizing consequences of devaluing daughters.

Some historians worry Asia's bachelor generations could even fuel wars in the decades ahead. Harvard University's Niall Ferguson, for example, wonders if it will incite Arab Spring–like uprisings, Brazilian-style crime, or worse. Europe's continent-wide wars and colonial conquests are sometimes seen as manifestations of population stresses. It isn't that hard to imagine how the unmet needs of young men might mix with perceptions that China's economy is rigged for the party elites. Try as he might to intensify Internet censorship, Xi will find it hard to keep China's struggling masses from learning how rich Communist Party members are becoming. Tens of millions of young, underpaid, and unloved men angry at their leaders is in no one's interest. Over the next decade, Xi will have to keep China's demographic sky from falling. Hence the Communist Party's move in November 2013 to ease the one-child policy somewhat.

■ ■ ■

India has its own gender crisis. In 2013, the lens of the world was on a series of brutal gang rapes, which precipitated huge protests over India's shameful record on women's rights in the world's biggest democracy. A longer-term problem is the dwindling odds of girls being born. In the 1990s, economist Amartya Sen drew attention to the phenomenon of "missing women." American feminist writer Mary Anne Warren goes ever further, calling the exploding number of sex-selection abortions "gendercide."

A key lesson Japan can teach the world is to find your demographic advantages where you can. It can be argued, for example, that Japan's demographics has its strengths as well as its weaknesses. A contrarian idea, indeed, but worth considering. It's not like Japan is doing anything about its population. Also, other rich nations will be in the same boat before long, making Japan a population prototype.

"Wealth is the best contraceptive," says Nicholas Smith, Japan strategist at CLSA Asia-Pacific Markets, who has long studied the supposed correlation between procreation and economic growth. "There is a well-known correlation between rising per capita GDP and falling fertility."

A dwindling workforce scares off investors such as Jim Rogers, Singapore-based chairman of Rogers Holdings. They say there won't be enough workers to pay off a massive and growing public debt. Smith, on the other hand, is enamored with Japan's "perfect demographics," or its surplus of retirees and women to keep the economy growing in the years ahead. This doesn't conform to the views of most economists. But Japan has all but run out of conventional ways to right an economy still suffering from the crash of the late 1980s. There's little room to boost growth with borrowing, and interest rates are already near zero.

Nor are officials in Tokyo taking obvious steps such as increasing immigration. After World War II, Germany thrived on comparatively liberal immigration policies, laying the foundations for the economic miracle of the 1950s. Today it is the world's second-biggest exporter, while Japan is only fourth. In homogeneous Japan, immigration is a taboo issue, leaving us to mull how it can fare with what it has, demographically speaking. The strategy seems to be morphing into Asia's Switzerland, proving that living standards needn't shrink as societies age. There also are environmental benefits to making do with fewer people. Can our planet really sustain nine billion people by 2050? Imagine the massive leaps in clean-energy technology required to make things even somewhat sustainable.

But for heavily indebted Japan, a low birthrate leads to other problems, including the nation's credit rating. Unable to balance work and family, more are putting off motherhood. That has sociologists delving, awkwardly at times, into Japanese culture both for answers and solutions.

Each year, the Japanese media works itself into a frenzy over condom maker Durex's figures. In 2010, then–Finance Minister Naoto Kan even asked his staff to work shorter days so they could have more time for dates. Let's not overstate things, though. If the correlation between sexual frequency, birthrates, and economic growth is so strong, why isn't Greece, one of the Durex list's top performers, booming?

Japan's supposed libido drought was back in the news in October 2013, with some rather dubious theorizing. An occupational hazard for foreign journalists is traipsing into the woods of "exotic Japan" and getting inexorably lost in its deep forests of stereotypes, fuzzy data, and pimped-up headlines.

Such is the case with the media's renewed obsession with Japanese giving up on sex. This canard emerges every couple of years, but it's snowballing anew thanks to an October 19, 2013, *Observer* headline screaming: "Why Have Young People in Japan Stopped Having Sex?" Its references to dominatrices-turned-sex-counselors, men who get turned on by robots, virtual-reality girlfriends, and the extinction of the Japanese people proved too much for Internet aficionados to resist. Editors, too; the *Observer*'s piece was followed by the *Huffington Post* quoting a documentary filmmaker asserting, dubiously, that "it's a strange thing that can only happen in Japan." The Japanese are really weird, don't you know, and this celibacy bubble imperiling the future must reflect their peculiar culture. Follow-ups are rolling in from the *Washington Post*, *Slate*, *Time*, and all over the Twittersphere.

At the root of Japan's supposed sex drought isn't culture, but economics. This distinction is important because it feeds into Abe's efforts to end Japan's 20-year bout with deflation. I, too, have been seduced at times by such data sets. As far back as 2001, I explored sex drives reports, citing findings that Japanese are the world's least prolific lovers. Such conclusions are quite paradoxical considering the society often seems more oversexed than prudish with its teeming red-light districts, massive porn industry, hard-core manga being read openly on subways, and a thriving love-hotel industry that can't turn over rooms fast enough.

But I've come to doubt sensationalist surveys suggesting young Japanese don't have sex. The real issue is that many avoid traditional, committed relationships out of worries about the future that are far more economic than cultural. If low libido were strictly societal, why do the Czech Republic, Poland, Singapore, South Korea, Spain, and Taiwan have low fertility rates comparable to Japan's? I don't see the global media characterizing them as sexless freak shows spiraling in a direction only contemplated in science fiction.

"This is the typical weird-and-wacky Japan story that overseas editors seem to gobble up and encourage," says Jeff Kingston of Temple University. "Of course Japanese have sex and if the number of love-hotels is any barometer, it seems like many are getting plenty of it. How do all those places stay in business if nobody is doing it?"

To Kingston, the basic premise is flawed. "Japan has a low birthrate and thus it must be a lack of sex," he says. "That's not exactly compelling logic that overlooks all the main factors behind couples' decisions not to have more children."

Part of the problem is cherry-picked data. Take the 2011 survey by the National Institute of Population and Social Security Research on which sex-drought stories are often based. Its finding that 61 percent of unmarried men and 49 percent of women between ages 18 and 24 were not in any kind of romantic relationship is mentioned up high. Rarely cited is this factoid on page 2 of the report: Almost 90 percent of respondents intend to marry someday. And what about international comparisons? A recent Pew study found that 71 percent of unmarried Americans aren't in committed relationships. Also, there can be big cultural and generational differences in the meaning of "single," "dating" and "having sex." And Japan's lack of immigration complicates demographic dynamics considerably.

Japan's low birthrate is about living costs, stress, and confidence. Even after two decades of deflation, prices in Japan for everything from rent to food to entertainment remain among the highest in the world. Economic stagnation and changes in labor laws have restrained wage growth and enabled companies to swap employees into low-paying part-time jobs with few or no benefits. That is excluding more and more Japanese from the lifetime employment system that's long been the cornerstone of Japan Inc., forcing many to work additional jobs. If you leave for work at 6 a.m. and get home close to midnight, including weekends, where is there time for dating?

Stress and worker insecurity is denting confidence. Young Japanese, especially men, don't feel financially secure enough to enter into long-term relationships, never mind getting married or starting families. At the same time, Abe has done little to address the institutionalized sexism that exacerbates Japan's low-birthrate problem. Hardships women face in balancing careers and family encourage many to delay marriage and motherhood. If Japanese felt better about the future, they wouldn't be so reluctant to start building their own.

■ ■ ■

Japan's demographics is indeed worthy of study. How it balances a fast-aging population, a gigantic debt burden, and a negligible birthrate—if it's even possible—will offer insights to officials in Beijing, Berlin, and Washington in the years ahead. But portraying Japanese as sexless

oddballs and looking for clues in their culture does more than dehu-
manize a nation. It misses Japan's pioneering role in one of the biggest
economic challenges of this century as developed nations mature.

Corporate Japan will have to get over its collective sexism. As it
does, women will play a bigger economic role. Retirees are another
potential staffing gold mine, Smith said. More and more of Japan's baby
boomers, born after 1945, are reaching the average retirement age of
about 63. Wage-cost reductions from their departure will kick in this
year and then accelerate. That's especially true of postwar boom industries such as iron, steel, shipbuilding, heavy engineering, and trading.

It's time to rehire many of these aging workers—at lower salaries,
of course. For many, an inescapable consequence of living longer is the
necessity of working longer. That's especially true of anyone whose
retirement loot was wiped out in the events of 2008. Companies can
trim costs while also tapping the intellectual firepower of retirees at a
discount to their previous pay packages. The good news is that companies most likely to enjoy a retirement dividend are in mature industries
that were the driving force behind Japan's meteoric growth after the
1960s. Those are now in need of aggressive restructuring. It may give
an unexpected boost to the economy.

Japan's demographic cushions aren't a cure-all. Without a rapid
increase in worker productivity, the nation will find it harder to
maintain its high living standards. The rise of China and India and
competition from Korea are direct threats to Japan's future. It may not
be all doom and gloom. Yes, Japan is bleeding people. Far from being a
crisis, Mark Clifford, executive director of the Asia Business Council,
thinks it may offer benefits and clues for other nations heading in
Japan's demographic direction. His chapter in McKinsey's 2011 book,
Reimagining Japan (p. 138), was perhaps most intriguing of all, characterizing the nation as an economic laboratory of sorts.

"Japan," wrote the former *South China Morning Post* editor, "is conducting a great experiment. No other significant country has ever seen
its population plummet so fast without disease or war." A Japanese child
born today, he argued,

> over the course of her life, will watch her country complete
> a fascinating two-and-a-half century arc. The journey so far

has taken Japan from a small, isolated nation to an industri-
alized phenom that peaked for a time as the world's second-
largest economy. Now, as China passed Japan in the GDP
league tables, Japan is charting a path that will see it once again
become a small nation on the periphery of a teeming, dynamic
continent. Therein lies Japan's greatest challenge in coming
decades: to ensure that its impending smallness is beautiful.
With the right leadership and the right policies, the country
can succeed.

Those policies include efficiently using its intellectual and physical
capital—its prowess in engineering, manufacturing, environmental sustainability, and supporting research and development. In the age of
China, India, and Indonesia, Japan has become a very expensive property
in a rather cheap neighborhood. Harnessing its internal strengths is the
only way Japan can keep its hard-won high living standards from adjusting downward toward Asia's developing-nation upstarts.

That's easier said than done, of course. It's just as plausible, Clifford
thinks, to picture a "dystopian spiral" amid daunting levels of government debt, scant growth in productivity, and an aversion to immigration that limits the economy's dynamism and the availability of labor to
care for a rapidly aging population—a labor pool that some think will
be falling by half over the likely 85-plus-year life span of that girl born
today.

"To avoid that outcome," Clifford argued,

> Japan must start now with a hardheaded look at how to cope
> with its extraordinary situation. There can be no more denial,
> no more pretending that the demographic ship will some-
> how dramatically alter course. Wise government policies must
> ensue, starting with measures to enhance output in some of
> the nation's least productive sectors, notably services, so that
> the falloff in the workforce does not deprive the nation of the
> resources its living standards require.

In the 1990s, Japan suffered a hollowing out of its industrial sector. High wages, overcapacity, and bloated corporate structures led to
painful downsizing. Factories closed, jobs went overseas, the lifetime

employment that formed the core of Japan's postwar boom lost traction, deflation deepened, rust-belt cities such as Osaka and Shizuoka lost their buzz, homeless shelters swelled, and the interest rates were cut to zero so that banks could remain solvent. The next phase of hollowing out will be of the human kind, as Japan literally runs out of young, able-bodied workers to replace retirees. The key is raising the productivity of today's workers and encouraging them to become more entrepreneurial and risk-oriented.

Yet driving this transformation requires fresh, forward-looking thinking and a strong political will of the kind that Japan hasn't seen in decades. As 2013 drew to a close, there were reasons to worry that, on Abe's watch, Japan's shameful gender gap could get even worse.

In December 2013, the month of Abe's first anniversary in office, I touched base again with Rina Bovrisse on what she made of the prime minister's gender policies. "I see absolutely nothing hopeful about his Womenomics," she lamented. "Abe will only talk, just like with Fukushima, as Japan's gender gap gets worse. Of course, empowering women in Japan, implementing Womenomics, will be harder than convincing dolphin eaters to become vegetarians."

Chapter 3

The
1,000,000,000,000,000
Yen Monster

*When a Debt Market Becomes So Big
It Dominates Everything*

I s Japan's central bank creating the biggest pyramid scheme in world history? It's a valid question as Governor Haruhiko Kuroda endeavors to do what monetary scientists from Milton Friedman to Anna Schwartz to Robert Mundell would surely say is impossible: creating inflation and sending stocks soaring, while also keeping bond yields below 1 percent, or at the very worst, 2 percent. Negligible borrowing costs is the only way a nation with an aging and shrinking population can service such a massive debt without becoming the next Greece or Argentina.

In August 2013, Japan's debt reached a dubious milestone: the 1 *quadrillion* mark, or 1,000,000,000,000,000 yen. That markets hardly noticed is a testament not only to Kuroda's skill as a policy maker, but to his gravitas. It's a balancing act that few could conceivably pull off, and a reminder that Abe chose well when filling the top job at the BOJ.

My favorite Kuroda moment was on a Tokyo-bound flight on March 13, 2011, two days after a gigantic earthquake and tsunami struck northeast Japan. I was in the Philippines when the quake hit and precipitated a nuclear crisis. On the first available flight back, the then-president of the Manila-based Asian Development Bank (ADB) sat near me on an almost-empty Japan Airlines plane. Manila-to-Tokyo flights are rarely made with a single empty seat, but no one likes to fly into a potential Chernobyl, not with tens of thousands in Japan, mostly non-Japanese residents, clamoring for the exits.

"We seem to have the whole plane to ourselves," Kuroda quipped, saying he was returning to Japan to "do what I can to help."

Those words came to mind two years later in March 2013, when Kuroda returned to his homeland to offer help yet again, this time to end deflation. It was a timely reappearance for a respected economist who had spent the previous eight years in Manila working to reduce poverty. It occurred to me then, as now, that this kind of selflessness made Kuroda an inspired choice to end Japan's two decades of deflation.

Long before he settled on Kuroda, Abe made it clear that, in his estimation, incumbent BOJ Governor Shirakawa had been a dismal failure and couldn't vacate his office fast enough. Abe also made it clear that his BOJ pick would open the yen faucet as widely as possible for as long as it took. If Abe were to say we need more liquidity, according to this view, his guy at the central bank would yell "Hai!" and dutifully boost the money flow. That perception created quite a paradox for Kuroda. Markets liked him because he was a steady hand when overseeing foreign-exchange issues at the Finance Ministry from 1999 to 2003.

Kuroda's 2005–2013 stint reducing poverty at the ADB also was intriguing. The whole challenge for the BOJ as it tries to defeat deflation is traction. Its policies had gotten little, and it was imperative that the next governor think outside the box and with a level of creativity that had long eluded Tokyo. A man who had spent the last seven-plus years searching for new and innovative solutions to broaden economic growth, and working with scarce resources, was just what the BOJ needed. Japan's monetary authority needed a fresh eye and toolkit; Abe found it in Manila.

But Kuroda's balancing act is just beginning. So far, he's done a truly supernatural job of increasing inflation expectations while keeping bond yields stable. Kuroda doesn't wear a wizard's hat when he arrives at BOJ headquarters each morning, but once inside I do half wonder if he dons a cloak, waves a magic wand, and concocts mysterious potions.

What is Kuroda's secret? Just how does he bewitch investors into suspending their disbelief and holding onto their government bonds? Janet Yellen over at the Fed would sure love to know as he does battle with the "bond vigilantes," that mysterious cast of characters who protest fiscal or monetary policies they deem dangerous. Kuroda is winning Bondland's obedience with two forms of trickery: (1) what economists call "financial repression"—essentially transferring money via monetary policy from citizens to the government; and (2) outright monetization of public debt.

Kuroda has to be cagey about engaging in either risky strategy so as not to anger Japanese households or attract the ire of credit-rating companies increasingly worried about Tokyo's debt trajectory. The longer Kuroda gets away with this dual-pronged magic trick, the better the chances Abe can pull off his own miraculous feat of deregulating the economy.

What would happen, though, if the bond vigilantes got a peek behind the curtain at what the wizard of Tokyo is really up to, and panicked? Japan would be ground zero for the worst debt meltdown in history. Forget Greece—Japan's debt burden is larger than that of Germany, France, and the United Kingdom combined. The entire world really does have a vested interest in Kuroda keeping the magic alive.

It's hard to exaggerate what an outsized role the bond market plays in Japan's stability. Government bonds are the main financial asset held by banks, companies, pension funds, institutions, the postal-savings system, and individuals—in other words, everyone. A one- or two-percentage-point jump in yields would send shockwaves across all sectors of the economy and export contagion overseas.

The magnitude of Japan's debt burden and the risks inherent in managing it make James Carville's 1992 observation about the United States seem almost quaint by comparison. The Clinton White House adviser said that when he dies he wants to be reincarnated as the bond market so he could come back and scare everyone. Bond vigilantes were indeed circling America's finances at the time. Yet even Carville, whose other famous pronouncement was "It's the economy, stupid," could never have imagined a government being as beholden to bond-holders as Japan's is today. Ten years after Carville's observation, for example, came news that the U.S. Central Intelligence Agency was examining the global implications of Japan's debt-and-deflation quandary. Press reports of the CIA's Japan inquiry emerged days after a prescient October 2, 2002, *New York Times* story exploring whether the United States could one day experience a slump like Japan's.

The most common argument for why Japanese government bonds won't plummet is their uniquely domestic character; well over 90 percent of public IOUs are held in Japan. And because everyone gets hurt if yields surge, there is little incentive for anyone to bid them higher. It seems counterintuitive that on hearing news that Japan now requires 15 zeroes to express its national debt, the Japanese doubled down and bought more rather than reduce their debt exposure. Indeed, what some might label a pyramid scheme, Japanese see as financial security. Yet mutually assured destruction isn't a viable strategy in the long run.

Count hedge fund manager J. Kyle Bass firmly among those betting Kuroda's ultraloose policies are hastening what he sees as Tokyo's inevitable demise. Thirty minutes with the head of Dallas-based Hayman Advisors LP leaves one tempted to buy a farmhouse in the middle of nowhere, pick up a gun or two, prepare for hyperinflation, and brace for a catastrophic meltdown. His claim to fame is making $500 million in 2007 betting against the subprime bonds that undid Wall Street. "In Japan, the situation is more compelling," he said.

Bass offers the following rationale: Any aging country that spends more than half of its central-government revenue on servicing its debt will be hard-pressed to finance itself at current rates as its workforce shrinks, never mind if debt yields surge. Kuroda doubling the monetary base and actively working to produce inflation may only accelerate the reckoning. So might Abe's plans to step up fiscal stimulus efforts at a time when Japan needs to be trimming debt.

"Abe and the BOJ face what I call the 'rational investor paradox,'" Bass says. "If JGB investors begin to believe that Abenomics will be successful, they will rationally sell JGBs to buy foreign bonds or equities." Carl Weinberg of High Frequency Economics in Valhalla, New York, thinks that in the years ahead, credit-rating companies will be accused of "criminal negligence" for not lowering Japan's debt to below investment grade.

The trouble with Japan's debt structure isn't just that you can't price risk properly. It's that it's ultimately unsustainable and there is no plan on the drawing board to address it. Japan has done a remarkable job keeping its pressure-cooker of a bond market from exploding. The clubby nature of the biggest bond market allows policy makers to maintain calm. Someday, though, Japan won't be able to get enough new money into its bond market to support the irrational expectations of investors. When that day comes, Bass says, the financial world will look back and agree that this was most obvious scenario it's ever seen. The lesson for developing nations is: Don't let the bond market dominate all else. And don't create a monster that requires constant feeding and obsessive maintenance that distracts you from building a more prosperous future.

■ ■ ■

The biggest flaw in Abe's revival plan is its inconsistencies. As investors ponder a reflated Japan, they will begin to bid up yields. Each sizable spike is prompting the BOJ to come to the rescue with a few trillion dollars worth of yen here and a few trillion there. With the increasing frequency, speed, and magnitude of these interventions, Kuroda is creating a moral-hazard pattern.

The trouble is this: The more liquidity the BOJ adds to the market, the more it feeds inflation expectations that drive up yields, the more it needs to do to stabilize the market. Picture a factory conveyor belt that speeds up faster and faster, making it harder for workers to keep up. Eventually, the BOJ gets trapped into this pyramid scheme. How does Japan expect bondholders to sit by quietly if inflation increases to 2 percent and beyond? They won't, of course, leaving Japan with rapidly rising debt-servicing costs and investors running for cover as sub-1-percent 10-year bond yields head to 2 or 3 percent. This is the first and biggest inconsistency.

Yes, Japan's financial system is unique, but the idea that Japanese banks, companies, pension funds, universities, endowments, insurance companies, government-run institutions, postal savings system, and individuals (many of whom are elderly and living on a fixed income) won't sell at some point is just fanciful. Unless government tax revenues surge along with bond yields, Abe and Kuroda will have some explaining to do.

Inconsistency 2: thinking you can derive strength from weakness. I'm always amazed by how virtually any Japanese you ask can tell you what the yen/dollar rate is on any given day. Pose the same question to my fellow Americans and you will get many blank stares. Exchange-rate-obsessed Japanese also have an emerging-nation-like view that weakness equals vigor.

Abenomics is basing a Japanese renaissance on the 20 percent drop in the yen since mid-November 2012. It proposes to generate higher consumer prices while thinking inflation-adjusted wages won't fall. The government is forgetting, too, that if companies need to dole out higher pay without an even greater increase in productivity—a very unlikely event—their global competiveness will drop. That's the opposite of what Abe purports to do.

Inconsistency 3: a wealth effect that won't come. Abe's plan is for BOJ largess to lift equity prices, fueling what surrogates call the "confidence effect." Tokyo was slow to realize that Japan's credit system was broken. The problem isn't the supply of yen, but uses for it. Banks are reluctant to lend; companies and households aren't borrowing. The multiplier effect that makes monetary policy so potent is eluding Japan. The missing ingredient is confidence. Until corporate executives and consumers believe the next 10 years will be more prosperous than the last, deflation will deepen. The government must do its job to create incentives to add jobs and raise incomes.

For a bunch of economists charged with boosting confidence, for example, BOJ staffers sure did seem gloomy as 2013 was drawing to close. On the surface, all was well with the BOJ's 2 percent inflation target for 2014 or 2015 when board members met on October

31, 2013. But the minutes of that meeting showed unmistakable signs of doubt among those who know more than we do about the breadth and mechanics of the world's most audacious monetary experiment. Three members dissented from the bank's preferred view. The gist of the meeting: Ending deflation is harder than the central bank expected.

Takehiro Sato wanted to add a line to the final statement declaring that consumer prices "are somewhat tilted to the downside" rather than that risks were "being largely balanced." Takahide Kiuchi proposed making the BOJ's 2 percent target more flexible. Sayuri Shirai wanted to highlight upside and downside risks to economic activity and price changes, which seems like code for *what happens with inflation is really anyone's guess.*

Why isn't the BOJ getting more traction? Blame "Scroogenomics," which is turning into a headwind that Abe probably didn't anticipate while devising his program to revitalize Japan Inc. The whole thrust of the first two waves of "Abenomics" was for massive monetary and fiscal stimulus to drive asset prices higher and the yen lower to boost corporate profits enough so that executives would raise wages. From there, as consumers spent more and a virtuous cycle of even greater corporate profits created vast amounts of new wealth, Abe would be able to engineer structural reforms to produce a genuine economic boom. But that plan is slamming into stingy corporate executives.

A Nikkei survey of chief financial officers from 241 listed major companies released on November 25 told the story. Companies were flush with cash, but reluctant to share it with workers. Executives are plenty keen on capital spending and research and development, but not on upping salaries. Publicly traded companies that end the fiscal year in March, Nikkei said, had record combined cash reserves of about $690 billion.

The bad news: Only 7 percent of respondents said they may use some of these reserves to raise salaries. "On the whole, however, major companies remain cautious about upping wages," Nikkei said. And for that, Abe must bear some of the blame, as roughly half of CFOs believe his government's green light to raise consumption taxes from 5 percent to 8 percent in April will hurt bottom lines.

The mention of Scroogenomics in the accompanying Nikkei article was partly a nod to University of Minnesota economist Joel Waldfogel's book titled thus, but also to the timing of Abe's first term in office. The day after Christmas, December 26, marked the one-year mark for Abe's term as prime minister and his attempt to end deflation. And, well, other than importing more inflation via energy imports—in other words, bad inflation—he had little to show for the effort. The problem, of course, is the very confidence BOJ officials want to generate. No matter how many times Governor Kuroda promises investors that inflation is on the way, he's talking to the wrong audience. It's the Scrooges in corporate boardrooms who need convincing, not to mention his own BOJ staffers.

Economist Richard Katz, editor-in-chief of the New York–based *Oriental Economist Report*, doubts rising equities matter much from a confidence standpoint in Japan in the long run. Much of the support for shares is speculative; it's not that Japanese companies are being more responsive to shareholder gripes. And it's largely an overseas-investor phenomenon. Too few Japanese own stocks, and for those who do, holdings tend to be too small to drive consumer spending. About 40 percent of stocks are owned by the richest 20 percent of the population; two-thirds of stocks are owned by people over age 60.

"The alleged wealth effect from the stock market rally is more of an advertising slogan from the PR firm of 'Abenomics Happy Talk' than a serious economic analysis," Katz said.

Inconsistency 4: exporting into a weak world economy. On May 29, 2013, Kuroda gave a timely speech about the world still struggling to shake off the effects of the 2008 crisis. Japan can drive the yen down all it wants, but we live in a "G-Zero" era that Ian Bremmer, president of Eurasia Group in New York, described in his 2012 book, *Every Nation for Itself*. It's one devoid of growth engines.

America's recovery is tepid, at best. Chinese growth is heading lower for the next several years. Europe's crisis is always just one credit downgrade away from resuming. To whom does Abe think Japan will be selling freighters full of goods? Also, Japan is importing more and more raw materials to meet energy needs with a falling currency. Even before Abenomics, Japan had little clout in global commodity markets. China is a prime maker; Japan is a taker.

Inconsistency 5: trading partners won't stay quiet. Nations like Korea are becoming more vocal about what they see as beggar-thy-neighbor policies in Tokyo. The outcry may increase as Asian growth slows and leaders struggle to support export industries.

■ ■ ■

Kuroda is indeed finding himself on a financial treadmill. The violent swings in government yields in May and June 2013 prompted him to crush the skeptics with overwhelming monetary force. The question is whether he can continue to up the ante. For now, at least, Kuroda's policies are keeping the peace in Bondland. That in turn is accelerating a huge redistribution of wealth within society from creditors (the people) to debtors (Japan's Ministry of Finance). That's pushing inflation-adjusted interest rates even further into negative territory and giving the government cheaper financing.

Debt monetization is clearly a part of the mix. Again, Kuroda can't really admit that the central bank has morphed into the Ministry of Finance's ATM. It's a fact, though, that the BOJ is now the dominant buyer of government debt at auction (more than 70 percent, in some cases) and a steadily growing one, too. What the BOJ does with much of that debt might never be known. Stick it in a file cabinet? Burn it? Doing so would be to take a page from Korekiyo Takahashi, the 1930s finance minister whose unconventional policies earned him a reputation as Japan's answer to John Maynard Keynes. Abe says Takahashi's exploits "emboldened" him to get radical. The unanswered question, of course, is just *how* radical?

If only Japan could get radical on another debt front: the nation's $1.2 trillion of currency reserves. Japan, America's closest ally in Asia, has long been an enthusiastic buyer of dollars. Yet Japan is at the center of the financial arms race that has swept Asia since the 1997 crisis. The stockpiling of dollars began in earnest to safeguard nations from turmoil in markets, but has taken on an unproductive life of its own. In December 1997, Japan owned $300 billion in reserves, one quarter of what it does today. This buildup has altered the financial landscape in two ways: (1) Asia is essentially America's banker, with China and Japan having the most at stake, and (2) Asia now has more cushions against market unrest than it knows what to do with.

The first makes Asia vulnerable to political shenanigans in Washington. In 1971, Nixon-era Treasury Secretary John Connally

famously observed that "it's our currency, but it's your problem."
Connally couldn't have foreseen how right he would be 40-plus years
on as Asia sits on $7 trillion in foreign reserve currency. Take Capitol
Hill's propensity for shooting itself—and markets—in the foot. It was a
pedestrian and pointless squabble over the debt ceiling that prompted
Standard & Poor's to yank the U.S. AAA credit rating in August 2011.
In the age of the Tea Party, where lawmakers think threatening to
default on America's debt is a reasonable bargaining chip, Japan, and
Asia in general, needs to stop considering huge reserve holdings a
financial strength. They are a trap that complicates economic policy
making. It's time the region devised an escape.

Why? The United States doesn't deserve Asia's money, not with
half of its government in financial jihad mode, and damn the global
consequences. The biggest economy has long taken its reserve-cur-
rency status for granted, but the events of recent days raise Washington's
hubris to entirely new levels. Chinese President Xi didn't mention
Ted Cruz, John Boehner, or the Tea Party in October 2013 when he
urged major developed economies to adopt responsible policies that
avoid negative spillover. He didn't have to. Their shutdown of the U.S.
government and the specter of U.S. default were written between the
lines in bold type. The United States is playing with fire here in ways it
might not recover from.

American politicians should be particularly worried about a conversation Xi had in October 2013 in Jakarta with Indonesian President
Susilo Bambang Yudhoyono. Xi proposed creating a regional bank to
invest in infrastructure in Southeast Asia and pledged funding from
China. Asia is also gradually building a neighborhood International
Monetary Fund. Where will all this cash come from? From Asia's
reserves, much of it currently in dollars.

Asians aren't panicking just yet. Many here think U.S. lawmakers aren't crazy enough to default on their nation's debt, no matter
how much they despise President Barack Obama's policies. They will
bicker, close the government, and embarrass the United States on the
world stage by forcing Obama to cancel visits to Asia in October 2013.
In general, America's banker, Asia, is betting bond guru Bill Gross of
Pacific Investment Management Co. is right that the risk of the United
States reneging on its debt is zero.

Is this a rational view? I'm not so sure. It's a bit surreal being an American journalist abroad these days as the tables get turned at interviews. After a few questions from me, the interviewee will inevitably ask some variation of: "What, oh, *what* is going on in Washington?" What disturbs officials in Asia the most is that this battle is over providing health care to Americans. How, they ask, could half your government take a stand against what other developed nations view as a basic human right?

The very nature of this question is what bothers me. This battle really is a political jihad, and congressional Republicans may very well think a default is a reasonable price to pay for stopping the Affordable Care Act, which they view as the end of Western civilization. Doing that would surely accelerate the end of the dollar's linchpin role in global commerce. But just as it takes a village to get big, history-making things done, Cruz and his friends in Congress may decide that it will take a crisis to get their way.

Another dangerous assumption: Washington's complacency about the primacy of its debt. Asia forgave Congress that first downgrade in 2011, prompted by Capitol Hill's last debt ceiling skirmish. Don't expect the region's central banks to look kindly on Standard & Poor's knocking the United States down another peg or Moody's Investors Service yanking away its Aaa rating.

While Congress takes Asia's continued support for granted partly out of smugness, it also reflects the Hobson's choice confronting reserve managers, meaning they have no real choice. China holds $1,000 of U.S. Treasuries for each of its 1.3 billion people. If traders sensed that China was selling large blocks of them, markets would plunge, resulting in huge state losses and less growth as surging bond yields slammed American consumers. And really, what other assets could the Chinese—or Japanese, for that matter—readily buy in such incredibly large amounts in a moment? So, to avoid the biggest foreign-exchange trade in history, central banks stay in dollars.

This pyramid-scheme-like arrangement is a bit Japan-like and explains why U.S. government bonds are rallying. Think about the twisted logic of a giant flight-to-safety trade based on fears that the very country to which you are rushing may soon default. You won't find that dynamic explained in Economics 101 textbooks. But the more the United States plays with fire with its Aaa rating, the more Asia will find an alternative. Researcher Zhang Monan at the National Development and Reform Commission surely spoke for many in Beijing in October when he said China "must" change the situation of holding "too much" U.S. debt. The Federal Reserve's easing program is one thing. It's quite another for lawmakers to hold U.S. finances hostage to score cheap political points in a farce that's even drawn comments from Lady Gaga on Twitter.

Xi's timing in proposing a regional bank can't be a coincidence. Beijing is also involved in efforts to build another institution that might challenge the IMF and World Bank among the BRICS nations (Brazil, Russia, India, China, and South Africa). Filling its vaults will come at the dollar's expense. Tea Party supporters should consider that they are helping enhance China's soft power around the world. Although China's currency reserve managers may have lost some sleep in late 2013, its leaders gained in global stature as they came across as serious and moderate in the face of the Washington frat-house spectacle. It's amazing to watch my U.S. tax dollars hard at work making Communists look like capitalist heroes.

Sure, this arrangement gives Asia some leverage over the U.S. government, as Japan demonstrated first. Bond traders still buzz about that June day in 1997 when Japanese Prime Minister Hashimoto made a startling admission. "Actually," he told a crowd at New York's Columbia University, "several times in the past, we have been tempted to sell large lots of U.S. Treasuries." One of those occasions, Hashimoto said, was during Japan's negotiations with the United States over auto sales. Or when "the exchange rate has suffered extreme movements and the American people have done little but look at domestic issues." Hashimoto summed things up this way: "We were very tempted on these occasions. However, in terms of fund management, we did not take the most advantageous road."

It's no coincidence that when Hillary Clinton made her maiden trip to Beijing as U.S. secretary of state in February 2009, she shelved human-rights issues in favor of debt. Her talking points focused on how the interest of the United States and China, the Group of Two, are "so intertwined" that "it would not be in China's interest" if America couldn't finance deficit spending to stimulate its stalled economy. Clinton may have said it best in a 2009 comment contained in cables released by WikiLeaks.org. To then-Australian Prime Minister Kevin Rudd, Clinton said: "How do you deal toughly with your banker?"

The United States might want to take a page from Japan and rethink its debt structure. What the Obama administration should ask is if it still makes sense for any major economy such as the United States to export more than 50 percent of its IOUs. Isn't there merit to countries building bigger domestic customer bases for their debt? Shouldn't they be more, well, Japanese?

This mere suggestion will strike the free-market fundamentalists as blasphemous, and it wouldn't be easy to do, anyway. Reversing financial globalization "would be akin to persuading a billion people not to use Facebook," says IMF head Christine Lagarde. Yet there are obvious ways in which nations, including the United States, might profit from a more Japan-style debt arrangement. In his 2012 book, *The New Depression*, economist Richard Duncan builds a compelling case for another Franklin D. Roosevelt–like New Deal to restore U.S. growth, strengthen competitiveness, and achieve energy independence. It could be paid for by tapping the vast amounts of private-sector cash sitting on corporate balance sheets. If executives sensed they were investing in future economic growth and profit potential, they might pull money out of tax havens and buy more Treasuries.

That's a longer-term discussion, of course. At the moment, the United States maintains considerable leverage. Were Tokyo to announce big Treasury sales, markets would quake, the yen would surge, and Tokyo's debt managers would have to explain the billions of dollars they just lost in the chaos. Finance Minister Taro Aso would both cannibalize Japan's economic prospects and find himself squarely in the hot seat when called before parliament.

The same goes for China, by far America's top financier with more than $1.3 trillion in dollar holdings. Washington's banker in chief, Chinese President Xi, is charged with overhauling China's $8.3 trillion economy. The balancing act facing Xi and Premier Li essentially calls for them to turn the entire economy upside-down on a scale that's never been tried before. Every economist understands why China must move beyond sweatshops and smokestacks to create jobs based more on ideas and innovation. The problem is a transition period that will be as destabilizing as it is unpredictable.

The only way to maintain stability is maintaining a reasonable amount of growth, which in China's case means at least 7 percent. The Communist Party's social contract with its 1.3 billion people is simple: We raise your living standards and you don't head to Tiananmen Square with protest banners or take to the Internet with grievances. For China, than means keeping the export engine alive and well, and padding incomes for as long as possible. That means China can no more afford a jump in U.S. yields that would unnerve the American consumer than could Japan. China would cannibalize its economic prospects by curtailing its U.S. debt purchases.

"While they're sure to make some loud noises about it, at the end of the day, they understand they have no option but to accept the hand they're given," says Leland Miller, president of China Beige Book International, a New York–based firm that does a quarterly survey of thousands of businesses across the most populous nation.

Japan faces a similar catch-22. Given its fiscal constraints, bringing a few hundred billion dollars back to Japan here and there could be used for infrastructure, education, research and development on cleaner energy, or any other vital investments in the future. But a key pillar of Abe's plan to end deflation is a weaker yen, and the policy has already reaped some benefits for corporate Japan as even down-and-out Sony Corp. is eking out some profits. The yen would surge if markets got wind Japan was dumping dollars.

Smaller economies might be able to pull that off. There would be a clear first-mover advantage for, say, South Korea (with $51 billion in Treasuries), the Philippines ($39 billion), or Malaysia ($12 billion). Each could try to sell dollars on the sly, but not bigger dollar holders in our hyperconnected, 24/7-news-cycle world; news of sizable dollar sales by, say, China or Japan would devastate world markets and drive up interest rates.

Still, Japan and the rest of Asia should stop feeding their dollar addiction and consider ways to bring more of those funds home. Never before has the world seen a greater misallocation of vast resources. And it's pure short-termism. Loading up on Treasuries helps Asia's exporters by holding down local currencies, but it causes economic control problems. When central banks buy dollars, they need to sell local currency, increasing its availability and boosting the money supply. So they sell bonds to mop up excess money. It's an imprecise science made even more complicated by the Fed's quantitative-easing policies.

Asia has mulled ways to shield itself from the kinds of shenanigans in Washington of which Connally warned before. The first serious one was a 1997–1998 effort to create an Asian monetary fund, a kind of regional IMF. When Thailand, Indonesia, and Korea turned to the IMF for about $100 billion of bailout packages, the payouts came with myriad ill-conceived and overbearing demands for austerity on the part of governments that made the crisis worse. Governments were expected to cut spending to reduce budget deficits, raise interest rates to support currencies, and let weak banks and companies fail. It was akin to yelling "Fire!" in a crowded theater.

The conditions that the IMF imposed on Asia had the fingerprints of Robert Rubin, Lawrence Summers, and Timothy Geithner, then–assistant secretary for international affairs. Kuroda was among those urging the creation of Asia's own bailout fund that would offer embattled economies breathing room with fewer strings attached. U.S. officials were apoplectic. They worried Asia's monetary fund would eclipse the IMF's influence and, by extension, America's say in how Asia retooled economies, which could prove dangerous.

In May 2011, the Association of Southeast Asian Nations, together with Japan, China, and South Korea, agreed on terms for the so-called Chiang Mai Initiative to pool funds to aid economies in times of trouble. Initially, its size was $120 billion. In 2012, it was doubled to $249 billion. Part of the impetus was irritation over America's generous Wall Street bailouts in 2008 and Europe's giant aid packages in 2012. It didn't escape Asian policy makers that the U.S. Treasury employed just about every tactic it refused to let Asia employ in the late 1990s, including bailing out banks. Nor did Asians miss how the IMF coddled Europe with generous amounts of aid and patience. The end justifies the means, though. It's wise for Asia to bring more of its savings back to the region.

One way Japan could do that is to start a sovereign wealth fund that could make far more productive use of state wealth. The demands that an aging population will place on the national budget are reason enough to get a better return on investment than low-yielding U.S. debt. Prudent sovereign-wealth-fund investments that generate steady returns also would negate the need for growth-slamming consumption and payroll taxes.

The temptation, of course, would be to use such a fund domestically to prop up stocks in times of turmoil, so-called *price-keeping operations*. Tokyo used that strategy in the early 1990s after the collapse of its bubble economy. Many speculated it employed similar measures during the banking crisis of the early 2000s. All this would prove counterproductive if sovereign-wealth managers saw their role as propping up equities. To avoid that, strict codes of conduct would need to be devised.

Perhaps the best reason for Asia to kick the currency-reserves habit is to escape another: an obsession with weak exchange rates. Here, Japan is a cautionary tale for a region that exerts an exorbitant amount of time, energy, and resources supporting exporters. Officials in Tokyo would be wise to consider something that Paul O'Neill said more than a decade ago. U.S. President George W. Bush's first Treasury secretary angered exporters when he said good chief executive officers don't live and die by exchange rates—they innovate around them. O'Neill, who had previously run aluminum giant Alcoa Inc. for 13 years, said the best CEOs adapt and move on.

That, after all, has been the experience of modern Germany. Japan's failure to understand O'Neil's point and embrace it more than 20 years after its asset bubble burst is a failure from which other economies can learn. Japan's obsession with a weaker yen is playing anew as Abe attempts to end deflation once and for all. Yet Tokyo's currency fetish holds the economy back in the long run. It's a short-term Band Aid, not a long-term cure for what ails the $6 trillion economy. The inordinate amount of time and energy Japan spends guiding the currency also tarnishes its capitalist credentials and has world markets fretting about a return to the so-called currency wars.

It's also a key reason Japan is sliding on competiveness league tables around the globe. Carmakers and electronics exporters should spend more time streamlining their business and focusing on research and development and less on blaming exchange rates. The consistent search for ever-more corporate welfare hasn't served Japan well. Exchange rates and monetary policy are important levers, but they shouldn't be used to delay fiscal or corporate reforms. It's another example of how Tokyo is still treating the symptoms of its malaise rather than the underlying disease. It's a lesson economies the world over should heed: If you rely too much on exchange rates as a growth strategy, you are doing more to hide your weaknesses than fix them.

■ ■ ■

What is a strong currency, other than a sign of confidence in your economy? Capital flows brought on by rising exchange rates boost equities and lower bond yields, giving companies more latitude to raise funds and benefiting Asia's rising middle-class. Yet even highly developed Japan is stuck in the emerging-nation mind-set that no good can come of a rising currency.

Japan raised currency manipulation to an art form in the 1990s and 2000s. In fact, those efforts even produced a bona fide financial celebrity in the form of Eisuke Sakakibara, a former Ministry of Finance (MOF) official (1997–1999), known as "Mr. Yen." With a snap of his fingers, Sakakibara could scare currency traders into driving the yen lower. Those snaps were backed up by the most sophisticated currency-invention apparatus world markets had ever seen. The overwhelming force the MOF would bring to bear left markets positively traumatized. MOF officials would continue honing that skill for many years to come.

Yet little attention is paid to how this yen obsession made Japan's malaise worse. In the years immediately following 1989, the top tick of Japan's bubble economy, bold action was needed to rid banks of bad loans and encourage deadbeat companies to restructure and sell off unprofitable businesses and increase productivity to raise Japan's competitive game. Instead, the government enabled banks and companies to muddle along with what amounted to massive corporate subsidies.

Take the events of 2003, when Tokyo deployed a record 20.4 trillion yen to cap the yen. In the first three months of 2004, it spent another 14.8 trillion yen. In a 15-month period, Japan poured roughly the annual GDP of Taiwan into currency markets to get its way. Those efforts were a huge boon to giant exporters like Toyota Motor Corp., Honda Motor Co., and Nissan Motor Co. Aggressive yen intervention lowered the cost of Toyota pickups, Honda sport-utility vehicles, and

Nissan sedans in key foreign markets like the United States, boosted companies' research and development efforts, and pumped up profits as they were repatriated back to Japan.

This all-gain-no-pain exercise is still playing out nine years later. Kuroda's first act as central bank governor was reminding traders who's boss with an unprecedented yen onslaught. By doubling the money base and keeping the bond market imbibed with steady shots of liquidity, Kuroda sent the yen spiraling lower and Japan Inc.'s spirits soaring in the opposite direction.

The smile on Kazuo Hirai's face two months later showed why the yen's drop below 100-to-the-dollar is as much a curse for Japan as a blessing. By mid-May 2013, the Sony chief executive officer was mugging for the camera as his beleaguered giant produced its first profit in years—43 billion yen for the fiscal year ended March 31, 2013. Yet how an executive pulls off an impressive feat can be just as important as the achievement itself. No, the company that once redefined consumer electronics with the transistor radio and the Walkman didn't suddenly dream up a new gadget better than Apple Inc.'s iPhone, iPad, or iPod. Nor had Sony raised productivity, halted dangerous infighting between departments, or cut costs and staff to compete in an increasingly dynamic marketplace. All Sony did was sit back and enjoy the benefits of the yen's 20 percent plunge since November 2012—and waste time.

Just when you thought Sony couldn't be any more distracted, the company comes up with the "SmartWig." Just because your gizmo designers make a hairpiece that aims to help its wearer navigate roads, check blood pressure, flip through slides in a presentation, or perhaps even take photos doesn't mean a company should admit it, never mind seek a U.S. patent. I can see the marketing slogan now: "The high-tech wig that will make you wish you were bald!"

If this is just a ruse for some bored Sony staffers to win an Ig Nobel Prize, then fine. This American parody of the Nobel Prizes, which honors 10 odd and trivial advances annually that do more to inspire laughter than serve humankind, is quite a phenomenon in Japan. Winners, like the Japanese researchers honored this year for using mice to study how opera affects heart-transplant patients, often become local celebrities.

But Sony seems too serious for comfort about its high-tech toupee. While Sony hasn't decided whether to commercialize this new technology, the publicity surrounding patent applications is often a trial balloon to see what the marketplace thinks. Analysts didn't miss a beat, instantly framing the wig as Sony's less-than-impressive answer to its competitors' wearable-technology products—from Google's eyeglasses, to Samsung's smart watches, to Apple's, well, everything.

This is no time for Sony to be dropping hints about a product that inspires only eye-rolling. The mockery is but the latest reminder that Hirai may have been a bad choice to restore Sony to relevance. It's easy to forget there was elation when Hirai replaced Howard Stringer in April 2012. Whereas Stringer, Sony's first non-Japanese leader, was a businessman brought in to trim fat and shake up Sony's insular culture, Hirai was a gadget man: a bona fide star in the tech community.

The real problem isn't Hirai. It's that Sony died years ago. The company goes through the motions and churns out new music players, flat-screen televisions, smartphones, and video-game players, but who cares? With each ho-hum product, Sony makes us nostalgic for the powerhouse that changed the world with the Walkman. It's been 13 years since Steve Jobs ushered in a new revolution with Apple's iPod, and Sony still hasn't come out with a globally viable competitor, never mind a rival to the iPhone or iPad. The remarkable thing is that Sony has what Apple sorely lacks: vast libraries of content, both music and films. And still Sony let Samsung, too, steal away its franchise. Its credit rating is spiraling toward junk.

What Sony and many investors don't get is that it's no longer an electronics company. Hedge fund manager Daniel Loeb of New York–based Third Point somehow missed that fact in May when he called on Sony to dump large chunks of its entertainment business and focus on electronics. Sony should be doing the opposite. It is to electronics what Microsoft is to the computer industry: a pulseless shell of its once-dynamic self.

All this explains why word of the SmartWig is such a buzz killer, not to mention potentially creepy. Japanese police are busy enough now chasing middle-age men sneaking naughty photos of schoolgirls. (Yeah, a hairpiece camera will *really* help that effort.) The bigger issue is what this says about Sony's mind-set. Sony needs to wow us all over again—to shock the world with a game-changer that has the folks at Apple, Samsung, and *Wired* magazine huddled around TVs (not Sony's, of course) taking in breathless news reports about its next revolutionary idea. Maybe I'm splitting hairs, but all SmartWig may do is win an Ig Nobel.

Kuroda's handiwork is taking the onus off Hirai and the rest of Japan Inc. to claw their way back through innovation and improved efficiency. Sony is emblematic of why Ezra Vogel's "Japan as Number One" argument in 1979 didn't work out so well. Akio Morita and Masaru Ibuka founded it amid the rubble of 1946. Their fabled success was a cornerstone of Japan's post–World War II resurgence. What many Americans feel about Henry Ford or Steve Jobs, Japanese think of the fathers of Sony. Morita's 1986 autobiography, *Made in Japan*, was a best-seller, as was the 1991 book he co-authored with politician Shintaro Ishihara, *The Japan That Can Say No*.

Then Sony, much like the national economy, grew complacent and lost its way. Moving from the rapid expansion and ballooning profits to a less-stellar growth environment proved difficult. After Japan's 1980s asset bubble burst, the once-formidable Sony found itself bloated, sitting on too much debt and devoid of the creative spirit that once revolutionized entire industries. Sony is now a microcosm of Japan's present—embattled on all sides by rising, nimble, and low-cost rivals.

Now that Abe and Kuroda are easing Sony's pain with a weaker yen, will Hirai push ahead to streamline his company and stop rivals like Korea's Samsung Electronics Co. from stealing its franchise? Or will Sony, Sharp Corp., and Nissan see a weaker yen as an all-clear sign to throttle back and stop reinventing themselves? Only time will tell, but a look at Japan's history these last 20 years doesn't offer much optimism.

■ ■ ■

A weak yen has other drawbacks, too. One is Japan's fast-growing need for energy with all but a small handful of the 54 nuclear reactors offline since the March 2011 earthquake and radiation crisis in Fukushima. That means resource-starved Japan has to buy more and more oil, coal, and gas from overseas. Abe's travel itinerary tells the story. An increasing number of his overseas trips are to energy-rich nations. The upshot is that Japan is beginning to have some inflation about which to boast, but it's the bad kind. That will undermine Abenomics, as higher energy costs are passed on to consumers. If the government saw fit to subsidize households and business, Japan's fiscal trajectory would grow even uglier.

Geopolitics is another flashpoint. Japanese officials work the phones to keep other Group of Seven members from publicly rebuking its yen policies. The pitch is, if you want our economy to become a growth engine in the long run, a lower yen is the price in the short run. But we no longer live in a G-7 world, but a Group of 20 world. Key G-20 powers, China included, won't sit idly by as wealthy Japan devalues its way to greater prosperity. As China's restructuring efforts slam GDP, officials in Beijing may devalue, too, taking political cover in Abe's own efforts.

Developing Asia must avoid Japan's fate. What officials in Tokyo see as savvy economic planning and crisis management, their peers around the region should see for what they really are: delaying tactics. A key failure of Abenomics so far is failing to inspire corporate executives to invest, expand, and fatten paychecks in a way that prompts households to save less and spend more. The evidence so far suggests that the weak yen has been a boon for corporate profits, but corporate executives aren't returning the favor. Getting companies to share profits by upping wages and boosting research-and-development budgets is a cornerstone of Abe's strategy. He's going to have to work harder and faster to spark that virtuous cycle—Asia, too.

The volatility seen in Asia in 2013 is a stark reminder that the region has come a long way from 1997, but not far enough. The speed with which investors lurched from the bullishness of Asia to negativity should be a wake-up call. Analysts were quick to explore whether Asia was on the verge of another financial meltdown, especially amid the uncertain fallout of the Fed ending its quantitative-easing program. But rather than 1997, it may make more sense to set our clocks back to 1994.

The year 1997 lives in infamy, of course: currencies in free fall; current-account deficits exploding; central banks scrambling to calm nerves; IMF officials parachuting in. But another 1997-like crisis is highly unlikely because exchange rates are more flexible, foreign-currency debt is lower, banks are healthier, countries are sitting on trillions of dollars of reserves, and economies are far more transparent. The differences between 1997 and today trump the similarities.

The same can't be said of 1994, the last time the Fed reminded the world its monetary policy is decided in Washington, not Bangkok, Jakarta, or Seoul. It also demonstrated how countries maintaining giant bond markets can experience control problems when markets spiral into turmoil. That was the year when Fed Chairman Greenspan began doubling benchmark interest rates over 12 months, causing hundreds of billions of dollars of bond-market losses and helping set 1997 in motion. The dollar's post-1994 rally made currency pegs impossible to maintain, leading to devastating devaluations across Asia.

The real problem was hubris. All that hot money coursing Asia's way in the 1990s made rapid growth too easy. Policy makers were too busy signing foreign direct investment deals, attending ribbon-cutting ceremonies for factories and flashy skyscrapers, and congratulating themselves for surging stocks to do their real jobs. Financial systems went neglected, unproductive investments accumulated, and cronyism ran wild.

Yet, in the years leading up to 2013, a different kind of smugness afflicted Asia. Governments believed their own press that they had decoupled from the West; how they nimbly steered around the 2008 global crash; how bankers abandoned New York and London for Hong Kong and Singapore; how Asian debt became a safe haven from turmoil in Europe; of the wonders of being in China's backyard as 1.3 billion mainlanders grow richer and drive Asian growth to new heights.

That's not to say Asia doesn't deserve a big pat on the back for its post-1997 reform efforts. But rapid growth and an impressive job surviving the global meltdown reanimated a hubris that Asia needs to own and analyze. The price of this cockiness is mounting as currencies in Indonesia, Thailand, and elsewhere suddenly seem toxic to investors. India is in chaos, at a time when China's growth trajectory is more uncertain than it has been in 15 years.

First up, we need a serious reality check on the myth of Asia decoupling from the West. Asia proved it can live without American and European consumers for four or five years, but thriving beyond that means creating more buoyant and self-supportive domestic economies. Also, if you are going to hitch your fortunes to another economy—China—it's best if it's not a developing one whose growth model is running out of steam. The test now, as it was in 1994, is what Asia does to modernize economies.

Examples of complacency abound. In Indonesia, President Susilo Bambang Yudhoyono forgot political stability only goes so far if corruption and inefficiency remain rampant. In Thailand, Prime Minister Yingluck Shinawatra was too busy tweaking the constitution to notice a potentially disastrous bubble in household debt. In the Philippines, President Benigno Aquino forgot that 7 percent growth only matters if you create lots of jobs. In Malaysia, Prime Minister Najib Razak has been too busy celebrating his recent election victory to tend to a current account swinging toward deficit.

"While the United States has been given a free pass on the twin deficit issue, emerging-market countries will not be so lucky," said Simon Grose-Hodge, head of investment strategy for South Asia at LGT Group in Singapore.

Take India, which has been too busy believing its own spin and relishing its status as a BRIC economy to notice the crisis brewing within its borders. Sure, the other BRIC members have their share of challenges, but none more serious than the second-most-populous nation. There was great excitement that respected economist Raghuram Rajan was tapped to helm the Reserve Bank of India in September. But the nation's problems are largely beyond Rajan's control. The central bank can't save a government that is as bereft of ideas and energy as it is corrupt and inefficient. Yet Rajan is already resorting to the Japan-like strategy of intervening more and more in the bond market to soothe investors. As he joins Kuroda on the debt treadmill, Rajan will have to be careful not to get stuck there.

Among the reasons it's not 1997 all over again is Japan. An underappreciated accelerator of Asia's meltdown is that Japan's then-shaky banking system held about $100 billion of loans to the five Asian economies hardest hit in 1997. When Japanese bankers pulled the plug, the crisis reached a fever pitch. Today, Japan Inc. is healthier than it was when Yamaichi imploded, the government is shoring up the economy, and the central bank stands ready to add new liquidity as the Fed's tapering process unfolds. China, meanwhile, will pull out all the stops to keep growth above 7 percent. As the United States ends its quantitative easing and credit markets tighten, cash-rich China may act to fill the void as a way of upping its regional prestige and power.

Yet as markets crack anew, Asia should remember the years it squandered between 1994 and 1997. Asia also must rethink the last few years, a period during which it should have been reducing vulnerabilities and avoiding the urge to hide its cracks, vulnerabilities, and tracks with opaque debt markets—not enjoying its headlines. This is something Japan did for way too long.

■ ■ ■

Developing Asia is not without its lessons for Japan, Europe, and even the United States. Observing Greece slide into chaos from 6,000 miles away has been painful and oddly familiar. This region, after all, was the last to experience what Europe is suffering through. Asia's crash toppled leaders, touched off riots, set back living standards a decade or more, and tarnished the IMF's reputation. Expect similar machinations if Europe's grand monetary experiment cracks.

Asia and Europe are half a world apart and it is true that the differences can be far greater than the similarities. Indonesia, Korea, Malaysia, and Thailand were much less developed 15 years ago than their euro-zone counterparts are today. China had yet to emerge as a dominant manufacturing economy. The United States was in a better position to offer international assistance than it is today. With that in mind, there are five lessons Europe might learn from Asia.

First, default may be unavoidable. Once Europe's crisis returns, bailouts will ultimately prove futile. The Greek public has been very consistent about one thing: the belief that it bears no responsibility for all the debt its leaders took on over the last decade. If that doesn't provide the backdrop for debt repudiation, what does?

As Greece runs through the funds its European neighbors throw at it and the bond market becomes the tail wagging the proverbial dog, other dominoes will fall. We saw that in Asia after Thailand devalued the baht in July 1997. Indonesia swore up and down it wouldn't get dragged into Thailand's mess—until it was. Korea assured the world it would avoid an IMF aid package—until it couldn't. The United States and Japan are near recession. As China's rise continues to squeeze wages in uncompetitive and highly indebted Europe, bond markets could turn hostile very quickly and push France and Italy toward the cliff's edge.

Second, recovery comes faster once debts are purged. Goldman Sachs's financial creativity helped Greece fudge its way into the common currency, leaving the government in Athens with a credibility gap. When it says the country can close its budget deficit with stopgap measures, traders are right to roll their eyes and policy makers are correct in canceling their vacation plans for 2014.

In December 1997, after Korea caved in and sought a $57 billion IMF bailout, it acted quickly to let weak companies fail, closed insolvent banks, clamped down on tax cheats, and came clean about the magnitude of its debts. Greece will have to continue restructuring its debt, and the fallout from this will increase pressure on Portugal, Spain, and Italy. If Greece had acted a year ago, markets might not have had to spend so much time and energy worrying about how and when a default will arrive. "Asia's crisis showed that the quicker you deal with the root of the problem, however painful that may be, the quicker you are likely to recover from it," said Grose-Hodge of LGT Group. "Europe could do worse than to heed that lesson."

Third, don't forget structural reforms. In all the obsessing over debt, European leaders are taking their eyes off the need to retool in a world increasingly influenced by China. Fiscal responsibility is important, of course, but so is altering policies to make economies more nimble, competitive, and conducive to entrepreneurs who create jobs.

In the years following its crisis, Asia worked to open service sectors to competition. It also cut red tape and took steps to limit cronyism. Asia still is home to many of the world's poor, market development is still a work in progress, and corruption is pervasive. What Asia got right is that crises can't only be about austerity. While you're trimming spending, you must be creative about generating new dynamism. Since euro nations can't resort to currency devaluation to revive growth, reform is the only way.

Fourth, growth beats taxes when repairing fiscal balance. Japan is a cautionary tale when it comes to rich nations getting incentives wrong. It issued mountains of debt, assuming for 20 years that it was just one stimulus plan away from 5 percent growth. That never happened. Then, amid a ballooning budget deficit, it increased consumption taxes in 1997. That killed a nascent recovery. In the current global environment, growth is the route to balanced budgets, not higher taxes. The latter would simply destroy the former.

Fifth, markets are quick to forgive and forget if you take the right recovery steps. Yes, there's a heavy price to pay for going hat-in-hand to the IMF. The key will be conditionality. There's much griping in Asia about how the terms of Europe's IMF packages are far less stringent than those forced on Indonesia, Korea, and Thailand. Fresh starts are possible, though, as the powerful gains in Asian markets over the last 16-plus years attest. So drop the denial, Europe. Let Greece do what it needs to do, even if it means default, and move on. Asia shows there is life after crisis.

Yet, one tax Japan should have implemented years ago is that on bond holdings. If Japanese won't buy and hold fewer government bonds on their own, the government should incentivize them with a special tax. Really, if Japan had taxed coupon payments on government bonds 10 or 15 years ago, its banks wouldn't be sitting on so many. If Wall Street is America's *chaebol*, an outsized bond market is Japan's. If bankers had made fresh loans instead of buying bonds, the Japanese recovery that just ended would have been more impressive.

Capitalism purists would surely object, but policy makers need to work harder to direct the money they create into the real economy. Without the so-called multiplier effect that can make monetary policy so potent, zero Fed and BOJ rates won't boost growth. The key lesson Fed officials need to learn from Japan concerns an exit strategy. Japan never had one when it began offering free money. The United States must devise one if it wants to avoid what economists call "Japan disease." It's never too late for officials in Tokyo to act, or Europe for that matter.

To economist Richard Koo of Nomura Research Institute, Europe has failed at every turn to learn from what he calls Japan's persistent "balance-sheet recession." Such a scenario occurs when the fallout from an asset boom that ended badly cripples companies and households with debt that must be reduced. Until it is, both companies and homeowners have little desire to borrow and spend even with historically low interest rates. Koo's recommended solution: Offset private-sector savings with government spending, the opposite of what German Chancellor Angela Merkel and European Central Bank President Mario Draghi have been advocating in the euro-area, one in which Portugal, Spain, and others are never more than a credit downgrade away from fresh turmoil.

Europe's cash-strapped peripheral countries are suffering the economic equivalent of pneumonia, which, just like the deadly lung infection, is most convincingly beaten by ensuring ample nourishment. To Tokyo-based Koo, a former Federal Reserve economist, the cure is greater fiscal stimulus to end the euro's confidence crisis once and for all. "The patient can have both, but the doctor has to cure the pneumonia first even if the treatments contradict those required" for other ailments, Koo said. The trouble is that "in Europe, austerity is the only game in town. When you look around Europe you see balance-sheet recessions."

Europe needs to heed the lessons from Japan, which has expanded less than one percent on average in the past 20 years and suffered falling consumer prices. Koo's views are made even more compelling considering the timeline of his career. The Taiwanese American was born in Japan in 1954 and studied at the University of California–Berkeley and Johns Hopkins University before winning a Fed fellowship. He was in Washington at the height of Ronald Reagan's supply-side reforms, which in some ways scuttled his career plans. Koo's hopes of staying on at the Fed in Washington ran into Reagan's public sector hiring freeze, and he ended up at the Fed Bank of New York where he dabbled in Latin America's debt crisis. He returned to Tokyo in 1987, at the height of Japan's bubble economy, and had a front-row seat to one of history's most spectacular, and some might say improbable, crashes. Through the 1990s and 2000s, Koo looked on with growing frustration as Japan's funk set in and deepened, a process he detailed in his 2008 book, *The Holy Grail of Macroeconomics: Lessons from Japan's Great Recession.* His conclusion: It's all about the debt.

Fed's tapering process began in earnest. It's only when the tide goes out, as Warren Buffett famously said, that you learn who's been swimming naked. Well, 2013 was a banner year for skinny-dipping among Asian leaders, central banks, and businesspeople. If Fed tapering gains momentum, Asian debt markets As 2014 began, Koo's conclusion took on even greater resonance as they could be in for a brutal reality check. It's not just Chinese companies overleveraging balance sheets in recent years. According to Standard Chartered, the average corporate debt-to-gross-domestic-product ratio in Asia, excluding Japan, jumped from 76 percent in 2007 to 97 percent in the first quarter of 2013, never mind all the borrowing since then. That's 20 percentage points higher than the United States and markedly above Latin America and Eastern Europe. And what about Japan, home to the world's largest debt burden? If quantitative-easing efforts drive inflation toward 2 percent by late 2014, as the Bank of Japan hopes, look out. At some point, markets will realize that 10-year government bonds yielding well below 1 percent do not compute given Japan's shrinking population. The years ahead could see the laws of finance reassert themselves.

The entire world has a vested interest in Kuroda keeping the magic alive. In July 2013, Deputy Economy Minister Yasutoshi Nishimura admitted something quite profound: "This is the last chance for Japan's economy." Many worry Kuroda is hastening what they see as Tokyo's demise. Hedge-fund manager Bass of Hayman Capital is now surer than ever in his bet on a Japanese crash. So far Wizard Kuroda has bamboozled and crushed skeptics with overwhelming monetary force. It's an entirely open question how long he can pull off this feat should the bond vigilantes James Carville feared 20 years ago rise up. Then, Japan's monster of a bond market may scare us all.

Chapter 4

The Fukushima Effect

How Rampant Cronyism Holds Japan Back

The coastal city of Natori is typical for northeastern Japan. Located along the fertile plains of the Masuda River, Natori is part of Miyagi Prefecture, one of six that make up the Tohoku region, a remote area known as much for breathtaking scenery and severe weather patterns as for its thriving fishing and agriculture trades. For Natori's 72,000 people, the morning of March 11, 2011, was one like any other. The forecast was for rain that Friday, the fish market was abuzz with activity, school buses shuttled children to class, and office workers were toiling away with thoughts of the weekend. No one could have known Natori was hours away from global infamy.

At 2:46 p.m. that day, a magnitude 9 earthquake, the biggest known to have ever hit modern Japan, struck roughly 43 miles east of Tohoku's Oshika Peninsula. The ground under Natori rumbled violently for an estimated six minutes. But that was just the beginning of the day's deadly events. Thirty minutes later, the first signs of water appeared in the city center. What started as a slow trickle morphed into giant waves as high as 133 feet. Within two hours, a city with known roots back to 1867 virtually disappeared.

Natori became ground zero for the world's first images of what Japanese call "3/11." It was featured in the first news footage that blanketed a world that had come to think of tsunamis as a concern for developing nations, not a first-world power like Japan. Petrifying images of cars, trucks, and even entire buildings being washed away had locals wondering if they'd been cast in some splashy end-of-the world Hollywood action flick. There was indeed an almost biblical quality to the way the nation shook on March 11 and the waters rose with supernatural speed to swallow entire cities, towns, and villages. Trains were thrown into the air like something out of a Godzilla film, roads turned to jelly, and nuclear power plants coughed out radiation. At times, many felt like producer Jerry Bruckheimer might suddenly yell "Cut!" as he finished up his latest apocalyptic box-office smash starring Nicolas Cage or Bruce Willis. Maybe John Cusack is in town filming *2012, the Sequel.*

All this was making for unprecedented theater down in Tokyo, where then–Prime Minister Naoto Kan was watching images on NHK, Japan's national broadcaster. The true magnitude of the devastation took time to set in. At his initial post-quake press briefing, Kan called it a "crisis," and for an hour or so, that felt right. That was, until more images poured in: waters were rising with horrible speed to swallow entire towns; shipping containers rolled like toys; bridges turned to tofu; schools brimming with children just up and disappeared; smoke was billowing out of nuclear reactors. As a sense of proportion settled in, "crisis" rapidly proved inadequate as the quake and tsunami precipitated the worst nuclear disaster since Chernobyl. What Japan had suffered was nothing short of a cataclysm.

It couldn't have come at a worse time for Japan, which had been gasping for economic life for two decades. The very next day, household-name economists like Nouriel Roubini, known as "Dr. Doom," said a "shock like this" would accelerate Japan's descent into a full-blown debt crisis. Others, however, had a different take on the same shock; they wondered about the cathartic potential of a natural disaster of this scale. Included in this camp was Malcolm Gladwell. "The only time you can get things done is in moments of genuine crisis and catastrophes—there's a small opportunity to do an extraordinary amount," the author of *The Tipping Point* and *Outliers* told Bloomberg Television on March 29, 2011. "Japan, a country whose politics were in deadlock and sluggish for many, many years, I hope they can seize this moment and accomplish a lot."

Pundits had been saying for years, after all, that it would require a huge crisis to end Japan's political paralysis. Temblors also had a complicated place in the Japanese psyche as change agents.

There's a widely held belief, a local mythology, that tectonic-plate shifts can coincide with big ones above the ground—in good ways and bad. An 1855 earthquake that destroyed much of modern-day Tokyo bookmarked the twilight of the Tokugawa period, during which Japan was isolated for two centuries. Rebuilding efforts after the devastation of 1923 coincided with the rise of Japanese militarism. Kobe's 1995 tragedy dovetailed with the end of Japan's postwar industrial boom and deflation. Might 3/11 also signal historic change?

The idea was that the complacency and distraction that had pervaded Nagatacho, Tokyo's Capitol Hill, for many a year was no longer an option. Politicians who spent the last two-plus decades doubling down massive borrowing to finance public works, with ultralow interest rates and lifetime employment, eschewing immigration, and with a rigid industrial structure favoring exports from a handful of behemoths, compliant banks, and clubby ties between the political and business worlds would have to roll up their sleeves to rebuild after the strongest earthquake on record. They would need to do so with fresh thinking and creativity and without the luxury of the massive borrowing that has been propping up the nation since 1990.

Economists have long argued that a crisis is a terrible thing to waste. That's particularly true of Nobel laureate Milton Friedman and his ilk. "Only a crisis, actual or perceived, produces real change," Friedman wrote in his 1962 book, *Capitalism and Freedom*.

> When that crisis occurs, the actions that are taken depend on the ideas that are lying around. That, I believe, is our basic function: to develop alternatives to existing policies, to keep them alive and available until the politically impossible becomes politically inevitable.

Naomi Klein explored the pros and cons of the strategy in 2007's *The Shock Doctrine*. While her emphasis was largely on how free-market ideologues exploit crises to impose rapid and irreversible change in nations around the world—like the Bush administration's misguided Iraq invasion—there are times when a major shock hands a people a chance to unleash the doctrine on themselves. The last few years have seen no better example of that potential than Japan. Clearly, 3/11 would catalyze the government to articulate a new and grand vision for the nation, overcoming bureaucrats' reluctance to make vital decisions and the realities of the deflationary forces that depressed both companies and consumers.

Instead of catalyzing change, the events of 3/11 demonstrated the stubborn resilience of Japan Inc. The best explanation for this may come from Elisabeth Kuebler-Ross and the five stages of grief outlined in her 1969 book, *On Death and Dying*. They aptly capture where the collective Japanese psyche has journeyed, and where it hasn't, since 3/11. Just as the terminally ill experience denial, anger, bargaining, despair, and ultimate acceptance, so have the Japanese people.

The first hints of denial came days after the tsunami erased entire communities and overwhelmed a nuclear facility 135 miles from Tokyo. As radiation leaked at the Fukushima power plants, authorities assured the nation, and indeed the world, that all was well. Tokyo Electric Power Co., whose negligence led to the worst nuclear mess since the Chernobyl meltdown in Ukraine in 1986, hid the severity of the crisis—and is still obfuscating today.

Anger arrived with the first press reports about how close the world came to losing Tokyo, home to some 13 million people and some of the biggest equity markets on the globe. Blood pressures rose with more details about how Kan stormed into Tepco headquarters and demanded that management abandon its plan to evacuate all staff from Fukushima. Kan commanded Tepco to gain control over the meltdown and, in the process, literally saved the city from extinction. The plight of hundreds of thousands in Tohoku also enraged the nation as reconstruction plans unfolded at a glacial pace. What the government missed was that the Japanese wanted change. They longed for greater transparency among leaders reluctant to disengage the autopilot that had been guiding the country for 20 years. They wanted someone at Tepco to go to jail and for the bureaucrats who enabled their incompetence to be fired. Public fury fueled the biggest street protests since the 1960s.

Increasingly, it dawned on the masses that engineering the kind of epochal change they crave was more than they had bargained for. News reports of shantytowns, radioactive schools, and squandered rebuilding funds became less frequent. Interest from abroad, which was once so intense, waned. Donations and public-service announcements poured in from the likes of Rihanna, U2, Cyndi Lauper, Sonic Youth, Norah Jones, and Lou Reed. Lady Gaga sold special bracelets on her website to fund relief efforts. Stories about the resilience of the Japanese people were eclipsed by curiosity about the role that ingrained conventions of culture and reflexive obedience played in the crisis.

Realization of how little would change led to the despair phase. Anguished pundits explored the depths and indeed the surreal resilience of the nation's political and social inertia and how many of the biggest risks Japanese face—earthquakes, Chinese pollution, North Korea's threats—seemed beyond the government's control. Disillusioned voters even moved to reelect the Liberal Democratic Party, which they had tossed out in disgust in 2009.

By the second anniversary of 3/11, in March 2013, Japan had gone full circle to acceptance. The clearest indication of that was voters' support for Prime Minister Shinzo Abe's return to the helm after a feeble 2006–2007 stint in the job. While Abe has had a good start this time around, only time will tell if his pledges of change, which are big on talk and small on bold action, will end in a new cycle of grief. For unless Abe deregulates the economy, improves a corporate-governance system that produced the fraud at Olympus, severs the incestuous ties between government and business that enabled Tepco's incompetence, and finds safer energy sources before the next giant quake, he will just produce Japan's next asset bubble. To understand how Japan got here, and what the rest of the world can learn from its experience, we must explore the "Fukushima Effect."

■ ■ ■

If ever there were a microcosm of what ails Japan, the omnipotent nuclear power industry with its legacy of fatal accidents, conflicts of interest, and failure to evolve is it. Too often, those writing nuclear-safety rules were also doing surveys and signing off on inspections.

It would seem an issue well worth the attention of Julian Assange of WikiLeaks fame and his ilk. After all, since oceans don't have boundaries, any nuclear crisis is an international incident. Were Japan's nuclear sites better inspected and maintained, we'd all be better off. Flippant as it may seem, Japanese found themselves wondering who had put Homer Simpson in charge of the nation's nuclear safety. Japan's nuclear safety record these last 15 years seems no sounder than that of the fictional Springfield Nuclear Power Plant, where on *The Simpsons*, Homer is head of safety. Only this was no laughing matter.

"There was certainly no shortage of critics," Richard Samuels wrote in *3.11: Disaster and Change in Japan*: "If Kan became the whipping boy in the discourse of leadership, Tepco became the consensus villain with regard to risk and vulnerability. It was an easy target." The governor of Fukushima, Yuhei Sato, for example, wasted no time in lashing out at Tepco and refused to accept a personal apology from company president Masataka Shimizu.

Japan's postmortem on the failures at Tepco and the regulators who oversee the company started out well enough. Rather than tap a physicist, engineer, or analyst to run an investigative panel, officialdom entrusted things to Tokyo University professor emeritus Kiyoshi Kurokawa, a medical doctor without significant ties to the energy industry. Kurokawa is a popular cultural figure, with a fluency in English, boisterous laugh, and bluntness that makes him a curious presence on TV talk shows. But if government officials were hoping for Fukushima whitewash, they didn't get it.

Kurokawa's 641-page report, released on July 5, 2012, had lots to say about Tokyo's many shortcomings, and the good doctor pointed fingers in directions that surprised the political establishment. His conclusion: The Fukushima meltdown was a preventable, manmade disaster stemming from the worst conformist tendencies of Japanese culture. And it seemed like a badly needed sign that a break with the errant ways of the past was in order. The first step to fixing a problem—and coping with grief—is identifying what the problem is, something Japan's government had stubbornly refused to do. Scant attention was paid, for example, to how government–industry collusion placed so much of Japan's population in danger, as did a reluctance to question authority and a reflexive obedience to process.

Much of the blame lies with the arrogance and incompetence of Tepco, which runs the Fukushima reactors now referenced in history books next to Chernobyl. But, as Kurokawa argued, it takes an insidious and toxic business and political culture to cultivate such a corrupt and dangerous system. Why, for example, is Tepco still in business? Why hasn't it been nationalized? Because of Japan's omnipotent "nuclear village," the nexus of power companies and pro-nuclear regulators, bureaucrats, and researchers that champions the industry, which came in for particular, and well-deserved, scorn in the Kurokawa review.

A particularly explosive suggestion was that it wasn't the tsunami that damaged the reactors and safety equipment, but the earthquake itself. It undermined Tepco's claims that the disaster was some act of God that it couldn't have foreseen or avoided. That storyline was meant to deflect attention from design flaws, shoddy construction materials, and insufficient training of reactor personnel—in other words, the human factor. At Fukushima, for instance, backup diesel generators that might have averted the disaster were located in a basement and swamped by waves. "This in the country that invented the word *tsunami*," quipped Ken Brockman, a former director of nuclear installation safety at the International Atomic Energy Agency in Vienna, on March 18, 2011.

Kurokawa's six-month investigation was a Japanese first, with wide-ranging subpoena powers and public hearings at which Kan and then–Tepco President Shimizu gave vastly conflicting accounts of the disaster response. The three previous government-led inquiries went easy on the nuclear village. Kurokawa's pulled no punches, warning against Japan's tendency toward cosmetic solutions, including replacing senior officials at regulatory agencies and power companies or just changing their names. It highlighted the dangers of lobbying and shamed regulators with tales of the difficulty panel members had getting documents.

"What must be admitted, very painfully, is that this was a disaster 'Made in Japan,'" Kurokawa wrote. "Its fundamental causes are to be found in the ingrained conventions of Japanese culture: our reflexive obedience; our reluctance to question authority; our devotion to sticking with the program; our groupism; and our insularity."

Of course, Kurokawa could just as easily have been taking about Japan's economy in the two decades after the asset bubble burst. But the real question was what the patient—Japan Inc.—would do with the doctor's diagnosis. Sadly, it's still stuck with the unhealthy ways that courted nuclear disaster. The prime minister who came after Kan, Yoshihiko Noda, largely shelved Kurokawa's report. Now that Abe's pro-nuclear LDP is back in power and enjoys majorities in both houses of parliament, the government's complete focus is on restarting the nuclear power plants mothballed after 3/11 amid safely concerns. Even the Nuclear Regulation Authority, created in September 2012 ostensibly to tighten oversight, is devoting more time and limited resources to recertifying reactors for restarts than monitoring the Fukushima cleanup and keeping the public safe.

Abe even helped Tokyo win the 2020 Summer Olympics by exaggerating the progress Japan has made in cleaning up Fukushima. The same week in September 2013 when Abe was in Buenos Aires addressing the International Olympic Committee, news was breaking back home about radioactive groundwater leaking into the Pacific Ocean. Another problem is over 1,000 spent fuel rods that are bleeding radiation into the atmosphere, and the threat of exposure is far greater than Japanese officials admit. Even so, Abe told the Olympic judges: "Let me assure you the situation is under control."

Japanese officialdom is being blinded not only by denial but also by dollar signs. In May, Abe jetted to Turkey to help close a $22 billion deal for Japan to build nuclear power plants in that seismically active nation. That kind of cash makes power companies virtually untouchable. And it raises doubts about Tepco's admission that 300 tons of water laced with strontium and other particles is pouring into the Pacific on many days. One can't help but wonder if the leaks are of much greater magnitude.

Instead of acting to decommission Fukushima, invite independent auditors from overseas to assess the magnitude of the damage, decide if the surrounding area is really safe for inhabitants, fishing, or farming, scour the world for innovative solutions, break up the nuclear village, and level with the Japanese about cleanup costs that will be in the hundreds of billions of dollars, Abe is focused on sales.

Three months later, reality intervened thanks partly to international pressure. Media reports from New York to London to Seoul pressured the Japanese press to return to a story that editors had been burying for many months. No longer able to downplay and refute environmental warnings from Greenpeace International, reports from the World Health Organization, and mounting evidence of radioactive groundwater gushing into the Pacific Ocean, Abe had no choice but to step up. In August, he admitted what much of the world already knew: Tepco isn't up to the task of containing the disaster. Abe pledged his government would "make sure there is a swift and multifaceted approach in place" to stop the leak.

Until that moment, Japan's leaders had been bewilderingly disengaged from their "BP moment." Abe's predecessors, Kan and Noda, virtually ignored the radiation leaks and spent fuel rods sitting out in the open air a short bullet-train ride from Tokyo. They entrusted the cleanup process to Tepco and felt little inclination to see to it that some of the company's executives go to jail for negligence or are at least shamed. BP's former chief executive officer, Tony Hayward, was at least fired and sued over the 2010 oil spill in the Gulf of Mexico. Tepco was leaking something far worse and lying through its teeth.

Yet Abe's Fukushima pledge hasn't been matched by action. Once he secured the 2020 Olympics for Tokyo, it was back to business as usual. That means official Japan is still stuck on *how* Fukushima became synonymous with Chernobyl, not *why* it happened or *what* it means for the world. The *how* is the stuff of the gods, according to conventional wisdom. The event Japanese call 3/11 was an act of the heavens that no one could have possibly foreseen. There was no way to plan for it, no way Tepco could have known not to place all of its backup generators in the same place underground, just steps away from the sea in a tsunami-prone nation.

This storyline ignores the *why*. Fukushima was a preventable, manmade disaster stemming from the worst conformist tendencies of Japan Inc. If executives got together globally and created a Hall of Shame for the greedy, corrupt, and clueless along them, Tepco would deserve its own wing. All Enron and Bernie Madoff did was manufacture fake profits. Tepco fudged its safety record and put the lives of tens of millions of people at risk, perhaps far more if its radiation continues imperiling the Pacific. In September, for example, Korea banned imports of fish caught near the site of the Fukushima nuclear accident. Radioactive traces have been found in bluefin tuna, not to mention on secondhand cars and auto parts imported by Russia from Japan.

Nuclear power enthusiasts argue that the science behind the reactors that prior to 3/11 provided 30 percent of Japan's electricity is sound. Where the trouble starts, though, is when we fallible humans get our hands on the most potent power source history has ever known in a system without inadequate checks and balances. Rigorous as it may be, nuclear science didn't stop the geniuses at Tepco from clustering all of Fukushima's backup generators in the worst possible place. Human error also came into play with the 1999 Tokaimura nuclear accident, caused by workers literally mixing radioactive materials in buckets.

Tell that to the devastated towns within a 100-mile radius of Fukushima facing extinction—or the nearly 100,000 people still living in temporary shelters for nearly three years now—that atomic power is safe, clean, and cheap. Until utility operators can elevate reactors on huge shock absorbers or construct them from rubber, Japan's people will fear them.

■ ■ ■

What can the world learn from the Fukushima Effect? Let's start with Indonesia, by far Southeast Asia's biggest economy, which is almost universally seen as a major economic power of the future. On any list of nations that might soon be invited to join the BRICS economies—Brazil, Russia, Indonesia, China, and South Africa—Indonesia warrants a place way up top. The fourth most populous nation in the world boasts an enviably young population, more than 26 percent of which is below 15. Not surprisingly, Indonesia is mulling a nuclear future. To keep growing in the 6 percent to 7 percent range, Indonesia needs energy, and lots of it. Hence the plan to build nuclear power plants.

Yet if a country as developed, technologically advanced, rules-obsessed, and earthquake-ready as Japan can't avert a nuclear catastrophe, what hope do developing nations have? Indonesia's regulatory environment is poor and its public sector far less tech-savvy than Japan's. Its disaster-response record needs work and it's a very seismically active place. Remember that Indonesia suffered by far the most casualties in December 2004, when a giant tsunami killed nearly 230,000 people.

Indonesia's nuclear-reactor plans might have raised few eyebrows on March 10, 2011, but in the post-Fukushima world, they need very careful consideration. If the ongoing drama in Japan tells the world anything, it's that earthquake-prone nations should be aggressively pursuing nonnuclear options to fuel growth. Granted, Japan's realities are a bit different. The Fukushima Daiichi power plant was 40 years old, almost as old as the median age of Japan's people. The technology going into today's reactors makes them far safer. The age of Japan's plants prompted some world leaders, like Germany's Chancellor Angela Merkel, to shut their oldest reactors.

Still, Japan's disaster was decades in the making thanks to falsified safety reports, underestimated risks, and plain old corruption. Incestuous ties between government and industry helped fuel the excesses behind the 1980s bubble economy. That same public–private collusion also plagued responses to the economic downturn that followed. A bad-loan crisis festered, deflation took root, and competition from China exploded. All the while, Japan Inc. circled the wagons and tried to stave off both change and tough decisions. Likewise, those writing nuclear-safety rules were also doing surveys and signing off on inspections.

Also to be avoided is the offensive practice of public servants getting cushy gigs in industries they once oversaw. You might expect there to be strict rules about former government officials gaining lucrative employment at Tepco after retirement—you know, just to ensure that nuclear plants are actually being watched with some semblance of objectivity. Nope; the practice that encourages bureaucrats to look out for their future employers and not the average Japanese household is alive and well. It's called *amakudari*, which means "descent from heaven." Decades of doctored safety reports and underestimated risks at Tepco were made possible by bureaucrats looking the other way. Far from heaven, it's made life a nightmare for farmers, fishermen, and millions living around Fukushima.

Wall Street should learn from this corrupt phenomenon, too. The revolving door from government to Wall Street is rife with potential conflict. Here, think Robert Rubin leaving Goldman Sachs to join the

Clinton administration, where he helped repeal the Depression-era firewalls between investment and commercial banking and precipitate the 2008 global crisis. After leaving the White House, Rubin rotated to Citicorp Inc. Or take Alan Greenspan and former U.S. Senator Phil Gramm, who worked with Rubin on that endeavor and then got plum jobs at Deutsche Bank AG and UBS AG, respectively. The list goes on.

Were Japan's nuclear sites better inspected and maintained and regulated with true independence and vigilance, we'd all be better off. Japan shows how difficult that balancing act can be. With scant energy deposits of its own, nuclear power became a national priority as Japan clawed out of the devastation of World War II, a conflict it fought partly to secure oil supplies. The irony, of course, is that the only nation ever attacked by nuclear weapons championed them to such an extent. It has 54 reactors, more than any country except the United States and France, to power its industries. This pits economic demands against safety concerns in one of the world's most earthquake-prone places.

The allure of nuclear power is obvious for developing nations from Indonesia to India to China. Yet, here's a number that should worry humankind: 114. That's Indonesia's ranking in Transparency International's latest corruption perception index, putting it behind Egypt, Tanzania, and Kosovo. Unless engineers can build remarkably shock-absorbent reactors, there's a question about whether they should find wide use along the Ring of Fire, that arc of fault-lines and volcanoes encircling the Pacific Basin. And that's before we consider the risks associated with corruption, shoddy regulation, and questionable safety standards.

If these things can go this awry in Japan, as efficient, tech-savvy, and work-ethic-oriented a nation as there is, where *won't* they? It's a question Indonesia and other economic upstarts should consider long and hard.

Did the Fukushima disaster turn Asia's economic upstarts against nuclear? Not as much as one might think, according to Vlado Vivoda, a research fellow at the Griffith Asia Institute. Before 3/11, Asia was widely viewed as the future of nuclear power as China, India, and the rest of this power-hungry region raced to build reactors. After Japan's crisis, that future seems very much in question.

"Some analysts suggested that Asia's nuclear renaissance was over while others remained cautiously optimistic about the region's nuclear power future," Vivoda wrote in a March 2013 report published by the East Asia Forum. "With increasing competition for oil and gas among Asian nations and the negative impact of carbon pollution, nuclear power is still considered by many regional states as a matter of survival, both in terms of growing energy demands and environmental security."

Fukushima turned a majority of Japanese against restarting the nation's reactors. Yoshihiko Noda, Abe's immediate predecessor, had pledged to phase out nuclear power by 2040. The moment he became prime minister in December 2012, Abe scrapped that plan. Yet, continued leaks and a series of accidents are pressuring Abe to return to Noda's pledge. Even after disclosures last summer about contaminated groundwater polluting the Pacific, a series of troubling mishaps came to light.

On October 9, 2013, Fukushima workers mistakenly disconnected a pipe near a desalination device, dumping another 10 tons of contaminated water into the surrounding area and exposing workers to radiation. Days later, heavy rains were blamed for tainted water overflowing dikes. A series of investigative stories also emerged to enrage the Japanese masses anew. On October 25, 2013, a special report from Reuters alleged Tepco was exploiting workers by paying them less than promised and exposing them to more dangerous conditions than agreed upon. Ten days earlier, the *Guardian* detailed how workers on the frontlines were plagued by health problems and fearful about the future under the headline: "Plummeting Morale at Fukushima Daiichi as Nuclear Cleanup Takes Its Toll."

Elsewhere in Asia, energy needs are trumping safety concerns. Take China, site of the world's most ambitious nuclear development program. On top of 16 existing nuclear reactors, according to Vivoda, 26 are under construction and another 51 reactors are being planned. Initially, Japan's 3/11 disaster prompted China's State Council to suspend approval of nuclear-power projects until it implemented new safety procedures. Those standards are expected to be in place, clearing China's path toward running history's biggest nuclear industry.

India responded quite differently. Within a week of Japan's meltdown, the government said its reactors—20 are in operation at six power plants—were safe and would continue running. "The government's message is that it's business as usual for nuclear power," Vivoda said.

New Delhi's stance is unsurprising in a country where power demand is surging and national electrification and grid integration programs are incomplete. Having passed the Indo–U.S. nuclear agreement in 2008, effectively ending a 34-year U.S. ban on supplying nuclear technology and fuel to India, and clearing the way for Australian uranium exports to India, New Delhi's plans to increase its nuclear capacity are moving faster than ever.

That isn't sitting well with populations near the reactors. In West Bengal, for example, the government is refusing to green-light a proposed plant that would feature six Russian reactors. While some of the resistance reflects disputes involving local land, labor, and the logic of importing reactors critics say could be built domestically, a large swath of the Indian public is at odds with New Delhi.

Korea, meanwhile, is a big user of nuclear power, with 20 operating reactors, or a potential exporter of it. But 2013 saw a sea change in the nation's nuclear ambitions as growing public opposition to atomic power after the Fukushima disaster met a domestic scandal over faked safety documents. In July, President Park Geun-hye called for tighter government regulation and monitoring of the industry. Three months later, the findings of a report by a working group of academics and state officials prompted a significant shift away from a technology that's been a mainstay of Korea's energy mix since its first reactor opened in 1978. Thirty years later, in 2008, Seoul had decided nuclear energy would account for 41 percent of power generation capacity by 2035. In October, it lowered that goal to between 22 and 29 percent.

A scandal involving faked quality-control certificates for parts and the indictment of 100 officials on corruption and bribery charges helped inform the decision by Korea's energy ministry. But so did the fallout from Tepco's incompetence, which prompted a steady erosion in public support for nuclear power. In March 2013, on the second anniversary of Japan's 3/11, 63 percent of Koreans said they consider domestic reactors unsafe in a survey by Hangil Research. A 2012 poll by the nonprofit Korean Federation for Environmental Movement found just 54 percent to be opposed to reactors.

"We should minimize social conflicts regarding atomic energy's role," the government panel said in an October 14 statement.

It's an open question how these social conflicts might affect Korea's nuclear export business. According to Vivoda, Korea is looking to sell 80 reactors abroad by 2030. "Korean enterprises are among those hoping to pick up overseas contracts at the expense of Japanese companies, and are pursuing opportunities in Jordan, the United Arab Emirates, Turkey, Indonesia, India, China, and Malaysia," Vivoda said.

Taiwan has seen its own Fukushima-related backlash. On March 11, 2013, the second anniversary of Japan's disaster, more than 68,000 protesters took to the streets to halt the completion of the island's fourth nuclear power plant. The state-run Taiwan Power Co. had already missed a deadline to start commercial operations on the nearly $9 billion nuclear power plant project at the end of 2012. Now, President Ma Ying-jeou faces a seemingly impossible balancing act: making good on a pledge to reduce carbon emissions to year-2000 levels by 2025, while also phasing out nuclear power, which generates one-fifth of Taiwan's electricity.

Like Japan, Taiwan lies on the Pacific Ring of Fire, an area bordering the Pacific Ocean that is tectonically active. Taiwan's three nuclear plants are near the ocean and the island sits on a variety of geological fractures, or faults. A 1999 earthquake southwest of Taipei killed about 2,500 people. Another in December 2006 halted Taiwan's number three nuclear power station and prompted inspections.

What about Indonesia, another Ring of Fire neighbor? The world's fourth-most-populous nation plans to run four nuclear plants by 2025. "With growing electricity shortages, Indonesia is unlikely to halt its plan to build its first nuclear-power plant," Vivoda said. "It claims its plants will be safe, thanks to the use of more advanced technology than the four-decade-old Fukushima reactors." Thailand, too, is keeping to its plan to build five plants over the next two decades. Vietnam has contracts with Russia and Japan to build as many as four nuclear plants. Malaysia and Bangladesh each plan to build reactors.

The lessons from Fukushima reverberated through Europe, even in nations like Germany that boast strong safety and negligible seismic risk. Pre-Fukushima, nuclear power supplied about a quarter of Germany's energy. Post-Fukushima, Chancellor Angela Merkel is seeking to get 80 percent of electricity from renewables by 2050 from about 23 percent now. While Merkel is bowing to a public backlash against reactors, she is struggling to contain the cost of renewable-energy subsidies stressing the national budget. Switzerland has taken a similar route.

■ ■ ■

Yet the biggest risks are in the developing world. Once developing nations do go nuclear, it's vital that marquee-caliber voices in the private sector speak out. Part of the problem in Japan is the near-absolute power enjoyed by Nippon Keidanren, a passionately pro-nuclear outfit. Anyone who crosses Japan's main business lobby will find himself on the outside—persona non grata in a nation in which relationships and access are everything. That's not to say a few mavericks haven't braved outcast status.

Masayoshi Son is the 56-year-old chief executive officer of Softbank Corp. The billionaire first cracked the monopolies that dominated Japan's telecommunications industry. Now he's working to shake up the utilities market with plans to invest about $1 billion to build 10 solar farms. That means crossing Tepco and other nuclear power merchants by offering alternatives.

Hiroshi Mikitani, 49, the president of e-commerce giant Rakuten Inc., has been more daring. In mid-2011, he sent shockwaves through Japan Inc. when he quit Nippon Keidanren and started a rival association. In part, his fight is about making corporate Japan nimbler and more entrepreneurial by creating spaces for long-neglected small-to-midsize companies to thrive.

Mikitani is targeting the "Galapagos syndrome" that plagues too many Japanese industries whose products are highly evolved but unable to survive beyond the water's edge. Rather than coddle such industries, the idea is to unleash the creative destruction emphasized by economist Joseph Schumpeter to encourage corporate Japan to adapt or die.

But Mikitani, whose birthday is, coincidentally, March 11, has made the most waves by taking on the Tokyo establishment's contention that the economy will collapse if Japan gives up on nuclear power. This canard is also being refuted by perhaps the unlikeliest of public figures:

Junichiro Koizumi, Abe's political mentor. Koizumi sent shockwaves through Nagatacho with an October 2 speech to business executives in Nagoya, in which he declared his opposition to nuclear power.

"There is nothing more costly than nuclear power," Koizumi said, marking an about-face from his early support of the industry. As prime minister from 2001 to 2006, Koizumi referred to Japan as "a nation built on nuclear power" and ended tax-funded subsidies for solar panel companies to preserve the supremacy of reactors. Abe was less than impressed, saying: "It's irresponsible to promise at this point to scrap nuclear energy."

Koizumi's siding with the anti-nuclear movement is important for two reasons. First, he's an extraordinarily perceptive politician with a unique ability to read the public zeitgeist and sell sweeping change to the masses. Second, and more important, he is calling for a kind of Manhattan Project in reverse. The reference here is to the U.S. project that produced the nuclear weapons that leveled Hiroshima and Nagasaki in 1945. What Koizumi envisions is an ambitious plan to do the opposite and rid Japan of the reactors the public has come to fear. What's more, Koizumi believes, Japanese are likely to rally around such a call for action.

"If the Liberal Democratic Party were to adopt a policy of no nukes, the public mood would rise in an instant," Koizumi declared. "The Japanese are masters at turning a pinch into a new chance." On October 25, 2013, Koizumi doubled down and called politicians who champion the nuclear industry "irresponsible."

Abe's failure to do just that is not only a blow to the success of his Abenomics, but a cautionary tale for other seismically active nations pursuing nuclear power. "Fukushima gives the opening that if they really want to get off nukes, then they really have to go and do something else," said David Suzuki, a Canadian author, environmentalist, geneticist, and Japan Renewable Energy Foundation board member.

Suzuki worries Japan is wasting a once-in-a-century opportunity to push alternative forms of energy. In the year ended March 2012, for example, only about 7.4 percent of primary energy came from renewables, with 3.4 percent from hydro and 4 percent from others such as solar, geothermal, and wind, according to data compiled by Bloomberg New Energy. In 2013, high-tech Japan trailed developing China in solar power.

The greatest hope for Japan may be its vast geothermal resources, which are mostly harnessed by the nation's hot-spring and tourism industries. "Geothermal can be a huge source of energy very quickly," Suzuki said. He believes Japan is also well positioned to take advantage of developments in tidal power on its way to being the "poster boy for renewable energy for the future."

Among its many advantages, geothermal energy offers a more stable supply of energy than, say, wind and solar, which fluctuate with breezes and clouds. In a May report, the Washington-based Geothermal Energy Association said Japan could potentially produce 23,000 megawatts of geothermal power. That promise, coupled with Koizumi's support for an already lively grassroots anti-nuclear movement, could be the catalyst Japan needs to become not only an energy leader but a role model.

To his credit, Abe is indeed moving to bolster clean energy. Some of the most promising projects involve giant windmills, some of which will be floating in the sea. An October 24 *New York Times* article detailed plans to generate over 1 gigawatt of electricity from 140 wind turbines by 2020—equivalent to the power produced by a nuclear reactor. According to the *Times*, the government will spend 22 billion yen building the first three wind turbines off the coast of Fukushima. After that, a consortium of 11 companies, including Hitachi Ltd., Marubeni Corp., Mitsubishi Heavy Industries Ltd., and Shimizu Corp., will commercialize the project.

While that sounds great, Abe would have to forsake the all-powerful nuclear village. One sign his party lacks the courage to do so is the proposals to combine 50 operable reactors into a single company that would be owned by Japan's nine regional utilities and wholesalers Japan Atomic Power Co. and Electric Power Development Co. The central government and local reactor makers would give financial and technical support. There's some merit to the idea. A portion of the profit from sales of electricity would go toward the cleanup of Tokyo Electric Power Co.'s wrecked Fukushima atomic station and victim compensation, which combined may cost more than 11 trillion yen. But such an endeavor would be about rebuilding the nuclear industry's clout and expanding the export of reactors, not finding alternatives.

Therein lies the lesson for less-developed nations eyeing a nuclear future: Don't give it so much clout and influence that it becomes the tail wagging the dog. That brings us to the *what*. Fukushima is a growing embarrassment for Japan on the international stage. Another earthquake—a live possibility—could damage Fukushima anew or take out another reactor between now and the 2020 Summer Olympics. The world won't give Japan a pass twice on what would have been a perfectly preventable disaster. Analysts are rating Abe on his success in cleaning up Japan's finances. Posterity will judge him on whether he cleaned up the mess Tepco and the nuclear village have created.

■ ■ ■

The plot thickens when you consider the government's efforts to make it harder for the public to know what's happening in Fukushima. It's perhaps the ultimate irony: Abe is so obsessed with China eclipsing Japan on the global stage that he's adopting some of his neighbor's policies. What else can we say about the secrecy law the prime minister's cabinet approved in October 2013 and the parliament passed in December 2013, an act that undermines and constrains his people's right to know?

LDP bigwigs say the move—which gives ministries the authority to classify as state secrets information on counterintelligence, counterterrorism, defense, and diplomacy—was necessary to protect the nation's people from any number of risks. It claims this is a necessary step toward creating a U.S.-style national security council and safely sharing vital intelligence with allies. And in the aftermath of the Edward Snowden/Bradley Manning leaks that have the United States reexamining its secrecy policies, why shouldn't Japan do something similar?

But the party didn't offer definitions or guidelines for what constitutes a "special secret." Compare that with the specifics about the jail terms journalists can expect for disclosing something that someone, somewhere, somehow might label national-security-caliber info: as much as 5 years. Government officials who blow the whistle on improprieties could get as much as 10 years. But the vagueness of this law, its disturbing ambiguity, will have a further chilling effect on a national media that are already too docile. If you think it's hard to follow the state of play with the Fukushima nuclear crisis now, just wait until the next radiation leak occurs and the media are kept out of the loop. It's a clear example of Abe borrowing a page from the Communist Party play-book. That page refers to curbs Beijing wants to impose on Hong Kong and the imprisonment threats it is using to police the Internet on the mainland.

Abe is no Mao Zedong, nor is he the rabid anti-free-speech cru-sader that current China President Xi Jinping is proving to be. But Abe's state-secrets edict puts Japan on a dubious trajectory that dam-ages its national governance and, ultimately, its global standing. It gives government staffers scope to protect anything they deem controversial or inconvenient. Ministries would have clear incentives to label every document they can "top secret." Sources will now become scarce on all manner of misdeeds and abuses of power involving everything from public safety to official corruption to government overreach.

"The most serious problem is that excessive secrecy creates the ideal environment for government wrongdoing," says Lawrence Repeta, a law professor at Tokyo's Meiji University. "This is the most disturbing lesson learned from the Manning and Snowden affairs."

Manning, of course, is the 26-year-old U.S. soldier convicted in August of leaking thousands of classified documents to Julian Assange's WikiLeaks. Snowden, 30, is the former computer-security contrac-tor accused of leaking classified intelligence information. Their actions made the United States even more reticent about sharing intelligence globally, and Japan's ability to keep secrets is far from airtight. Abe may believe the new law will endear Japan to its most important ally.

But the potential for abuse, overreach, and corruption from this China-like step abounds. It means that a government bureaucrat or regulator who, say, discloses details of a radiation leak at the crip-pled Fukushima power plant could end up in handcuffs, as could the reporter. Might the same fate befall an employee at Tepco who reveals a new mishap? That remains to be seen. The Japanese media are already prone to self-censorship for fear of alienating advertisers or losing access to sources.

All this means that a reporter who gets wind of a Japanese politi-cian running a massive slush fund might be wary of writing a story the nation needs to read. It means a government official miffed about a major Japanese company or bank having links to organized crime would keep quiet, or that a public-health crisis might never come to light. What about a report about the Bank of Japan's behind-the-scenes maneuvers to avert a bond-market crash? Again, we can't say. How about a journalist detailing the specifics of what Abe told President Obama at a bilateral meeting? Would that be a crime? There are many implications to what Abe is proposing. For one thing, it dovetails with his desire to rewrite Japan's postwar constitution, which was drafted by the United States in ways that put civic duty before civil rights. For another, it has uncomfortable parallels with the secrecy state that prevailed before World War II.

No one is saying this law will transport Japan back to those dark days. But it's an unsettling development. At the very least, Abe needs to detail very specifically where the boundaries lie: what exactly a "special secret" is; how such a secret is defined and designated; who gets to decide; the statute of limitations; and the legal process that would make sure justice is preserved. The prime minister needs to ensure there is a robust and transparent independent review process. Limits must be set on the period of confidentiality. The ability to protect secrets forever corrupts. For all Abe's rhetoric about standing fast against China, he seems happy to emulate his rival to the west in state-control policy and add new momentum to the Fukushima Effect.

Cronyism also impedes Japan's corporate sector, of which Tepco's relationship with the government is a microcosm. The workings of Japan Inc. often resemble an M.C. Escher drawing more than what Harvard MBAs are taught. The level of public-/private-sector collusion might make officials in the Philippines and Indonesia blush. If Tepco is Exhibit A, Olympus, home to a $1.7 billion accounting fraud, is easily Exhibit B.

It says a lot when world-weary investors hardened by the shenanigans at Enron Corp., WorldCom Inc., Parmalat SpA, and Wall Street are aghast at a scandal. The cast of characters at the proud Japan Inc. icon founded in 1919 pulled off that feat and more in a drama that became public in late 2011 and played out through 2012 and into 2013 even as Abe pledged to raise Japan's corporate-governance game. The sordid tale began in October 2011 when Briton Michael Woodford was ousted as chief executive officer amid vague accusations of cultural insensitivity. His firing made for quite a spectacle. Woodford was that rarest of things in a hyper-homogeneous business culture: the non-Japanese CEO, and a press-savvy one with a colorful personality. The mainstream Japanese media were happy to take Olympus at its word. The *gaijin* just didn't fit in amid a culture steeped in *not* being the proverbial "nail that sticks up."

Not disposed toward going quietly, Woodford reached out to the foreign media. It turned out that Woodford was looking into reports by Japanese magazine *FACTA* questioning outsized payments associated with a 2008 acquisition of the United Kingdom's Gyrus Group PLC. *FACTA* even alleged that some Olympus payments may have gone to "antisocial" elements, a euphemism for organized-crime groups. Far from being rewarded for trying to clean up the 94-year-old Olympus, Woodford was shown the door. He then reached out not only to foreign journalists, but to America's Federal Bureau of Investigation. Eventually, Olympus bigwigs, including former chairman Tsuyoshi Kikukawa, were arrested and convicted. And in September 2013, Olympus was charged in the United Kingdom for allegedly deceiving auditors. Woodford detailed his own side of the story in his 2012 memoir, *Exposure*.

You might expect this turn of events, dovetailing with the Tepco scandal, to prompt a wholesale reassessment of Japan Inc.'s clubby ways—and you would be wrong. Not only did Kikukawa receive a suspended sentence, but Abe is backing away from initial pledges to require companies to name outside directors as a means of internationalizing Japan's corporate culture and attracting more overseas investment. Abe's latest proposal only requires companies to justify the lack of outside directors without forcing them to appoint any.

The reversal is a sizable blow to Abenomics. If Japan wants to double foreign direct investment in Japan to 35 trillion yen by 2020, it must force companies to have at least one outside director and preferably several. According to the Board Director Training Institute of Japan, roughly 90 percent of countries in which global investors trade equities have some form of corporate governance code. Japan basically has none.

As Abe aids corporate Japan in circling the wagons, the aforementioned iron triangle remains alive and well to squander shareholder value. Why is Japan so reluctant to take steps that would be obvious after the most cursory reading of Peter Drucker's work? It is partly due to the stubborn belief that the strategies that worked so well for Japan in decades past hold just as much potential today, and that Japan Inc. is still just one government stimulus package of yen depreciation away from reclaiming its former glory.

Master's of Business Administration programs the world over should add a new course: Olympus 101. For budding business magnates, it would be a timely exercise in how *not* to handle a crisis, run a major company, or manage the third-biggest economy. This, too, is proof of the durability of Japan's way of doing business even after 3/11. Even in modern times, says Temple University's Jeff Kingston, "many influential advocates in the iron triangle believe that introducing risk through market-oriented, structural reforms involving deregulation and privatization is the cure for ongoing economic stagnation and low growth in productivity. These advocates believe Japan's economic problems are due in significant ways to muting of market forces and minimization of risk, and argue that the nation's prospects are dire if it fails to embrace sweeping reforms that boost productivity and change the inefficient way companies do business and the government runs the economy. It is not obvious to many Japanese, however, that less government intervention, reduced social welfare spending and the unshackling of business from regulations that protect workers' rights will achieve these goals."

Rather than iron triangle or M.C. Escher, Woodford prefers to think of corporate Japan through the lens of Lewis Carroll's 1865 novel, *Alice in Wonderland*. In many ways, it's an apt analogy. Japan's endemic cronyism can indeed seem like a through-the-looking-glass world of fantasy and illusion. After tumbling down the rabbit hole, investors are on their own to make heads or tails of Tokyo's policies. It often seems like economics in its most surreal form.

Woodford's own hopes that his experiences and disclosures would shake Japan Inc. to its core have been disappointed. That seemed clear enough in August when Sony Corp. rejected billionaire Daniel Loeb's proposal to raise cash by selling part of its entertainment business. The frustration felt by Loeb's Third Point LLC hedge fund was emblematic of how many investors view Sony's failure to stop Apple Inc. and Samsung Electronics Co. from driving it further toward irrelevance.

"The club, meaning corporate Japan, will do everything it can to mask and hide what's wrong," Woodford told me when I asked about

Sony ignoring advice from a non-Japanese shareholder. "That's what's most important."

The Olympus board also had market pundits questioning whether its shareholders are stupid, xenophobic, or both. It's an entirely valid question after Woodford was sent packing for the last time in January 2012. After being vindicated in the news media, Woodford raised his hand to return to Olympus and try to salvage a little credibility. Shareholders gave him a definitive "no." Bizarrely, they preferred to stick with the board that presided over one of corporate Japan's most shameful scandals rather than a chief executive—Woodford—who showed the courage and transparency Olympus needs to survive this affair.

The explanation may lie in shame itself. In 1946, Ruth Benedict, author of the influential book *The Chrysanthemum and the Sword*, famously dubbed Japan a "shame culture." Failing, either in the political or corporate realm, can carry a debilitating level of embarrassment, one many Japanese try at all costs to avoid. It explains Japan's lack of entrepreneurship. Huge Japanese companies can be plenty innovative and have long prided themselves on being world leaders in new patents. Less common is a few young Japanese sitting in a garage, Mark Zuckerberg–style, with a laptop, a dream, and ambitions of starting their own game-changing company. Fear of failure is a powerful thing in Japan. At Olympus, it wasn't greed or enriching cronies that had executives hiding losses, but fear of losing face. How fascinating it is that Olympus executives would rather risk jail and the total destruction of a 94-year-old company than simply fess up that they, like so many before them, got suckered on some toxic bonds. Consider, too, how Tepco executives hid safety infractions over the years in ways that led to today's radiation crisis. We will leave the dynamics behind the economics of shame to the psychoanalysts. It's clear, though, that in Olympus's case, it played a dominant role in ways the news media have yet to explore.

Woodford's experience explains so much about what's wrong with corporate Japan: why it's standing still as the rest of the world races forward; how opacity destroys dynamism and wealth; the groupthink that prizes the status quo over change; how a compliant Japanese media don't hold leaders accountable; the lack of women in places of power; the antipathy toward foreign ideas; and a culture that believes a public apology for missteps is punishment enough. All this could be applied as much to Japanese politics as to corporate life.

One reason cronyism is so rampant is Japan's culture of apology. It's known as the "corporate money shot," which I alluded to earlier with Yamaichi's Nozawa and Toyota's Toyoda. Many in the Japanese media seem to live for scenes of corporate executives or government officials bowing in shame before the cameras. Tears are often part of the show as the high-and-mighty fall on their proverbial swords to take responsibility for some misdeed or scandal. The practice is meant to break with the past and progress forward. And it's a lot of bunk, really. It has become a cynical public relations tool to offer the perception of contrition and change before returning to business as usual.

It's intriguing, then, that some want Wall Street titans to learn from this custom and be more Japanese. "I've suggested it wouldn't be a bad thing that the leadership of these institutions would take a Japanese-style approach to corporate governance," U.S. Senator Charles Grassley was quoted as saying in October 2008 by Iowa's *Daily Nonpareil*. "And I'm not talking about going out and committing suicide as some Japanese do in these circumstances, but I am talking about scenes I've seen on television where in belly-up corporations the CEOs go before the board of directors, before the public, before the stockholders and bow deeply and apologize for their mismanagement. Something like that happening among Wall Street executives would go a long way toward satisfying my constituents" worried about legislation that seems to bail out rich investors.

It's hard to decide where to start. First, what the Iowa Republican suggests isn't going to happen; Wall Street lawyers wouldn't allow it. Second, Grassley's faith in the sincerity of apologizing bigwigs is misplaced. For Japanese executives at confectionary companies selling tainted food, tire companies shilling defective treads, or nuclear-power plants playing loose with safety requirements, bowing publicly is about deflecting blame, not repairing problems. Of course, Grassley does have a point about the appalling lack of shame on Wall Street. The pinstripe set did itself no favors by wearing an air of entitlement as unemployment rose, 401(k) accounts shriveled, and politicians used, as of the date of Grassley's comments, $700 billion of public funds to patch up their recklessness. It would be grand to see America's biggest corporate villains of the time—Edward Liddy of American International Group, Lloyd Blankfein at Goldman Sachs Group, John Thain of Merrill Lynch, and Richard Fuld of Lehman Brothers—ask for forgiveness at a time when even then–Pope Benedict XVI complained the financial system is "built on sand" and the massive bank bailout seemed immoral.

What clues does Japan's lost decade offer? There are some definite similarities even if the magnitude was different. Richard Katz of the *Oriental Economist Report* estimates that Japan's bad loans amounted to about 20 percent of GDP, while Congress's bailout is closer to 5 percent of GDP. What of Grassley's views on Japanese corporate governance? Is Japan's system any better? The most important lesson nations can learn from Japan's experience during the 1990s and early 2000s is the importance of acting quickly and forcefully. And while Japanese banks avoided the worst of the 2008 crisis that began with subprime loans, they were more lucky than right. The conservatism that kept Japanese capital away from hard-to-value securities such as collateralized debt obligations (and according to Finance Minister Aso, bad English skills) explains why Asia's biggest economy was so vulnerable once global growth slowed.

As Wall Street reeled in 2008, there was a triumphal air coursing through Tokyo. Japanese banks even saw themselves as financial white knights, buying sizable stakes overseas, a trend highlighted by Mitsubishi UFJ Financial Group Inc.'s $9 billion investment in Morgan Stanley. That missed the point on two fronts: First, the phenomenon highlighted Japan's desire to have globalization both ways. Just imagine the uproar if the tables were reversed and amid a global crisis Morgan Stanley sought to buy a 21 percent stake in Japan's biggest bank. The reluctance to welcome foreign investment holds back growth. Second, Japan's vulnerabilities were rapidly coming to light. Even with short-term interest rates near zero, banks are stingy about making new loans, while businesses and consumers are reluctant to borrow. Japan was simply too reliant on exports as global growth slid.

Another problem with Japan's apology culture is it helps corporate miscreants escape responsibility. Almost three years after an earthquake in Japan touched off the worst nuclear crisis since Chernobyl, many are still asking this simple question: Who's going to jail? The news media have been distracted by the obvious and safe questions: How well did the government respond? Whither the devastated northeast? What's the economic effect? When might nuclear reactors mothballed since then reopen? Yet the "anniversary" articles sure to fill newspapers on March 11 are sure to miss the point. Anniversaries commemorate events in the past, ones for which there is a modicum of closure. Radiation is still venting into the air around Fukushima and spent fuel rods are still sitting out in the open air. Makeshift equipment, some held in place by tape, is keeping vital reactor systems operating. Is Japan's 3/11 history? Not unless we change the definition. And the government's new secrecy law will make reporting on the true state of Fukushima impossible to assess independently.

■ ■ ■

What the third anniversary of the disaster requires is a dose of accountability. We need a few good perp-walks by current and past Tepco executives, whose arrogance, negligence, and corruption sent radiation clouds Tokyo's way. Next on the docket should be the government officials who enabled what more closely resembles an organized-crime syndicate than an energy sector. For years, this crowd ignored warnings of a 3/11-like catastrophe. When it occurred, they claimed the tsunami was beyond anything anyone ever imagined. In March 2012, then–Prime Minister Noda disappointed the nation when he concluded that no individual could be held responsible for the nuclear fallout and that everyone should "share the pain."

It was a jawdropping comment. In the darkest moments of the Fukushima meltdown, Japan considered evacuating Tokyo's 13-million-plus people. Consider where the Dow Jones Industrial Average and the Stoxx Europe 600 Index might be if the financial capital of one of the three most international currencies were an uninhabitable wasteland. This isn't the stuff of John le Carre novels or Tom Clancy's imagination. It's the reality that Tokyo navigated in 2011. What much of the world forgets about 3/11 is how Noda's predecessor, Naoto Kan, saved Tokyo. In the days after the earthquake, he got wind that Tepco wanted to evacuate all workers from Fukushima. That would have ensured apocalyptic radiation leaks from more than 10,000 spent fuel rods, which the bright minds at Tepco stored in relatively unprotected pools near the reactors.

On March 15, 2011, Kan stormed into Tepco's headquarters and demanded that its engineers stay on and handle the crisis. Culturally, it was a very un-Japanese thing to do in a nation programmed for propriety. Yet desperate times call for culturally questionable measures, and Kan saved Tokyo. Was his overall leadership state-of-the-art? No; he failed to offer the transparency the citizens of any democracy deserve. Yet Noda's first act after becoming prime minister in September 2011 was to reverse Kan's most important policy shift: reining in the nuclear industry and finding energy alternatives in one of the most seismically active nations. With the benefit of hindsight, it's clear that Kan was a goner the second he took on the alliance of politicians, bureaucrats, and power companies promoting reactors. His proposal to halt plans for 14 new reactors shook the nuclear-industrial complex to its core. The knives came out for Kan, and Japan's docile media played along.

Noda made life safe again for the nuclear mob, letting it go with a few public apologies. He gave them a Get-Out-of-Jail-Free card that ensured Japan would learn little from 3/11. It's funny how the world fixates on Japan's organized-crime groups. Even the Obama administration is freezing assets of Japan's largest *yakuza* network, the Yamaguchi-gumi. What about the nuclear mob? Its members might not have full-body tattoos and missing fingers, but they're far more dangerous to our planet. Noda says the entire Japanese establishment had been taken in by the "myth of safety" and it's all a do-over. At the same time, that establishment also propagated the now-laughable argument that nuclear power is clean, safe, and cheap. Clean? Ask Japanese schoolkids who are afraid of the vegetables on their plates. Safe? Not unless we build reactors out of rubber and elevate them on huge shock absorbers. Cheap? Japan will spend hundreds of billions of dollars cleaning up Tepco's mess.

But no worries—we're going to share the pain. Why should the nuclear industry and its shareholders pay the bill when Japanese taxpayers can? People are going to jail at Olympus for cooking the books. In 2007, Internet entrepreneur Takafumi Horie of Livedoor Co. was locked up for book cooking. In the 1970s, even a former prime minister went to prison in the Lockheed Corp. scandal. Why is no one in handcuffs for cooking northeastern Japan? Most Japanese don't want a nuclear future, yet they're being strong-armed into submission. If that's not a crime, I'm not sure what is. And if this isn't an ominous lesson from which the rest of the world should learn, what is?

The fascinating thing about Kiyoshi Kurokawa's report on the Fukushima Effect is how the problems he highlighted aren't confined to the power industry. It takes a village to breed a system corrupt and dangerous enough to create a Tepco, which got away with its negligence for years because of the cozy ties between companies, regulators, bureaucrats, and supposedly independent researchers. Backed by its connections, money, and control of the media, Tepco has brazenly continued to cook its radiation data for the last two and a half years. It matters little that the government is finally commandeering Tepco's cleanup: The government *is* Tepco.

Chapter 5

Galapagos Nation

How Isolation Stunts Japan's Evolution

N o modern nation would fascinate Charles Darwin more than
Japan. It's the highly developed economy that time forgot. It
may be sitting amid a sea of epochal change as Asia's upstarts
rise, but its business and political systems generally behave as if the world
has been sitting still for decades. Japan is the market equivalent of the
endemic species Darwin found on the remote Galapagos islands off
Ecuador's coast. Its products and business customs are highly distinct
from anything found elsewhere, but not particularly suited to thriving
beyond the water's edge. Even as deflation has deepened, Japan has refused to turn away from the fossilized policies that are walling it off from
an Asia region racing forward. All too many if its companies still have a
sepia-toned view of a rapidly globalizing world, refusing to think bigger
and more internationally. Welcome to "Galapagos Nation."

"Around 1990 Japan was self-satisfied with the economic success, and Japanese people thought that they have nothing to learn from anybody," Masamoto Yashiro, a legendary banker and private-equity expert, said at a University of Tokyo symposium on October 19, 2013. "This time is over now, and Japan and Japanese corporations must change to regain growth and become competitive again."

Japan, first and foremost, is a nation of paradoxes. Everywhere you turn you find a startling mix of the old and the new, the traditional and the novel, the past and the future. Thousand-year-old temples sit in the shadow of hypermodern skyscrapers. A traveler walking through a modern city of steel and neon can turn a corner and find a narrow alley of classical wood-and-tile buildings. Rustic red lanterns sit in the shadow of the nation's high-rise future. Japanese will fly across the country and pay $50 for the perfect taste of fish and then wait in line for an hour for Krispy Kreme doughnuts. Japan is home to what is arguably the most refined cuisine, as evidenced by UNESCO's recently naming its food culturally important and its abundance of Michelin-starred restaurants, but it's also one of the biggest markets for McDonald's and Spam! Japan is the third-biggest economy in the world, and yet Korea seems to get more headlines.

In a nation of paradoxes, Japan's lack of innovation is a standout. In its latest Global Competitiveness Index, the World Economic Forum ranks Japan ninth after the Netherlands and Hong Kong and just ahead of the United Kingdom. Such surveys, and that goes for the Economist Intelligence Unit and others, often rank Japan as one of the most innovative countries based on the number of patents per million of population and other criteria. The trouble is, the vast majority of those patents are held by Japan's biggest companies. The regulatory structure favors giants over startups, which exacerbates the concentration of new ideas in a handful of corporate boardrooms. Technology is an area to which the so-called Galapagos Syndrome is most immediately applicable. The industry often gives little regard to tapping new markets overseas. It makes, for example, cutting-edge mobile phones with more functions than the average user could ever need, yet with features and functions that differ markedly from global standards. As the population shrinks, Japan needs to think bigger and more internationally. Why? Globalization is causing a commoditization of the things Japan long did well; now good cars and electronics are coming from virtually anywhere, including China. The only way Japan can thrive is to innovate as rarely before. What Japan lacks is a bunch of sleep-deprived, caffeine-driven Steve Jobs wannabes perched over laptops around the nation creating game-changing products and new industries.

■ ■ ■

Technology was the first industry to get trapped on Galapagos. Seduced by a large population of technophiles and enthusiastic shoppers, mobile phone makers saw little reason to go truly global. Any search for explanations why Finnish and Korean phone makers succeeded globally where Japan failed has to consider their much smaller domestic markets. Why has Korean pop music made bigger inroads globally than J-pop? Japan's large domestic consumer base seemed success enough for singers and record companies. Japan's business model got more traction in the analog age when all that mattered was making good products. But in the digital age, where networks and connectivity through the Internet matter even more, Japan Inc. has found it hard to compete. Here, think Google Inc. and Yahoo! Inc.

Where did Japan first go wrong? "Due to language, culture, comparatively small interchange between Japan's markets and foreign markets, some technologies and some products evolved in Japan differently than in other markets," said Gerhard Fasol, president of Tokyo-based technology consulting firm Eurotechnology Japan.

> In part, Japan chose unique Japanese technology standards for mobile phones, mobile TV, and mobile payments in the hope to achieve global adoption of these Japanese standards, and at the same time to make market penetration of Japan's markets more difficult for foreign companies in these fields—thus giving a competitive advantage to Japanese companies in their home market, Japan.

The ways in which the strategy backfired and walled Japan off from greater global markets should be lessons for less-developed markets like Korea and developing ones like China. "In this globalized world, it's all about making sure what you design, make, and do has relevance and utility far beyond national borders," said Naomi Fink, founder and CEO of Europacifica Consulting. "It's the only way to compete and thrive."

It's ironic when you consider how far ahead of the West Japanese mobile phone makers were in the 2000s, including in sending e-mails, accessing the Internet, the ability to make payments, watching television, and global-positioning systems. But Japanese phones worked on different systems than much of the outside world and brisk sales at home fed complacency. Once smartphones hit the market, Japanese tech companies were caught flatfooted. Apple's iPhone came out in 2007, and no Japanese carrier has produced a globally plausible competitor.

In 2010, Sharp Corp. even paid homage to this phenomenon, introducing a Galapagos line of tablet computers. The Osaka-based company consciously chose the name to accentuate the device's Japaneseness—that its features and functionality stood completely apart from anything else abroad. Yet Sharp fell prey to the economic zeitgeist. Within a year, it announced it would stop selling the line amid dismal sales. Several months later, Mikio Katayama, the Sharp leader who oversaw the introduction of the Galapagos, was out as president, too.

This arrangement served Japan well until around the late 1990s. As deflation set in and the population aged, domestic profits began to suffer. Since then, *Galapagos* has become an umbrella code word for Japan's uniqueness and its growing isolation from an increasingly dynamic world.

The Galapagosization of Japan can be found beyond the corporate boardroom. Fewer Japanese, for example, are studying or living abroad. A September 2010 survey by Japanese graduate school Sanno Institute of Management was indicative of the trend, finding that two-thirds of white-collar workers don't want to work overseas—ever. This reluctance to leave Japan is creating an odd generational quirk: Today's young Japanese are often less international than their fathers.

The reasons for this are many, including a general lack of English proficiency. Safety concerns often come up in surveys; Japan is, after all, among the world's most crime-free nations. Perhaps the biggest reason is rigidities in the labor market. Today's college graduates are chasing a dwindling number of coveted lifetime-employment jobs and students begin lobbying for them in their junior year, or even their sophomore year. Fear of missing out on this recruitment process dissuades many from studying abroad or taking time off to travel before joining the ranks of the salarymen.

The good news is that some mavericks are working to get Japan off of Galapagos, including Tadashi Yanai.

So this is what it has come to for Japan Inc.: a future in underwear instead of cars, color TVs, or industrial robots. Long before 2010, when China surpassed it to become Asia's biggest economy and Apple unleashed the iPad, Japan fancied itself a nation fated for global primacy. Its technology was second to none, its banks dominant, its car assembly lines envied and imitated, its corporate chiefs giving Jack Welch a run for his money.

Deflation and political paralysis have changed that narrative in a manner that was made crystal clear in 2011, when corporate Japan was shut out of *Forbes* magazine's ranking of the top 50 Asian companies. Claiming many of the spots on the list was always a matter of national pride. Japan's economy may be weak, its leaders lacking, and the population aging, but the country sure has some amazing companies. Yet, recent *Forbes* lists have found plenty of room for Chinese, Filipino, Indian, Indonesian, Korean, and Thai companies, but not for Japanese brands.

Rather than despairing, Japan ought to look beyond the aging industrial mainstays to learn how to thrive in a dynamic world economy: I offer up Yanai's Uniqlo brand. The graybeards who control Japan Inc. have been slow to embrace Fast Retailing Co.'s expanding brand, or to recognize what they might learn from it. Japan liked being a technology powerhouse, not a bargain clothier that relies on cheap Chinese labor. Yet Japan can use all the fresh thinking it can muster these days and, financially, the end justifies the means. On another list, *Forbes* ranks Fast Retailing's president Yanai as Japan's richest man.

The lessons to draw from Yanai and Uniqlo are obvious. The markets of the future are outside Japan, and the provincialism that rules Japanese management perpetuates the forces of deflation. To avoid the "Galapagos syndrome," Yanai is opening 200 to 300 new stores worldwide each year. Japanese have been reluctant to go big overseas since their chastening in the late 1980s. That foray was an exercise driven by hubris. Buying Rockefeller Center and the Pebble Beach golf course had more to do with bragging rights than rational investing. Company presidents didn't bid on every Van Gogh, Picasso, and Monet up for auction to make money. It was to celebrate new wealth. This time, venturing abroad will take on more strategic significance.

■ ■ ■

There are other things Yanai's peers can learn from Uniqlo. One is the need to think big and out of the proverbial box. Few are his equal at framing the debate about what ails Japan. When I chat with Japanese executives about Uniqlo, many are dismissive. Responses are often some variation of "It's a Japanese version of Gap Inc., not so impressive." Or Uniqlo represents a race to the economic bottom, while Japan needs to move steadily upmarket. Yet Yanai understands that deflation isn't a cyclical phenomenon, but a secular one. Rather than sit around and hope consumer prices will suddenly rise and growth return, Yanai is reshaping the retailing world. Uniqlo has brought more *kaizen*—the process of continuous improvement—to the apparel industry than meets the eye. Its underwear that helps wick away sweat has been a godsend to those struggling through sticky summers from Tokyo to New York. Call it Japan's underwear model of economic growth.

The company breaks any number of hidebound Japanese traditions. Meetings are held in English, a very rare practice in Japan. Fast retailing isn't hung up on seniority-based hiring; if you're 26 and smart, the job can be yours. The company has few qualms about poaching talent from competitors, which can run afoul of local etiquette. It is working to increase the ratio of foreign staff and employs edgy advertising campaigns. The company seems more serious than most about corporate social responsibility. In 2011, Yanai joined hands with Nobel Peace laureate Muhammad Yunus to create a textile company in Bangladesh to help poor women gain the financial independence society often keeps beyond their reach. Yanai also was an early and generous provider of aid after Japan's earthquake.

All isn't perfect with Uniqlo, of course. There's always a risk it will overexpand in this chaotic global environment. And the company's fortunes are disproportionately linked to the charismatic and hands-on Yanai. If he bowed out tomorrow, it's not clear where Uniqlo would be. Yet here is an example of how Japan—amid deflation, natural disasters, and a shrinking population—can stoke growth and change the landscape in global markets. The world needs more of it from a country that once thought being on top was its destiny.

"We shouldn't depend upon technological advancements in one narrow sector of the economy, such as manufacturing, to single-handedly drive growth, which is a mistake Japan has made for way too long," Fink of Europacifica said. "Structurally, productivity growth is the greatest driver of output growth." In other words, Japan needs to allocate more capital and energy to ideas and innovation, not making old-economy cars or ships. "The idea is to cut down on unproductive capital quickly, otherwise, depreciation costs start killing you and marginal product of capital declines and you have deflation."

Japan's English problem, meanwhile, deserves more attention than government officials realize. Paradoxically, Japan spares little expense boosting its economy. It has amassed the largest public debt, lowered interest rates to zero, and bailed out banks and companies like Japan Airlines Co. Now, it's time for Japan to put its mouth where its money is.

Tokyo wants to be a global financial center. It's busily upgrading infrastructure and considering a similar zoning approach as London's Canary Wharf to attract hedge funds, banks, and other institutions. While that's all well and good, a key ingredient is missing: English. Call it the "Economics of Engrish," as did C. H. Kwan, senior fellow at Japan's Research Institute of Economy, Trade and Industry, in a May 2002 article. The idea was that Japan needs to improve its English proficiency to stay at the forefront of business in an increasingly globalized world.

Fast-forward more than a decade and Japan is still tripping over what many observers call its "English-language deficit." Considering its economic success and the frequency with which Japanese travel abroad, the country's English-fluency rate is surprisingly low. I feel a bit uncomfortable tackling this issue. Arguing Japanese need to learn English might strike some as an attempt to advance America's cultural hegemony. My own challenge learning Japanese after 12 years in Tokyo also makes me skittish about judging others' language abilities. We Americans aren't known for our passion for learning other tongues.

Yet English, for better or worse, has become the lingua franca of finance, business, science, and the Internet. The longer any nation resists the need to improve its English skills, the more it limits its potential. This argument would be valid if the global business language were French, German, Mandarin—or Japanese. Even world leaders known for acrimony toward the West, such as former Malaysian Prime Minister Mahathir Mohamad, grudgingly acknowledge as much.

"A genuine global financial center needs to bring together players of every nationality, and from a variety of disciplines: accountants, lawyers, IT specialists, traders, due-diligence guys, etcetera," says Louis Turner, London-based chief executive of the Asia-Pacific Technology Network. "There has to be one working language to bring all these people together and, like it or not, that language has to be English."

In Asia, Mandarin may eventually establish itself as a working second language for business and science. For now, though, the focus is on English. In 2011, native-Japanese speakers taking the paper-based Test of English as a Foreign Language (TOEFL) placed among the bottom 3 out of 33 Asian nations.

Japan is beginning to move in the right direction. The education ministry introduced measures in recent years to improve its language program and encouraged public school teachers to undergo fresh training. Abe wants to compel students to begin English classes much earlier and with greater fluency. That would help repair some of the damage Abe's government did to Japan's language programs during his first stint as prime minister from 2006 to 2007. Abe's education minister, Bunmei Ibuki, shifted the focus back to teaching traditional values and patriotism to young Japanese. It was an untimely distraction in tackling what's arguably a curriculum problem. The emphasis has long been on passing written English exams, not verbal communication. Japan's mistake has been to view English as a curriculum subject, not as a tool for greater competitiveness.

Japan's English challenge becomes downright farcical at times. In June 2013, Finance Minister Taro Aso prompted considerable eye-rolling when he suggested corporate Japan's poor language skills are actually an asset. Japan escaped the worst of the 2008 financial meltdown, Aso claimed, because its bankers were mystified by subprime loans: "Managers of Japanese banks hardly understood English, that's why they didn't buy."

The English issue is becoming a serious liability. It was moot in the 1980s, when foreigners lined up to do business with a Japan very much on the ascendancy. Today, Japanese companies compete more with international executives, often boasting better communication skills, than with domestic rivals. All this can lead to heavy costs for corporations. Teaching English to employees is an expensive, productivity-killing process. It also can lead to faulty decisions. Hiring someone primarily for his or her language skills may mean missing out on a far more skilled candidate. The language debate has met with some resistance in Japan. It's at the core of concerns about globalization watering down culture and tradition. Japanese is an incredibly complex language with thousands of characters, layers of honorifics to master, and a proud literary history. Many worry a greater emphasis on English will devalue Japanese skills in future generations. A happy medium must be struck here. Embracing English need not come at the expense of tradition or culture. The stark reality is that the rise of China and India is making this debate moot. It's leaving Japan with a choice: Either improve English proficiency, or get left behind by fast-growing economic upstarts.

"It would definitely help to brand Japan and rebrand the country," said Martin Roll, chief executive officer of Singapore-based consulting firm VentureRepublic and an expert on branding.

Generally, people find Japan a very nice place to visit and Japanese very friendly. I actually think people's general English proficiency has increased in the last 10 years, but there is still lots to be done. People's English proficiency will help brand a country due to the enhanced perception of a country by visiting tourists and business people who find it easier, more seamless, and more approachable if they can navigate/communicate with ease. It would be perceived easier by businesspeople, other governments, and associations of all sorts to conduct business/activities with Japan, and will help the impression of professionalism, international perspectives, and similar issues, if the English proficiency is higher. On the internal aspects, so will an enhanced English proficiency encourage/motivate especially younger generations to interact and embrace the global world, as they would feel more confident visiting other countries, study internationally, interact with foreigners, and connect themselves on a larger scale than today with the global world.

Singapore's example is instructive, Roll said. Its population is predominantly Chinese, but the government policy spanning back from the 1970s made English the norm throughout the government and society. It was among the signature achievements of Lee Kuan Yew, the nation's founding father and former prime minister. Singapore's level of English proficiency helped Singapore connect into the fiber of global business and today it's a key Asian financial center.

"The Japanese government would therefore contribute lots to the future of Japan and its people by enhancing the usage and proficiency of English across all platforms in schools, universities, and government," Roll said.

English isn't everything, though. It's not a magic wand that will suddenly rid Japan of its long-term problems. Something even deeper is at play, something Robert Dujarric, director of the Institute of Contemporary Asian Studies at Temple University's Tokyo campus, calls Japan's *deglobalization*. "Around the world, students at the best universities are experiencing a more international upbringing than their parents," Dujarric said. "Japan, however, stands apart because of its continued seclusion. In particular, the decline of the number of Japanese students at leading U.S. institutions is startling."

The findings of Dujarric's research with Shin Woon, an economics student at Barnard College at New York's Columbia University, in 2013 are startling indeed. Between 1998 and 1999, 705 Japanese students were enrolled at the three top U.S. universities they analyzed: Columbia, Harvard College, and Massachusetts Institute of Technology. But by the 2011 to 2012 period, that number had fallen to 339. More broadly, enrollment over the preceding seven years also dropped markedly at Yale University and University of California–Berkeley. Overall there were just 19,966 Japanese studying in the United States between 2011 and 2012 compared with 46,872 between 2000 and 2001. Dujarric and Woon went even deeper, looking at doctoral candidates in several renowned, mostly U.S.-based English-speaking universities with an emphasis on business, economics, and science—disciplines where moderately proficient English speakers can excel. Out of all Northeast Asians enrolled, Japanese accounted for less than 10 percent. And of the 1,306 faculty members, 6 were Japanese, whereas more than 60 were from Northeast Asia. While some of the decline in Japanese studying in the United States reflected some students enrolling in other nations, the basic direction is abundantly clear: Overall Japanese participation in international education is declining dramatically. That's an ominous trend on several levels.

"First, Japan's national security requires Japanese who can interact with the rest of the world," Dujarric and Woon argued.

It suffers from a paucity of officials, politicians, journalists, and public experts who can engage foreigners. Its national security apparatus is woefully short of men and women who can participate in international meetings, negotiate with foes, work with allies, and understand the outside world. The situation will worsen. Second, the country is not producing enough internationalized Japanese when corporate Japan is embarking on a new wave of expansion, fueled by a falling demographic at home, increasing costs of production, temporarily lowered by "Abenomics" but nevertheless high, and growing opportunities overseas. But unlike Korea, Japan lacks the internationally minded young men and women who are best suited for these tasks. And third, Japanese academia needs to integrate with the rest of the world, starting with Japanese studying and teaching abroad. As other countries engage in "brain circulation," Japanese schools are stagnating because of their isolation. This happened in the Edo period (1603–1868), when the lack of sufficient intercourse with the outside world led to Japan falling behind in every area of science, technology, and administrative efficiency.

Will Japan change? Dujarric and Woon aren't optimistic, even as Abe's team urges greater globalization on the part of young Japanese. One problem is the rising cost of tuition, a burden exacerbated by Abe's efforts to weaken the yen. Runaway university tuition in the United States has been climbing into the stratosphere and acts as a barrier to Japanese. But it's far from the whole story, considering the increased numbers of students from much poorer nations flocking to the United States, even with the arduous visa process. While some of these students receive government assistance or scholarships, many pay their own way. In other words, students committed to studying in America tend to find a way to fulfill those goals.

What's more, surveys indicate that young company employees in Japan are increasingly more reluctant to work overseas than, say, their fathers' generation. Japanese diplomats, for example, often bemoan the unwillingness of new recruits at government ministries to be posted abroad. That reluctance will increasingly hold Japan back in the international arena.

"With some exceptions in the natural sciences, Japan's universities play in the national leagues, not in the Olympics," Dujarric and Woon said.

> This is not due to a lack of intellectual firepower, but is a result of the evolution of Japanese tertiary education since the nineteenth century. For elite Japanese schools, a globalized Japan would be like bringing in a T-Rex to roam free in their erstwhile-protected enclosure. Good students and the best faculty would leave and globally oriented funding would flow elsewhere. Also, the elite will suffer because their power comes from their Japanese credentials—education, experience, recognition, connections, etc. . . . Globalization would make status far more dependent on international social and educational capital. Thus those whose capital is solely Japanese would see their assets trade at a discount. This explains why many Japanese feel that spending too much time overseas will be detrimental to their career prospects, as they will miss out in the race to acquire Japanese credentials.

Here, too, there's even a role for gender. In the globalized workplace, Japanese women often outperform men. Japanese females outnumber men both at the United Nations and as a percentage of managerial roles at foreign-owned businesses. All this means is that the internationalization of the economy will benefit women most. The paradox, of course, is that Japan is a nation run by conservative men who tend to think women belong in supporting roles. These incentives inherent to this arrangement argue against greater Japanese globalization.

Is there even a Japan psyche angle worth mentioning here? "An internationalized Japan would delegitimize the idea of the archipelago as a unique harmonious, homogeneous, and 'Japanese' homeland and open the door to a more liberal society with different values and new elites. This runs contrary to Prime Minster Shinzo Abe's cabinet's emphasis on Japanese values and history," Dujarric and Woon argued.

This deglobalization is decidedly at odds not just with the direction of the world economy but at key turning points in Japan's history. When the Tokugawa Shogunate gave way to the Meiji period in 1868, the Japanese embraced ideas from abroad with voracious enthusiasm as the country began its march toward industrialization. "Today, those who decide Japan's destiny benefit from a system that is much stronger than that of the Tokugawas," Dujarric and Woon concluded. "The institutions that define the country are old and powerful. Those who rise to the top of this system are rarely revolutionaries, but mostly diligent functionaries who fear reform."

■ ■ ■

Fast Retailing isn't alone in compelling employees to speak English. Tire giant Bridgestone and Honda Motor Co. are joining a small group of companies using language to declare their global ambitions. The same goes for e-commerce giant Rakuten Inc., whose president, Hiroshi Mikitani, is on a personal mission to get Japan off Galapagos.

In mid-2011, Mikitani caused shockwaves when he left the main business lobby, Nippon Keidanren, and started a rival association. He's fighting to make corporate Japan nimbler and more entrepreneurial by creating space where long-neglected small-to-midsize companies can brainstorm and make policy recommendations that are getting Abe's attention (the prime minister met with the group in April 2013). Mikitani loudly condemns Japan's insularity and favors letting the creative destruction emphasized by economist Joseph Schumpeter play out.

That also goes for SoftBank Corp. president Masayoshi Son, who is defying the powerful nuclear lobby by investing $196 million in renewable-energy projects and promoting an Asia-wide "supergrid" to link cities from Mumbai to Tokyo. His $21.6 billion bid for U.S. mobile giant Sprint Nextel Corp. in 2013 also marked a bold foray overseas.

In October, Japan was treated to the juicy spectacle of two of its richest and most innovative entrepreneurs brawling in public over Internet market share and visions for the future. But what's most important about the fight between Son and Mikitani is the example it sets.

The two men have much in common. They are self-made billionaires who founded game-changing technology companies—Son with mobile-phone carrier SoftBank, Mikitani with Japan's answer to Amazon.com. Each is his company's largest shareholder, fully fluent in English (a rarity in corporate Japan), and U.S.-educated (Son at the University of California–Berkeley; Mikitani at Harvard University). Both are married with two kids. Both make splashy investments in overseas Internet companies (Son in Alibaba Group Holding Ltd.; Mikitani in Pinterest Inc.). Both are sports nuts who own baseball teams.

Son and Mikitani are also the faces of New Japan and unapologetic critics of Japan Inc.'s clubby, insular ways. They oppose nuclear power, a stance that puts them in direct conflict with the ruling Liberal Democratic Party and Japan's powerful business lobby, Nippon Keidanren. Above all, both share a passion for change and are the kind of creature Japan needs more of as it tries to end a 20-year funk. As they mix it up and make headlines around the globe, they are adding some much-needed energy to Abe's revival plans.

Their latest tiff was instigated by Son, who is also chairman of Yahoo Japan Corp. Son eliminated fees that the search and shopping business had charged for online stores, a direct challenge to Rakuten, Japan's largest Internet shopping mall. Rakuten's model is based on charging businesses such fees to operate shops on its site; by contrast, Yahoo Japan is a portal and retail site that gets more than half its revenue from advertising. Son figures lower fees will increase market share and, eventually, ad sales.

Japan's conservative business culture is somewhat aghast by the budding price war: At one point, investors had wiped out as much as $4.3 billion in both companies' market values. Japan Inc. has always encouraged firms carving up territory and staying out of each other's way. When rifts emerge, they're handled over whiskey and secret handshakes. How could Japan's second- and third-wealthiest men scuffle publicly like this? The indignity!

But Son and Mikitani are showing young, would-be entrepreneurs that they can be more than docile, corporate drones in dark suits mindlessly working their way toward retirement. They are injecting competitive juices into an economy that's known all too little. They are, by example, inspiring contemporaries to take risks, think globally, and act in the best interests of shareholders.

Theirs isn't the perfect rivalry. A better one would pit New Japan against the old guard. The last time that happened in a widely publicized way it didn't end well for Internet guru Takafumi Horie of Livedoor Co. In 2007, the then-35-year-old Horie, an outsider in corporate Japan, was locked up for accounting irregularities, though his real crime seemed to be speaking out against Japan Inc.'s blinkered ways.

Contrast his fate with that of Kikukawa, on whose watch a $1.7 billion fraud at Olympus resulted in an 80 percent plunge in market value and global shame. The scrappy, brash, T-shirt-wearing Horie went to prison for engaging in practices that are widely employed in Japan accounting circles. And Kikukawa, as Japan Inc. as an executive can be, got to go home—a suspended sentence.

Still, there's great value in having the two faces of Japan's new guard locking horns. More fights like this would have executives looking over their shoulders, unable to hide behind the cross-shareholding arrangements that kill competition, the poison pills that breed complacency, and the insularity that stifles rapid growth.

Does Abenomics deserve some credit for this Son–Mikitani spat? I would argue the opposite. Sure, their businesses are benefiting from the first two phases of Abe's revival plan: monetary and fiscal pump-priming. But these innovators are taking phase three—shaking up Japan's staid business culture—into their own hands. Abe would be wise to respond to their impatience by getting on with deregulating the economy.

For all their differences, Mikitani and Son personify the kind of visionary and unconventional leadership Abe hopes to inspire. Mikitani wants to be the world's next Jeff Bezos, the Amazon.com founder who is now rescuing the *Washington Post*. Son, meanwhile, is expanding globally with his acquisition of U.S. wireless provider Sprint Corp.

As these two titans face off and roil the claustrophobic confines of Japanese society and business, they're giving Abenomics just the boost it needs.

There's no shortage of pundits eager to tell Abe how to shake up Japan's economy. Instead of looking to academics for advice, though, the prime minister should get into the trenches with some of the nation's more unconventional corporate heads. Even so, enough top executives have successfully challenged the status quo for Abe to take note. They have proven how much change is possible, even within the claustrophobic constraints of Japanese society and business. Abe should absorb the lesson.

Yet the appeal of argumentativeness can have its limits in a nation that favors harmony. That's particularly true of politics, as Osaka Mayor Toru Hashimoto learned the hard way. The words "future prime minister" routinely accompany discussions of Hashimoto's rapid rise. At 44, he's young and telegenic in a nation where 26 percent of the population is over 65 and the other best-known regional leader, former Tokyo Governor Shintaro Ishihara, is 81. Hashimoto is unusually blunt in his criticism of national leaders, and his vision is often at odds with the prevailing wisdom in Tokyo. Some have even gone so far as to call the brash Hashimoto Japan's answer to Adolf Hitler. Certainly not the majority of the 2.7 million people in the western Japanese city. Many Osakans love their mayor's crusade against Tokyo's dysfunction and absolute power over the country. It has Japan's old guard running scared and comparing Hashimoto to Europe's most notorious genocidal fascist.

If the world needs anything, it's a moratorium on Hitler analogies. As much as one may dislike Barack Obama or George W. Bush, neither bears even the most fleeting resemblance to the maniacal German leader. Suggestions to the contrary are beyond ignorance and vandalize history. Yet for Japanese to turn to a man in this rarefied company speaks volumes about where Japan finds itself in a volatile global environment.

The desire for change reached a fever pitch after the 2011 earthquake and tsunami. Even before the earth shook, the waters rose, and radiation leaked on March 11, 2011, Japanese sensed Tokyo had lost its way. Many just hadn't realized how much. Hence the Tea Party–like dynamic inherent in Hashimoto's popularity. His drive for greater accountability, decentralized decision making, and fresh ideas is as well-timed as it is frightening to the establishment.

Frankly, I find some of Hashimoto's platform borderline creepy. His party's training program for aspiring leaders, the Restoration Politics Institute, smacks of nationalism. His inquisition against teachers who refuse to stand and sing when the national anthem is played—some worry it celebrates Japan's militaristic past—is right-wing silliness. Giving the third degree to city workers with tattoos is just weird. Yes, Japanese traditionally associate body art with members of *yakuza* organized-crime groups. But in 2013, is it anyone's business if some desk clerk inked Mickey Mouse on his back?

Yet at a time when Japanese are grasping for change, Hashimoto is what passes for a breath of fresh air. Take his stance against relying on nuclear power, one that enraged the national government. Hashimoto is doing what any elected leader should: heeding the will of the people. The large majority of Japan's 127 million people no longer trust power companies and bureaucrats to protect them from another Chernobyl.

All Abe's LDP has done is remind voters that the nuclear industry holds the puppet strings even after the Fukushima disaster. Hashimoto is fighting for people, not companies, and good for him. This gives us a sense of how dangerous divergent views are to vested interests in Tokyo—and why Japan needs more of them. Hashimoto's calls for greater accountability and competition are particularly welcome. His Japan Restoration Party favors direct elections for prime minister, which would be a genuine revolution in Japan that could reduce official corruption and increase accountability. It wants to scrap one of the two chambers of the Diet to hasten decision making and reduce the grid-lock that stops virtually all change in Japan.

The dark side of this would be a charismatic leader becoming too powerful—even dictatorial. That has opponents calling the movement "Hashism," a play on *fascism*. This is a minor risk in a nation with so many checks and balances embedded in its postwar system of government. What really worries the establishment is new ideas that leave its carefully built fiefdoms out of the loop. This really is the point. Japan is a prosperous, safe, and politically stable place. Yet, it may be a little too stable and in turn change-averse. Public debt is more than twice the size of Japan's economy, the population is aging rapidly, and its global competitiveness is waning. How is the government responding? It is adding to the debt. In May 2012, Fitch Ratings cut Japan's sovereign-debt rating, calling the government's fiscal strategy "leisurely." Well, that description applies to everything from energy policy to raising productivity to boosting the birthrate to encouraging entrepreneurship to lowering trade barriers to improving corporate governance to increasing female participation in the labor force to liberalizing immigration.

Love the Tea Party or hate it, it challenged the status quo in Washington in unpredictable ways. The same goes for the Arab Spring, which not only shook the Middle East and North Africa, but also sent waves of fear through the halls of power from Beijing to Mexico City. Japan, it has long been said, needs a new generation of leaders to step forward and engineer a major course correction. Hashimoto, love him or hate him, personifies it, and the extent to which he makes the establishment squirm, and play the Hitler card, suggests this political upstart is on to something.

■ ■ ■

The Galapagos Syndrome manifests itself elsewhere in the economy. Insularity plagues its entertainment industry, one that's never thought seriously about going global. It's fascinating, for example, that the one Asian pop star to go truly global in the last 30 years wasn't Japanese but a performer from a nation whose population is more than two and a half times smaller: Korea's Psy. His 2012 hit, "Gangnam Style," went global in a way none of J-pop's biggest acts ever did. Psy became a YouTube smash, earned gigs on *The Ellen DeGeneres Show* and NBC's *Today Show*, and single-handedly strengthens Korea's global brand and "soft power."

Why is this so? The reason is found in the insularity of Japan's entertainment industry. Just like Japan's mobile phones, its music travels badly outside the nation. For this, there are two main explanations: One is the formidable size of Japan's domestic market. Its lucrativeness reduces incentives to heading overseas or bothering to record songs and videos in English. The other is that large swaths of Japan's entertainment business are controlled by the mafia.

The first phenomenon also can be seen in the movie industry, and a 2005 Hollywood film about Japan tells the story. Roger Ebert put it well in his scathing review: "I suspect that the more you know about Japan and movies, the less you will enjoy *Memoirs of a Geisha.*" So began the late *Chicago Sun-Times* critic's take on a film that created more hard feelings than buzz in Asia. It wasn't the reception director Rob Marshall anticipated; he thought completing the first big-budget Hollywood production with an all-Asian cast would endear him to Asian audiences.

Yet Japanese were put off by the casting of Chinese in main roles and made claims of cultural insensitivity. And Chinese were outraged that actresses Zhang Ziyi and Gong Li appear in a film that romanticizes Japan during World War II—and that Zhang did a love scene with a Japanese man, played by Ken Watanabe. Americans, meanwhile, were indifferent, if tepid box-office receipts are any guide. The dustup actually offered insights for Asian governments trying to get along, corporate executives struggling to compete, and investors grappling to make sense of it all.

The film at the center of this controversy, as the late Ebert said, wasn't a very good one. A highly simplified adaptation of Arthur Golden's 1997 novel, it told the tale of a poor fisherman's daughter who is sold into quasi-slavery in Kyoto in 1929 and, against all odds, eventually becomes the city's reigning geisha. The subtleties of Golden's book, its almost Flaubertian attention to detail and historical context, were lost on the film. It's less about Japan or the stillness, grace, and traditions of one of its most rarefied cultural icons than backstage bitchery. Above all, it was a movie about beautiful, exotically dressed women hissing and backstabbing to become Kyoto's premier geisha and win the men they love. At first glance, it seemed like a Jane Austen tale with some Charles Dickens tossed in. But the end product played more like *Desperate Housewives* in kimonos.

Oddly, though, *Memoirs of a Geisha* became an unlikely flashpoint in Japan–Chinese relations, and a timely one, too. Asia's boom is fraught with risks, including power struggles, high energy prices, terrorism, pollution, and economic competition from the West. Sadly, the leaders of Japan and China can't even get in a room together and talk without trading recriminations over World War II. Just like director Marshall, the leaders of Japan and China missed the real story and focused on the theatrics surrounding it. Japan's qualms with *Memoirs of a Geisha* miss a bigger point relevant to Asia's largest economy. Yes, a film with so specific a setting should star Japanese. While many seethe that major roles went to Zhang, Li, and Malaysian actress Michelle Yeoh, Marshall also had a point. His casting decisions reflected a dearth of internationally known Japanese actors who can speak English.

Hollywood wouldn't have made the film if it thought it wouldn't appeal to the lucrative yet subtitle-averse U.S. market. One reason there are few globally known Japanese actors: Japan's large domestic market creates few incentives for film studios and actors to search for audiences or projects abroad. There's a lesson here for Japan Inc. Japanese are ravenous consumers and, until now, its market seemed big enough. As sales soared in the heady 1980s and stayed reasonably brisk during the recession-plagued 1990s, companies were slow to look abroad, the mobile-telephone industry being among them.

Yet, you can't use the vast majority of the phones or their functionality overseas. That insular focus is a problem amid Japan's rapidly aging population and competition from countries such as Korea, home to Samsung Electronics Co. and its dazzling line of Galaxy products. The real story behind the *Memoirs of a Geisha* ruckus is that corporate Japan needs to think more globally. Japan Inc.'s future prosperity depends on looking to new markets.

Chinese critics missed the point, too. Seeing homegrown actresses eclipse Japan's should be reason to celebrate China's rising dominance not only in the area of economics, but culture. Instead, nationalist tendencies spoiled the moment in the spotlight. When it comes to Asia's past, there's plenty of blame to go around. Japan needs to go further to apologize for its atrocities and its prime ministers should stop visiting a Tokyo shrine honoring some convicted war criminals among the war dead. China isn't blameless, either, as it foments a volatile strain of nationalism that increasingly unnerves its neighbors in Asia.

Finally, there's a lesson here for investors. While it may come as a surprise to folks in the West, Chinese, Japanese, and Koreans don't tend to think they look alike. Hollywood's who'd-know-the-difference mind-set in casting films is comparable to how many investors and executives view Asia. Some see it as an undifferentiated collection of nations that is hard to get their arms around. Asia's economies are incredibly diverse. Those who think China's rise is a repeat of Japan's do so at their own peril. The same is true of India's development versus China's. If you think Europe is having a tough time getting the 18 euro-zone economies on similar footing, just wait until Asia tries. Foreign filmmakers can take artistic license with their casting decisions. They are free to make assumptions about Asians' appearances and sensibilities. Such oversimplification isn't an option for those looking to make money in the region. Respecting the vast differences that exist here may help investors find the Hollywood ending they seek.

Part of the problem is that Japan just isn't very good at marketing itself. In 2009, for example, one of then–Prime Minister Taro Aso's plans to attract foreign tourists was schoolgirls. His government sent a teenage girl wearing a miniskirted uniform abroad to enhance Japan's international profile and, by extension, the economy. Never mind that at 19, actress Shizuka Fujioka was no longer a schoolgirl. She traveled the world with two other young women as cultural envoys. The plan was to capitalize on Japan's long-running craze for all things cute. Many found the campaign creepy. Fujioka was joined on the road by Misako Aoki, dressed in the doll-like "Gothic Lolita style," and Yu Kimura, who showed off the "Harajuku style." Such fashions attract armies of amateur paparazzi in Japan, an uncomfortable number of whom are middle-aged men. More recently, post-2011 earthquake, the government dispatched members of a girl group called AKB48 to the United States and elsewhere as emissaries of Japan. It was an odd choice, given their whole shtick: 20-year-olds dolled up like 14-year-old schoolgirls and performing for middle-aged men. Is that really the best Japan can do to promote itself?

There's a trying-too-hard quality to much of Japan's international marketing apparatus. Oddly, one of the best boosters for tourism, at least temporarily, was a 2003 American film that at times poked fun at Japanese culture, Sofia Coppola's *Lost in Translation*. Many Japanese quibbled, and often appropriately, with the triteness of some of the movie's observations—including a few too many jokes about the inability of Japanese to pronounce the letter *L*. All too often, the depiction of Japanese was cartoon-like.

But the film, starring Bill Murray, also managed something extraordinary: It helped many foreigners operationalize their notions about Japan.

After seeing it, many felt Japan didn't seem so foreign anymore. It succeeded in showing the different faces of Japan. Japan has never really harnessed the vast potential of tourism as a growth industry. With its multitude of temples, World Heritage sites, quirky cities, incredible cuisine, and reputation for convenience and safety, Japan should be a people magnet.

Yet in 2012, it didn't even break the top 20 tourist destinations in the UN World Tourism Organization's annual ranking. China, Korea, Macau, Malaysia, Singapore, and Thailand stamp more foreign passports each year than Japan.

The economic potential of films shouldn't be dismissed. The *Lord of the Rings* franchise, for example, did wonders for New Zealand, where they were filmed. Tourists continue to flock there to see where J. R. R. Tolkien's books were brought to life for moviegoers the world over. The good news is that Japan is waking up to the potential of culture exports. With gross domestic product being such a yawner in recent years, entrepreneurs and even government officials have been promoting Japan's "gross national cool" instead.

That phrase was reportedly coined by Douglas McGray, who penned a 2002 *Foreign Policy* magazine piece about Japan reinventing itself as cultural powerhouse. "Over the course of an otherwise dismal decade, Japan has been perfecting the art of transmitting certain kinds of mass culture," he wrote. And the government wasted no time coming up with a "Cool Japan" campaign, hoping a bigger global footprint would offset domestic gloom. But the decade since then hasn't been encouraging, as the obsession with schoolgirls attests.

Still, the ideal is perfectly understandable. If Seoul can cash in on the "Korean Wave" movement, why can't Japan? For all its paradoxes, controversies, idiosyncrasies, and hypocrisies, America does very well from its cultural exports. It's the business of globalization, after all. Nation-states are increasingly obsessed with branding. In 2013, for example, Japan launched the state-backed Cool Japan Fund Inc. Led by former Carlyle Group manager Koichiro Yoshizaki, the $560 million fund will promote products the nation deems internationally trendy, from sushi and ramen noodles to manga comics to anime to pop music to *kawaii* fashion to cosplay (costume play). But as pundits like Nancy Snow, a visiting professor at Keio University, point out, Japan's efforts are more often than not lost in translation.

"Cool Japan is anything but," Snow wrote in a November 7, 2013, op-ed in Tokyo's *Metropolis* magazine.

> A fundamental rule of persuasion is that if you have to iden-
> tify yourself or your institution as "cool," then you aren't and
> it isn't. Frank Sinatra and Sammy Davis Jr. would have never
> made the Rat Pack such an American cultural phenomenon
> if they had announced their coolness at every stop. "Hey cats.
> Aren't we cool? Look how we dress, drink on stage, and have
> bromance banter with one another. Cool, huh?" The Rat Pack
> allowed others to define their style and manner.

One recent example came from Ikuo Kabashima, governor of Kumamoto Prefecture in western Japan, who in November 2013 tried a little mascot diplomacy. Perhaps no country is more obsessed with "cute" than Japan, and the place is awash in furry mascots. Some of these cuddly critters would travel poorly outside Japan, of course. Fukushima Prefecture's bizarrely named "Fukuppy"—blend-ing the first part of "Fukushima" with the last part of "happy"—is a case in point. Beat cops in Boston would surely chuckle at seeing the Tokyo Metropolitan Police Department's orange "Peepo" amulet. Still, Kabashima thought he'd take his "Kumamon" to Harvard in November, where he lectured on how to "maximize the overall happiness" of a city's residents. That left many Harvard students and faculty asking a very valid question: *Huh?*

The concept can flop at home, too. In June 2010, the Ministry of Finance launched a truly desperate advertising campaign arguing that women are seeking men who invest in government bonds. "Playboys are no good," the ad had a young Japanese woman declaring. "I want my future husband to be diligent about money." She's one of five buxom women featured on the page, which says, "Men who hold JGBs are popular with women!!"

The ministry hoped the ads would appeal to citizens at a time when record government borrowing threatens to outstrip demand. The government's plan to attract marrying-age men comes after a campaign aimed at retirees started in August 2009. That push fea-tured Junko Kubo, a former anchor on Japan's public broadcaster NHK, in ads placed in the backs of taxicabs. Kubo followed Koyuki, an actress and model who in 2003 appeared in *The Last Samurai* with Tom Cruise as well as posters for government bonds. Talk about desperation.

"It doesn't take a Chinese female astronaut to conclude that Cool Japan is a government and industry production directed predominantly by men with a feminine ideal that doesn't exist," Snow said.

> Where are the images and ideas of the women scientists and financial executives, as well as the geek girls who don't want to be viewed through the narrow confines of pubescent cuteness? I'm not against cuteness, just its monopolization. Why not fund the next film giants like Akira Kurosawa or Yasujiro Ozu rather than the next AKB48 spinoff?

And then there's the *yakuza*. Hollywood has long fetishized Japanese gangsters with their full-body tattoos, missing pinkies, and harems of buxom groupies. Ever since Sydney Pollack's *The Yakuza* in 1974, they have provided periodic fodder for directors from Ridley Scott to Quentin Tarantino. Yet, curiously, studios are suddenly abuzz with a flurry of Japanese mob films. Warner Bros. is developing *The Outsider*. Robert Whiting's 1999 book, *Tokyo Underworld*, which has gotten nibbles from Martin Scorsese, is being made into a cable-television series. Perhaps most timely of all, Jake Adelstein's 2010 memoir, *Tokyo Vice*, is coming to the big screen. Its star, Daniel Radcliffe of *Harry Potter* fame, will ensure wide release around the globe.

Adelstein's life story as a crusading Tokyo reporter exposing the mob's infiltration of the mainstream economy (and being out under police protection) dovetails remarkably well with recent events. Tokyo is aghast as banking giants like Mizuho Financial Group Inc. get busted making *yakuza* loans and the U.S. Treasury Department freezes assets. It's time Japan stamped out gangs Adelstein calls "Goldman Sachs with guns." "There's a lot in the book about organized crime's ties into the political and financial sphere, and as the years have passed, much of it has proven to be prescient," Adelstein said.

It may surprise many to learn that, unlike America, the *yakuza* operates legally and in plain sight. Japan's roughly 63,000 organized-crime members hand out business cards and have office buildings, fanzines, out-in-the-open control over large chunks of the entertainment trade, and significant political influence. When they aren't collecting protection money, shaking down shop owners, or running prostitution rings, the *yakuza* are dabbling more and more in mainstream finance, including stock dealing, flipping real estate, and acquiring companies.

Take Shinsuke Shimada, who is often called "the Jay Leno of Japan." Tongues wagged around the nation in August 2011 when one of television's most famous faces was found to be in the orbit of a notorious organized-crime gang, Yamaguchi-gumi.

"But Shimada is only one of many celebrities with yakuza ties," Adelstein wrote in a September 23, 2011, *Daily Beast* article.

> In the last few weeks, extensive evidence has emerged that Japanese show business is saturated with the yakuza's influence. Police records and sources, along with testimony from current and former yakuza members, have revealed that many powerful Japanese talent agencies and production companies are not simply fronts for the yakuza—they are the yakuza. For instance, Rikiya Yasuoka, a Japanese movie star, was allegedly once a member of an organized crime group, and attended and sang at a birthday party for the former don of Japan's entertainment business, Tadamasa Goto, the John Gotti of Japan.

The entertainment business has long been dominated by the *yakuza*, who push for romanticized depictions of their brethren. They also wield tremendous power over Japanese talent agencies, which form the core of the entire industry. That has Japan cracking down, partly at the behest of the United States, partly as a necessary element of Abe's drive to increase Japan's competiveness. But Japan must go much further and dig much deeper to separate its gray economy from the formal one. Many industry observers believe Japan's inclusion in the U.S.-led Trans-Pacific Partnership would shake up the nation's entertainment cabal as never before by, at least in theory, forcing more international norms on it.

■ ■ ■

Oddly, much of the recent pressure to crack down on the gangsters originates with Barack Obama. In a post–September 11 world, the United States is concerned that Japan is too lax on cross-border

organized crime and the huge, opaque sums of money the *yakuza* send
zooming around the globe. The U.S. Treasury Department estimates
that Japan's biggest crime family, the Kobe-based Yamaguchi-gumi,
alone generates "billions of dollars annually."

Japan's few enforcement efforts all too often lack teeth. In 2011,
the Financial Services Agency enacted ordinances making it harder
to do business with the *yakuza*, but didn't outlaw such groups outright. Then something unexpected happened: Obama's White House
pounced with an executive order demanding that financial institutions freeze *yakuza* assets. In 2012, Washington blacklisted the
Yamaguchi-gumi. The Treasury started small, freezing about $55,000
of *yakuza* holdings, including two American Express cards, according
to documents obtained by Bloomberg News under the Freedom of
Information Act. The move was a clear slap in the face of Japan's government, though, not to mention the *yakuza*.

Yamaguchi-gumi is the reason Adelstein, 45, is a household name
among the underworld. In 1993, the Missouri native became the first
non-Japanese to work as a police reporter for Japan's *Yomiuri Shimbun*,
the world's largest newspaper. His snooping landed him in serious
trouble with Tadamasa Goto, the twisted, Yamaguchi-gumi-affiliated
crime boss. Adelstein learned that in 2005 Goto and three other *yakuza*
had somehow received lifesaving liver transplants in California, abet-
ted by U.S. authorities. Adelstein has been under police protection ever
since. If Yamaguchi-gumi were listed on the stock exchange, Temple
University's Jeff Kingston wrote in his 2011 book, *Contemporary Japan*,
it "would be the Toyota in its sector." Morgan Stanley economist
Robert Feldman once called the gang Japan's "largest private-equity
group."

In 2007, Feldman wrote a report detailing how the *yakuza* held
Japan back:

> The influence of organized crime in both political and corpo-
> rate/financial circles remains a barrier to an efficient economy
> and efficient financial markets. The loser has been Japan's com-
> petitiveness. It seems unreasonable to expect foreign companies
> and investors to expand activity in Japan while the issues with
> organized crime remain so troubling.

Six years on, the situation is only modestly improved.

Abe should use his second stint as leader to accelerate the crack-down on Japan's crime syndicates. You can bet the *yakuza*'s vast and detrimental role in the economy will be a sticking point in Japan's negotiations to join the U.S.-led Trans-Pacific Partnership. A burst of Olympics-related spending between now and 2020 will offer all-too-many opportunities for graft and extortion. Why not just go ahead and made the mobsters formally illegal now and round them up? Their ranks are thinning—there were 87,000 gangsters in 2004—but not nearly fast enough.

I asked Adelstein a question he gets often these days: How does it feel being played by Harry Potter? The answer was a bit surprising. "I can't think of anyone else I'd rather have be me," Adelstein said. "If they reissue the book with his picture on the cover, I can fade into obscurity rather nicely, I imagine." Even if that doesn't work, Adelstein remains hopeful that his life can one day return to normal. "By 2020, I think their day will be done. That's not so far away." It's not so close, either. For Japan's sake—not just Adelstein's—Abe should start hasten-ing the *yakuza*'s day of reckoning.

Why hasn't Japanese officialdom been more aggressive? Public opinion, for one thing: Many Japanese harbor romantic notions of *yakuza* as Robin Hood–like folk heroes who, by keeping crime orga-nized and centralized, help maintain the peace. Political connections, for another: In his book, Whiting explored how crime figure Yoshio Kodama was instrumental in the creation of the Liberal Democratic Party that's currently leading Japan.

The opposition Democratic Party of Japan has its own *yakuza* problems. In October 2012, when the DPJ was ruling, Justice Minister Keishu Tanaka resigned after attending a gangster's wedding and accepting donations from a foreign-run company. Around the same time, Finance Minister Koriki Jojima was fending off allegations in the press that he received gangster support while campaigning. Even then–Prime Minister Yoshihiko Noda had to return $20,000 in politi-cal donations after one his supporters was arrested as part of a fraud involving a *yakuza*, according to Adelstein.

In other words, it can sometimes be hard to tell where parts of the government end and the *yakuza* begins. Mobsters, for example, played an unappreciated role in prolonging Japan's bad-loan crisis of the 1990s. Loans linked even tangentially to the criminal underworld were virtually impossible to collect. On the one hand, bankers were afraid to call many loans. In 1993 and 1994, some bank collections officers were assassinated. On the other hand, the LDP bigwigs were dissuading banks from collecting. In a 2002 exposé, the *Far Eastern Economic Review* called the lost decade of the 1990s "The Yakuza Recession."

It's easy to blame corporate executives for preferring to stay on Galapagos than to venture out of their comfort zones. But in some ways, corporate executives are proving to be gutsier than Prime Minister Abe, who talks much of change but has delivered little thus far: SoftBank's Son expanding abroad with a bold acquisition of a U.S. wireless provider; Rakuten's Mikitani taking on the fossilized ideas of Japan's business lobby and the nuclear industry; Fast Retailing's Yanai plotting world domination for Uniqlo; Honda's Takanobu Ito making English the company's official language.

While all of these moves might sound obvious to Harvard MBAs, they are out of the norm for Japan Inc. and should be championed and facilitated by Abe's administration. Add Takeda, a Japanese drug maker that's more than two centuries old, to the list, as it moves toward naming its first-ever non-Japanese chief executive. The company has hired 20-year GlaxoSmithKline veteran Christophe Weber as chief operating officer with an eye toward having him succeed CEO Yasuchika Hasegawa and, hopefully, pulling off a "Ghosn."

The reference, of course, is to fellow French passport holder and Nissan chief Carlos Ghosn, the CEO Japanese call "Le Cost Killer." When he took over the faltering automaker in June 2000 and began cutting jobs and downsizing everything in sight, Ghosn was derided as an evil foreigner running roughshod over the Japanese way. Three years later, Nissan's turnaround assured, Ghosn had attained rock-star status in both business and culture. His battle to resurrect a corporate zombie even inspired a manga comic book series.

Drug maker Takeda's problems are a microcosm of Japan Inc.'s: an economy in the doldrums, an aging population, rampant price competition from abroad (in Takeda's case, cheap generic drugs, too), and a corporate culture protective of its clubby ways. The hope is that Weber will shake up the corporate culture, cut costs, and reach abroad to find growing markets. Insularity is a long-standing problem in Japan, and non-Japanese CEOs—only two currently run Nikkei 225 companies—themselves can seem like the business equivalent of the endemic species that Charles Darwin found on the remote islands off Ecuador's coast. Ghosn is one; Eva Chen of Trend Micro Inc. is another.

To his credit, Abe recognized this early on and talked about compelling companies to welcome at least one outside director and a female board member, too. But intense pressure from Japan's powerful business lobby, Nippon Keidanren, has made Abe water down pledges to make companies more vibrant and responsive to shareholders. Perhaps Abe senses it is counterproductive to cross the CEOs he needs to raise salaries if Abenomics is to have a fighting chance.

One reason a Ghosn-like hire might work for Takeda is the wild-card dynamic it tosses into a company almost as old as America. Weber is an outsider to Takeda, making it easier to close businesses, fire workers, and ignore the seniority-based promotion system that restricts the size of a company's talent pool and, by extension, its profits. Competing in global markets means pulling together an A-team, not a bunch of clock-punchers next in line for a corner office.

The hiring of outsiders as CEOs, while common in markets like the United States, is incredibly rare in Japan. In the United States, Yahoo! Inc. recruited Marissa Mayer from Google Inc. and Hewlett-Packard Co. appointed Meg Whitman. While Ford Motor Co.'s choice of former Boeing Co. executive Alan Mulally is among the success stories, there have been failures, including J.C. Penney Co.'s recruitment of Ron Johnson from Apple.

Of course, success will depend as much on Weber as Takeda's board. Japan's more recent experiments with *gaijin* CEOs went awry. Welsh-born Howard Stringer, for instance, got the top job at Sony in 2005 amid great fanfare. He fired thousands of workers but failed to fix Sony's notorious "silos problem"—several divisions jealous of each other's resources, looking in different directions, barely talking to one another, and sapping the company's once-fabled innovative spirit. In 2012, Stringer stepped down after four straight annual losses.

Michael Woodford's experience made for even worse headlines. In April 2011, Olympus president Tsuyoshi Kikukawa thought he'd found the ideal corporate lackey in Woodford, a Briton. He would offer the illusion of outside, international thinking, but be a pushover in the boardroom. Instead, Woodford discovered the camera maker was an Enron-esque mess that had spent 13 years hiding losses that snow-balled to at least $1.7 billion. Rather than reward him for trying to right the company, the Olympus board fired Woodford for "cultural insensitivity."

To succeed, Takeda must embrace change in a survival-of-the-fittest world that's quickly evolving beyond Japan Inc. If Abe's exhortations can't do it, perhaps the private sector can show stuck-in-time vested interests how to escape Galapagos. Japan shows unambiguously that the islands that so beguiled Darwin and changed our understanding of nature are a great place to visit. You just don't want your economy getting stuck there.

Chapter 6

Hello Kitty Isn't a Foreign Policy

How Amateurish Diplomacy Undermines Japan

I n May 2013, Shinzo Abe did a goodwill tour of the tsunami-devastated Tohoku region. He visited local government offices, aid workers, schools, and displaced inhabitants along Japan's northeastern coastline. Keen on making the most of the trip and buttressing his bona fides as a strong leader, Abe's advisers added a stop at Matsushima air base. There, Abe would be photographed conferring with senior military brass. It would be photo-opportunity heaven. Little did Abe's people know it would also precipitate an international incident.

The Matsushima base is home to "Blue Impulse," Japan's Air Self-Defense Force's aerobatic display team. Created in 1958, the squadron is the pride of Japanese military culture and their Kawasaki T-4 training aircraft painted in white-and-blue colors are instantly recognizable throughout the nation. Abe's aides couldn't resist having their boss climb into one of the cockpits for the cameras. Unfortunately, the plane was emblazoned with the number "731."

The Imperial Japanese Army's Unit 731 tested chemical and biological weapons on human prisoners during the 1937–1945 Sino–Japanese War and World War II. It was located in the city of Harbin, the largest city of Manchukuo, the Japanese puppet state that is now northeast China, and run by General Shiro Ishii. A microbiologist by training, Ishii is often called Japan's answer to Josef Mengele, the brutal doctor of Auschwitz infamy. Needless to say, Chinese and Korean officials were outraged. Japan insisted it was all an unfortunate coincidence, but no one in Beijing or Seoul bought it. Just 10 days earlier, Abe wore a baseball jersey to an event honoring slugger Hideki Matsui bearing the number "96." In China and Korea, it was read as a reference to "Article 96," the clause in Japan's constitution that spells out the process of revising the pacifist document. Altering it to enable Japan to maintain an offensive military is one of Abe's biggest priorities.

"Abe's Pose Resurrects Horrors of Unit 731," screamed *Korea Joongang Daily*'s headline. Chinese cyberspace buzzed about Abe's latest "numerical provocation." The episode showed how raw and close to the surface tensions are in North Asia—and how hard feelings over the past could derail Asia's future. Even something as seemingly innocuous as tourist attractions can raise blood pressures. One generalization that's safe to make about the Japanese people is their love of World Heritage Sites, both at home and abroad. Walk past any travel agency and you will see reams of banners pitching "UNESCO Tours." Visit any place that the United Nations Educational, Scientific and Cultural Organization stamps as globally important—Cambodia's temples at Angkor, Greece's Acropolis, Jordan's Petra, Tanzania's Serengeti, or, of course, Ecuador's Galapagos Islands—and you will see busloads of Japanese. But national pride has prompted governments in recent decades to win as many UNESCO certifications as possible. In 2013, for example, Mt. Fuji became such a site, while UNESCO put Japanese food on its list of important world cuisines.

So, in September 2013, when the government said it was requesting that 28 historic sites that formed the nucleus of Japan's industrialization be recognized by UNESCO, officials in Tokyo expected little flak. However, nearly a dozen of those "Sites of Japan's Meiji Industrial Revolution," clustered mostly on the island of Kyushu, served as World War II labor camps for Korean prisoners. It prompted an immediate and fierce rebuke from Seoul. According to *Korea Joongang Daily*, thousands of Koreans worked as slaves at the sites, which included a Nagasaki shipyard and coal mines and steel mills in Fukuoka. Few Koreans were known to come out alive or healthy.

The dustup is another reminder of how Asia's past gets in the way of what should be a bright and cooperative future. But it's also but one small example of how insular and amateurish diplomacy undermines Japan's designs on playing a key geopolitical role in a world that's already moving on to China. "What is necessary for Japan's renewal is a powerful catalyst that will restyle the old Japan and make the 'new' Japan even stronger," Abe told an audience at Guildhall in London on June 19, 2013.

Yet, how possible is that when so much of the old thinking permeates Tokyo, particularly in foreign policy? Never mind World War II; Japan's Liberal Democratic Party can't even relegate the nineteenth century to the past. It may be 2013, with the world surrounding this island nation changing at a blistering pace, but Japanese officialdom seems oddly stuck in the late 1800s. Back then, reformers adopted the slogan "rich nation, strong army." This rabid nationalism culminated, of course, in World War II and a crushing defeat. Fast-forward a hundred years or so. Here is the hauntingly similar motto Abe used to win the premiership in December 2012: "Build a strong and prosperous Japan." Few can know for sure what's in Abe's heart or that of his Liberal Democratic Party (LDP), but such views are emblematic of the rightward lurch in Japanese politics at a time when an ascendant China is challenging Japan's very relevance in the region. The implications for Asia and Barack Obama's second presidential term are enormous.

■ ■ ■

Abe's nineteenth-century nostalgia has complicated roots that began at his grandfather's knee. Nobusuke Kishi, the former prime minister who brought the 1964 Olympics to Tokyo, was Abe's maternal grandfather and, by all appearances, his personal hero. In his 2006 book, *Towards a Beautiful Country*, Abe writes glowingly of the man who inspired his brand of conservatism. That's why securing the 2020 Olympics for Tokyo was such a sweet victory for Abe—a family legacy bookend. The 1964 Games confirmed Japan's phoenix-like rise from defeat in World War II. Its bullet trains, avant-garde stadiums, and neon-lit skyline advertised a country and an economy prepared to take the lead in Asia and indeed the world. Abe is clearly gunning for a similar rebirth so that the world's attention swings back Tokyo's way.

The family also hails from Yamaguchi Prefecture, on the western-most tip of Japan's main island, Honshu, and proudly so. There, you will find a small city of immense importance to Abe's worldview, called Hagi. The white-walled medieval castle town was the stomping ground of the sixteenth-century samurai warlord Motonari Mori, who tried to teach his sons unity by showing them a single arrow could be snapped easily, while three together were hard to break. This local bit of home-spun wisdom is the inspiration for the "three arrows" about which global markets are buzzing.

To the Abe-Kishi clan, Yamaguchi has an almost spiritual energy coursing through it. It's a place with a history of deep conserva-tism, but also a knack for reinvention and reformist zeal. Clans from Nagato, the city of Abe's birth, were instrumental in the fall of the Tokugawa shogunate, the last feudal government, and the rise of a new imperial one. Abe is deeply proud of Yamaguchi's propen-sity for comebacks prior to the start of the Meiji Restoration that marked Japan's opening to the world and its industrialization. Those powers of reinvention may have driven his grandfather's redemptive journey from a suspected war criminal to prime minister. Abe's, too; few would have ever predicted his return for a second chance as prime minister.

Yet it's the events long before 1964 that fill Abe's mind. In the mid-1930s, Kishi was a senior administrator in Manchukuo, a key indus-trial site. He later served in Hideki Tojo's wartime cabinet overseeing commerce and industry. After Japan's surrender in 1945, Kishi found himself doing time in Sugamo Prison near Tokyo's Ikebukuro district amid accusations of exploiting Chinese labor. He was never charged or tried by U.S. Occupation officials as a war criminal, ostensibly for lack of evidence. Once freed, Kishi managed to resurrect his career in ways few peers thought possible, helping to form the LDP on his way to the prime minister's residence, where he resided from 1957 to 1960. Even so, Kishi's reputation never shook off the baggage of the past.

In his 1999 Pulitzer Prize–winning occupation history, *Embracing Defeat*, John Dower called Kishi "brilliant and unscrupulous" as part of his blistering attack on the way U.S. officials carried out the war-crimes trials. His conclusion was that it's impossible to "defend the American decision to exonerate the emperor of war responsibility and then, in the chill of the Cold War, release and soon afterwards openly embrace accused rightwing war criminals like the later prime minister Kishi Nobusuke."

For Abe, Kishi personified the humiliation of defeat and the post-war order: the emperor stripped of god status, a constitution written by the United States, and a nation unable to have conventional military forces. Anger over this "victor's justice," in the parlance of Japan's right wing, is what informed Abe's first stint as prime minister from 2006 to 2007. The concern in Asia has been that as Abe feels more secure in his premiership, he would shift anew to his obsession with a "Beautiful Japan." That's the catchall phrase that Abe trotted out early in his first stint as prime minister in 2006. The euphemism encompasses a wide range of controversial policies—from downplaying or denying Japan's wartime atrocities to scrubbing textbooks of embarrassing history and inserting more patriotism into school curriculums to rewriting Japan's pacifist postwar constitution to flexing muscles in Asia. It also encom-passes official visits to Tokyo's Yasukuni Shrine, which honors several convicted war criminals along with Japan's war dead, that cheer local nationalists and enrage an Asia that believes the government has never properly atoned for its wartime aggression.

It's hard to exaggerate how devastated the political establishment in Tokyo was to see China's economy surpass Japan's in 2010. That Japan shares the same credit rating as China is a deeply sore point for the conservative lawmakers who make up Abe's LDP. Abe is anxious to restore the pride drained by two decades of economic stagnation, and in the postwar period before that. Visiting Washington in February 2013, he pledged to "bring back a strong Japan." He went even further in a speech to the U.S. foreign-policy establishment: "Japan is not, and will never be, a tier-two country," he declared ominously.

In the spirit of harmony, Japanese place great emphasis on deciphering the difference between *honne*, the officially stated position one feels obliged to state publicly, and *tatemae*, one's true opinion. Figuring out which of these default positions you are getting in a conversation can be as challenging as it is maddening. For much of 2013, Japan observers bought into the *honne* coming from Abe's cabinet. Abe dropped few hints that he would go to Yasukuni, focusing instead on his electoral mandate to end deflation. Yet that changed on December 26, 2013, the one-year anniversary of his second premiership, when Abe betrayed his true intensions—his *tatemae*. On a crisp Thursday morning, with television-news helicopters circling overhead to air the event live, a tuxedo-clad Abe went to Yasukuni in defiance of global opinion. Afterward, Abe tried to finesse the gesture by declaring, "Japan must never wage war again. This is my conviction based on severe remorse for the past. It is not my intention at all to hurt the feelings of the Chinese and Korean people."

But hurt Asia's feelings is exactly what Abe's shortsighted action did, provoking immediate and strong condemnation from China's state media as Chinese consumers took to social media to call for a boycott of Japanese goods. "Japan has no future if it continues on its revisionist path," *People's Daily*, the Communist Party mouthpiece, said in a December 27, 2013, editorial. The *Global Times* demanded that Abe and senior Japanese officials who visited Yasukuni be barred from the mainland. The *China Daily* labeled the pilgrimage an "intolerable insult" and urged Beijing to reconsider its relationship with Japan on everything from trade and security to diplomacy.

In Seoul, giant protests besieged the Japanese embassy. Korean Culture Minister Yoo Jin-ryong called Abe's move "deplorable" as Park Geun-hye's government scrapped plans for a series of defense meetings that held the promise of cooperation to rein in North Korea. In a December 27, 2013, editorial, *Chosun Ilbo* said Abe "crossed the final line" and urged Seoul to devise "completely new ways" to deal with Tokyo. *Dong-A Ilbo* characterized the visit as a "serious act of provocation" to Asians who suffered from Japanese imperialism.

For Asia, Yasukuni is about as charged an issue as there is, and the divide between Japan's official view of politicians paying respects at

Yasukuni Shrine and the rest of the region continues to widen. The shrine honors the military's dead, including 14 World War II leaders convicted as class-A war criminals such as Hideki Tojo, who in addition to serving as prime minister was war minister in the 1940s.

Until Abe's December 2013 visit, the spin in Tokyo, the *honne*, was about Abe's restraint—how he had kept his eyes on the economy and his nationalist tendencies in check. In September 2006, he arrived in office energized to revise past apologies for wartime offenses and alter the U.S.-imposed pacifist constitution, so Japan could more freely deploy military assets. During that abbreviated 12-month term, Abe challenged Japan's 1993 apology by then–Chief Cabinet Secretary Yohei Kono for the military's use of foreign women as sex slaves before and during World War II and legislated making patriotism a key goal of education. He also passed a measure to allow for constitutional change. But in the first 12 months of his current premiership, Abe appeared to leave these aspirations on the backburner.

Turns out, it was all a head fake, and a terribly timed one. The six weeks prior to Abe's provocation were unusually good ones for Japan's normally ham-handed diplomacy. The nation was riding a wave of global support following a series of missteps by China. One came in mid-November 2013, when China made an absurdly chintzy aid offering to typhoon-devastated Philippines, one that dented its "soft power" in Asia. Japan, by contrast, led international relief efforts, showering the Philippines with tens of millions of dollars of cash, supplies, and a small army of medical personnel.

Yet China's biggest blunder was in late November 2013, when Beijing unilaterally declared a wide "air-defense identification zone" across the East China Sea, including over various islands and rocks claimed by Japan and Korea. The confrontational move revived fears of China as a bullying hegemon, gave Japan and Korea something on which to agree, and allowed Abe look downright statesman-like. That Japan had regained some of the moral high ground in Asia that Abe so coveted was apparent during a December 13–14, 2013, summit with southeast Asian leaders in Tokyo. There, Abe unveiled plans to lavish some $20 billion in investment on the region and pitched Japan as an alternative to Beijing's bullying ways. With one impetuous visit to a Tokyo shrine, though, Abe squandered all the goodwill Japan had amassed. That may go for Washington, too. No relationship is more vital to Abe than that with the United States, and yet his Yasukuni jaunt irked the White House. Jen Psaki, a State Department spokeswoman, said the United States was "disappointed that Japan's leadership has taken an action that will exacerbate tensions with Japan's neighbors," echoing comments from Ambassador Caroline Kennedy. Abe's act also put a damper on what otherwise would have been a moment of joint celebration in Washington and Tokyo: a deal to end a tussle over the location of a Marine base on the island of Okinawa.

In retrospect, it's clear that Abe's deputy prime minister, Taro Aso, was setting the stage for his boss with his own visit two months earlier. Accompanied by three other cabinet members, and about 160 lawmakers, Aso went to Yasukuni on October 18, 2013, during Japan's annual autumn festival. That visit, along with Abe's decision to make a personal $500 offering to the Shinto shrine, prompted fast and furious reactions. The *People's Daily* in China sniffed that Abe's offering was no different from visiting in person.

"The Yasukuni shrine is a Japanese militarism symbol," Hua Chunying, China's Foreign Ministry spokeswoman, said on October 18, 2013. Visits to the shrine are "a blatant attempt to whitewash the Japanese military's history of aggression."

Korean officials were no less apoplectic. Yet even before this most recent Yasukuni dustup, President Park said she wouldn't meet with Abe unless his grasp of history improved. She demonstrated her resolve at a testy meeting with U.S. Defense Secretary Chuck Hagel in Seoul in September. When Hagel encouraged Park to get along better with Tokyo, Park, according to a November 24, 2013, *New York Times* report, shot back: "If Germany had continued to say things that inflicted pain, while acting as if all was well, would European integration have been possible? I think the answer is no." Park reportedly lectured Hagel about Japan's "total absence of sincerity."

Park's steeliness is partly about family baggage. In 1965, her father, former dictator Park Chung-hee, signed a treaty normalizing relations with Japan on terms many Koreans believe went too easy on Tokyo. Lashing out at Japan helps buttress Park's bona fides with conservatives and rally her 50 million people. But the events of World War II are very close to the bone for many Koreans. That explains why the "731" jet photo enraged the nation. It also explains why comments from Osaka Mayor Toru Hashimoto—a man few outside Japan had ever heard of before—so enraged Park's nation.

In May 2013, Hashimoto shocked the world when he said that "anyone could understand" brothels—of the kind for which Japan is infamous during World War II—were needed for soldiers facing battle. He later tried his hand at damage control at a Tokyo press conference, saying that holding sex slaves was "inexcusable" and Japan should express a "heartfelt apology" to victims. But then he doubled down, complaining that Japan shouldn't be singled out because other countries' militaries had also violated women's rights. In July, Aso again dragged Japan back into the weeds of World War II, when he was quoted in the *Tokyo Shimbun* as telling a seminar in Tokyo that Abe's government, which wants to overhaul the pacifist constitution, should learn from Germany's Weimar Constitution, which he said was amended quietly, leading to the rise of the Nazis. Neither the Chinese nor the Koreans were amused.

"It's Abe's revisionism that is the crux of the problem," said Rikki Kersten, a politics professor at the Australian National University in Canberra.

> By questioning Japan's guilt for war crimes in WWII and playing word games with volatile concepts such as "aggression," Abe is cancelling out more than 60 years of Japan's peaceful, positive contribution to the international community. Instead, revisionism puts Japan squarely back into the frame of WWII and evokes negative and suspicious responses from Japan's neighbors who were Japan's victims in that conflict.

Even some of Japan's domestic rhetoric feels a bit too Gestapoesque for comfort as senior government officials suggested those protesting the secrecy bill are unpatriotic. No less than Shigeru Ishiba, the LDP's secretary-general, said demonstrating against the legislation was akin to a "terrorist act," a comment he later tried to retract amid public anger. But then, is it appropriate for a democracy to essentially make a secret, well, secret and to do so largely in secrecy?

"Welcome to the new Dark Ages of Japan, brought to you by Prime Minister Abe Shinzo's Liberal Democratic Party" and his coalition partners, wrote *Tokyo Vice* author Jake Adelstein, who also runs the Japan Subculture Research Center, in a November 30 *Japan Times* op-ed. Thanks to the state secrets law, "Japan's press freedom ranking is expected to sink to nearly Uzbekistan or China levels. Welcome to the land of the setting sun. Let's see how much darker it will get."

This isn't as hyperbolic as it sounds. Japan's press freedom index was in freefall even before Abe's December 2012 return to the premiership. In 2013 alone, its standing dropped a precipitous 31 places from 2012, to a new low of 53 out of 179 countries, according to Reporters Without Borders. The main culprit was weak reporting on radiation risks at Fukushima, something that's sure to get even worse as incentives for media self-censorship increase.

The secrecy bill, Adelstein pointed out, has been compared to Japan's pre–World War II Peace Preservation Law, which gave the government wide latitude to arrest and jail any individual out of step with its policies and ideas. This, from a political party with a disturbing track record of cover-ups: the Minamata mercury-poisoning episode of the 1960s; the HIV-tainted blood scandal in the 1980s; the Ministry of Economy, Trade and Industry's heavy-handed efforts to manipulate nuclear-safety problems at Fukushima before and after 3/11; and now this.

"How can the government respond to growing demands for transparency from a public outraged by the consequences of the Fukushima nuclear accident if it enacts a law that gives it a free hand to classify any information considered too sensitive as a 'state secret'?" Reporters Without Borders said in a November 27, 2013, statement.

> By imposing heavy penalties on those who obtain classified information and then publish it, Parliament is making investigative journalism illegal, and is trampling on the fundamental principles of the confidentiality of journalists' sources and public interest.

Noriko Hama, an economics professor at Doshisha University in Kyoto, likened Tokyo's secrecy drama to an episode of the popular 1980s BBC sitcom *Yes, Minister*. In it, a bigwig from a fictitious branch of the British government opining on the public's right to know declared: "He that would keep a secret must keep it a secret that he hath a secret to keep." To Hama, this axiom aptly explains the mind-set of Abe's LDP.

Japan's government, as I mentioned earlier, is one run mostly by nameless, faceless career bureaucrats building their own fiefdoms and power structures. This arrangement already leaves the government notoriously opaque. At best, the secrets bill means even less transparency. At worst, it could nudge Japan back in the direction of the prewar period when draconian restrictions on speech enabled generals to pull Japan into war.

"This may not quite take Japan back to wartime days, but way too close for comfort," said Temple's Jeff Kingston. "The absence of an oversight mechanism to review classification of special secrets is a blank check for bureaucrats to cover up inconvenient documents and their own misdeeds."

Asked whether it's fair to compare the secrecy act to the George W. Bush–Dick Cheney power grab that was the Patriot Act, Kingston said:

> It's just as scary and an extremely disturbing development that runs counter to global trend towards greater transparency. This bill will foster a cocoon of impunity that is always and everywhere an anathema to good governance and democracy. Strong public opposition is due to citizens knowing all too well that officials operating in secrecy often act against the public interest and their right to know. It will send a shot over the bow of mass media and have a chilling effect on reporting due to risks of imprisonment.

Legal scholar Colin Jones of Doshisha Law School in Kyoto put it this way:

> The Patriot Act was more about surveillance and law enforcement techniques, whereas the secrecy act is about secrecy itself, so I am not sure I would call it a mini–Patriot Act. What is driving this so soon after an election when it was barely mentioned is a mystery; I suspect that there is U.S. pressure behind it, but also Edward Snowden may have been a wake-up call. The urgency with which it is being brought about is certainly disturbing. Granted, their government side may have a

point—that they do not have anything like an "espionage act" and they've been trying to pass one for a while. At the same time, I think that the vagueness of the act reflects a basic theme of Japanese governance, which is "I work for the government, therefore I know more than you, therefore you should do what I say." It helps them if the "I know more than you" part is institutionalized.

■ ■ ■

Back in power again, Abe is one of the three most important politicians in Japan—the others are Shintaro Ishihara, 81, and Hashimoto, 44. In a striking bit of generational serendipity, both men largely agree on where to take their nation. It's too bad that, like Abe, they have the wrong direction in mind. They want to take Japan inward, not outward into a dynamic global environment that is rife with opportunities.

At 59, Abe straddles the generations between Ishihara and Hashimoto. All three are hell-bent on drawing a nationalistic line in the sand between Japan and the rest of Asia. Their views aren't in sync on every challenge facing Japan. Where their ideologies overlap is a more confrontational stance in a region where China is overshadowing Japan. Many Japanese support this pivot to the right. China, let's face it, hasn't distinguished itself as a reasonable stakeholder in the so-called Pacific Century. Its territorial claims to a bewildering number of islands, atolls, and rocks in the sea are antagonizing Filipinos, Koreans, Taiwanese, and Vietnamese.

Japan is anxious to recover the clout drained by 20-plus years of economic stagnation. It irks Japan that President Obama, UK Prime Minister David Cameron, or Brazil's President Dilma Rousseff would dare set foot in Asia without visiting Tokyo. Or that *Japanization* has become a catchphrase among economists warning about the evils of falling prices and political gridlock.

It's true, too, that Japan doesn't get enough attention for what it does right: industrial quality that ranks among the best anywhere; negligible crime; universal literacy; an enviable environmental record; one of the narrowest rich–poor divides; generous aid programs for developing nations; one of the longest life spans; and a commitment to world peace.

But the answer for Japan isn't to do away with this last attribute. It isn't to ramp up its military or pursue a more muscular and unilateralist foreign policy. That, remember, was Abe's undoing when he first occupied the prime minister's residence. His predecessor Junichiro Koizumi fleshed out a plan to revitalize Japan's economy and politics and then entrusted it to Abe, who promptly put that plan in his desk drawer and opted for creating a "Beautiful Japan." It meant revamping the education system to encourage nationalism, upgrading the defense agency to ministry status, and myriad statements and actions that annoyed China and Korea. Now that he's back in power, Abe has a second shot at doing all of this and then some.

Under Abe, Japan has become an unlikely spoiler in Obama's desire for a united front to denuclearize the Korean Peninsula. Traditionally, China has played this irksome role. The six-party talks over North Korea's nuclear program—suspended since 2009—never got anywhere largely because China refused to put the screws on its ally. No matter how many missiles the Kim Dynasty fired off, how many nuclear tests it conducted, or how many North Koreans starved or ended up in prison camps, China remained convinced that the alternative of a possible regime collapse was worse.

Yet even the Chinese are now fed up with the antics of North Korean leader Kim Jong-un. Officials in Beijing have openly chastised the North for its provocative behavior and have supported United Nations sanctions against the country. At their one-on-one California summit in June 2013, Obama and Chinese President Xi Jinping found more common ground on the issue than ever before. Most dramatically, China Construction Bank Corp. ended business with North Korean lenders Korea Kwangson Banking Corp. and Golden Triangle Bank—a slap across the face for strapped Pyongyang.

Kim's government has responded with transparent diplomatic ploys, first seeking talks with South Korea—most likely to satisfy Chinese demands—and then with the United States. As Bradley Martin, author of the book *Under the Loving Care of the Fatherly Leader*, said: "I'd be very surprised if this were anything but the usual divide-and-conquer tactics." Officials in Seoul and Washington have displayed admirable unity and discipline. For months, they have treated the erratic Kim with benign neglect, refusing to react to his every threat and each unhinged comment by government mouthpiece Korean Central News Agency. The line is consistent: The outside world will not engage with the North until it does something meaningful to halt its nuclear program and returns to talks with denuclearization as the goal.

With both China and Russia—which has its own differences with the Americans over Syria—echoing the same line, Kim faces a narrowing set of options. Yet now, when presenting a united front is more critical than ever, Shinzo Abe threatens to go rogue.

In May 2013, Abe sent a top aide, Isao Iijima, to Pyongyang for an unannounced four-day trip to meet senior North Korean officials. Iijima hoped to make progress on the issue of Japanese citizens abducted by North Korea years ago, and possibly to lay the groundwork for a summit meeting between Abe and Kim. Since then, Japanese officials have hinted that Japan may resume bilateral talks with the North. Abe's government reportedly plans to elevate a specialist on the abduction issue to the top bureaucratic post in the Foreign Ministry.

"It's a very amateurish kind of diplomacy," said Robert Dujarric of Temple University. "Japan is going to get very little out of it, and it won't strengthen Japan's global standing."

North Korea has acknowledged kidnapping 13 Japanese nationals in the 1970s and 1980s; Japan says North Korea abducted 17 people as part of a plot to train spies. It's impossible to exaggerate how big an issue this is for Japan's right wing, a group the ruling Liberal Democratic Party has long coddled. In 2002, Abe himself accompanied Iijima and mentor Koizumi, then Japan's prime minister, to Pyongyang to pursue it.

Privately, Abe advisers argue that resolving the dispute will enable them to join the international community in isolating the Kim regime. Yet even this limited outreach to Pyongyang has already proved a public relations disaster. The Korean Central News Agency exposed Iijima's supposedly top-secret trip, gleefully driving a wedge between America and its closest ally in Asia. If Abe persists, he's sure to alienate not just the Americans but also the Chinese and South Koreans. "Bad feelings could intensify very quickly if Japan feels emboldened to pursue narrow interests at the expense of global progress," Dujarric said.

This seems to be developing into a pattern with Abe. When Japan most needs to build bridges to its neighbors, the government remains fixated on parochial issues that fuel regional resentment. Abe's economic policies have driven down the yen, angering Korean and Chinese exporters. How have Japanese officials responded? By visiting the controversial Yasukuni Shrine. At a time when markets want to hear about serious structural reforms from Abe, he seems more interested in talking about revising Japan's pacifist constitution.

Optimists still hope that with majorities in both houses of parliament, Abe will worry less about nurturing his right-wing base. Perhaps then he could start more serious economic reforms, stop talking about the constitution, and wholeheartedly join the international effort to isolate North Korea. Or perhaps his party's hold on power will embolden him to go his own way and possibly even visit Pyongyang, as his predecessor, Koizumi, did in 2002 and 2004. Such a trip would be aimed more at learning about the fate of Japanese abductees than world peace.

This would be a dangerous path. Few nations would benefit more from a stable, denuclearized Korean Peninsula than Japan. Its export-focused economy is heavily dependent on the goodwill of its neighbors: China and South Korea alone import some $443 billion worth of Japanese goods annually. If Abe really wants to revive Japan and make the country stable and secure, he should take a lead role in working with his neighbors rather than against them to foster greater peace and stability.

The true state of affairs in Pyongyang grew even more uncertain in 2013. On December 12, 2013, Jang Song-thaek, Kim Jong-un's uncle and number two, was executed. Rarer still than a Kim purging a family member was the fact that the official North Korean media publicized it and even explained the rationale behind it (Jang allegedly was lining his pockets and plotting a coup). Jang's inglorious downfall sent shockwaves through the halls of Asian power because he was close to China, the Kim dynasty's main benefactor, and the only government official with real leverage over Pyongyang.

Jang had long been associated with Chinese-style economic innovations such as the series of special economic zones planned in the north, steps thought to hold the greatest potential for change on the Korean Peninsula. The hope was that Jang had the gravitas to prod Kim, a newish and rather untested leader, toward opening the world's most isolated economy. When he succeeded his father, Kim Jong-il, who died in December 2011, many Pyongyang watchers hoped Kim would shift his impoverished nation of 24 million people onto a less ruinous path.

When he took over, Kim the younger was an untested twentysomething—a callow, Swiss-educated Michael Jordan fan at the top of the world's most repressive regime. And Jang, the thinking went, would serve as regent to guide the young leader through the thickets of Pyongyang politics and international challenges. The true source of their falling-out may never be known. But the execution of Jang suggests that Kim is instead digging in his heels and doubling down on the Kim family playbook of blackmailing the world for food and financial support with nuclear-weapons tests, missile launches, and threatening to rain fire on Seoul and Tokyo at the slightest provocation. This is no time for Abe to be acting unilaterally for limited domestic gains.

"The hope all along was to persuade the North Koreans to reform and open," said author Bradley Martin. "With Jang dead, who in Pyongyang is going to argue for that now? Anyone who does is automatically part of Jang's conspiracy and probably in receipt of Chinese kickbacks, by definition." Bottom line, Martin added, is that it's anyone's guess where Kim plans to take his nation in the years ahead. "If ever there were an issue that deserved international cooperation," Martin said, "it's this one." To outsiders, Asia's tit-for-tat diplomacy seems as arcane as it does counterproductive. Can't the region move past its squabbles over shrine visits, history books, and how far this apology or that one went? The obvious lesson from Japan's experience is that denying the past and hoping the world will forget about it won't endear you to the aggrieved. There's a lost-in-translation problem here that Japan refuses to acknowledge. Japanese officialdom, for example, contends, with U.S. support for the most part, that the San Francisco Peace Treaty of 1951 settled the matter. Tokyo believes the document ended all controversies over its wartime actions and reparation agreements with China, Korea, and the rest of Asia.

Officials in Beijing have very different interpretations, particularly on the right of individuals to seek compensation. China and Korean officials, meanwhile, still want their Willy Brandt moment.

In December 1970, then–German Chancellor Brandt dropped to his knees in contrition before a monument to the Warsaw Ghetto uprising of 1943. His gesture of apology, repentance, and humility moved the world and created a very high bar for Japan. In 1995, as the fiftieth anniversary of Japan's surrender approached, then–Prime Minister Tomiichi Murayama sensed Japan needed to say more about the past. His famous statement was that Japan, "following a mistaken national policy, advanced along the road to war . . . and, through its colonial rule and aggression, caused tremendous damage and suffering to the people of many countries, particularly to those of Asian nations."

Better, Asia thought, but still no Brandt-style cathartic break with the enmity of the past. To the Japanese, Murayama's heartfelt declaration was bold, sweeping, and final. To Chinese and Koreans, it was woefully vague. *What specifically about Japan's aggression was mistaken?* Asians asked. Explain what you mean by *aggression,* observers wanted to know. And toward whom was it directed and why? And when will Tokyo start writing checks to individuals, families, and businesses? The question for many Japanese is, Why do we still have to apologize after six-plus decades of peace and contributions to the global community?

"That may well be, but there is something in the world today that I call a 'global memory culture,'" Carol Gluck, a professor of Japanese history at New York's Columbia University, told the *Wall Street Journal* on September 17, 2013.

> This refers to the new international norms that have developed over the past half-century about what a country is expected to acknowledge about its past actions. A main factor in the evolution of this global memory culture was Europe's coming to terms with the Holocaust. What we now routinely call the "politics of apology" is itself almost completely new. Heads of states in the 1950s were not expected as a routine matter to say "I'm sorry" to other countries, even when reparations were involved.

Here, too, we see another example of the world changing rapidly around Japan, but Japan remaining on Galapagos. "Japanese politicians avoided public acknowledgment of Japan's wartime past in Asia for a very long time, partly because of the Japan–U.S. relationship, which had frozen memory of the Pacific War with little emphasis on the China War or indeed on China, which of course was Communist and thus in the other camp," Gluck said.

> But after the end of the Cold War, the Japan–U.S. relationship was no longer the only relationship that mattered. Japan had increasingly to deal with Asia and China and their demands, which compelled the Japanese government to face war memory in a different register in the early 1990s. And when the government did so, it encountered a world where the norms of war memory had changed since the 1950s. . . . The LDP may want to make domestic political use of the wartime past, but the international context has changed rather dramatically. One evidence of this is the series of U.S. congressional resolutions that have been passed since the 1990s demanding that Japan deal with the issues of the comfort women, the Nanjing Massacre, compensation for victims, and so on. And this is the United States, not South Korea or China.

In the current Asian climate, with China surging ahead and Korea rapidly catching up, nationalism among Japanese politicians is proving toxic. And for better or worse, Yasukuni sits at the center. Temple's Kingston calls it "ground zero for an unrepentant view of Japan's wartime aggression." In Kingston's view, the shrine itself is less radioactive as an issue than the accompanying Yushukan museum.

"The museum presents a selective and sly reinterpretation of Japan's shared history with Asia—one that is antithetical to reconciliation, convinces few Japanese, and offends neighboring nations that endured the brunt of Japan's imperial aggression," Kingston said. "Politicians who insist that they are only paying tribute to those who died for their country when they visit Yasukuni are not telling the truth. If that's all they wanted to do, they could walk five minutes down the road to Chidorigafuchi National Cemetery, which is, like Arlington, Japan's officially designated war cemetery."

Yasukuni is simply a diplomatic dead end. Announcing a moratorium on visits by any serving Cabinet ministers would be a good start. From there, active lawmakers of all parties should abstain from going. "If Abe is truly looking for a new beginning—for himself, and for Japan's relations with its neighbors—that's where he should start," Kingston said.

That would go a long way toward enhancing Japan's soft power. So would ending deflation once and for all and opening the economy. But successive Japanese governments have damaged Japan's international standing to curry favor with the nation's political right wing. What's the point of driving down the yen if two of your biggest customers boycott your goods? Japan has a daunting and well-known catalog of challenges, from long-term economic stagnation to removing limits to trade to rebuilding the part of the country devastated by the tsunami to political dysfunction. The LDP must tackle each problem with an urgency few past prime ministers displayed. Yet Abe's LDP seems more interested in flexing muscles in Asia than building them. What the party doesn't understand is that the way for Japan to thrive in the twenty-first century isn't by reviving the ideas of the nineteenth. A more humble and pragmatic foreign policy would be focused on greater leadership in the decades ahead and threats as varied as China's growing navy to North Korea's nukes to America's pivot east.

■ ■ ■

Too often, Japan thinks marketing campaigns and slogans are enough. Japan has long had trouble capitalizing on its soft power around the globe. Abe certainly tried in New York in September, with references to baseball star Ichiro Suzuki, sushi, bullet trains, and advances in maglev rail technology, which Japan is itching to export to America's Northeast corridor. It was in keeping with Abe's efforts during his first 2006–2007 stint as prime minister, one followed closely by Lam Peng Er of the East Asian Institute at the National University of Singapore. In an October 2007 report on what many observers deride as "Hello Kitty diplomacy," Lam agrued that "despite the attractiveness of Japanese pop culture and other more traditional forms of public diplomacy, Tokyo's pursuit of 'soft power' and a good international image is undermined by its failure to overcome its burden of history."

It's a ploy to which many of his predecessors resorted. In 2010, the government set up a creative-industries office to accelerate things to raise Japan's profile. The hope was that growing interest in Japanese food, fashion, animation, comics, films, music, and global phenomena like Hello Kitty and Pokemon would do the government's work for it.

No cultural icon has gone more global than Hello Kitty, and the tale of how Sanrio Ltd. brought the all-but-featureless character world-wide fame is fascinating in itself. It's become not just a staple of the *kawaii*, or cute, segment of Japanese popular culture but of global-ization. But the soft power Japan might get from its ubiquitous kitty doesn't amount to a foreign policy. Nor does anime, cosplay, or comic books. In 2009, when he was prime minister, Taro Aso championed the construction of a manga museum to boost Japan's global brand. His government's schoolgirl tour, remember, did more to turn Japan Inc. into a punchline than capitalize on Japan's all-things-cute craze.

Nothing would sell Japan Inc. globally like organic economic success. Revive the economy, reinvigorate your biggest corporate names, unleash a wave of innovation among young people, and the international clout Japan craves will follow. Abe's clumsy sales job in September was emblematic of Japanese governments past and present. Something was definitely lost in translation when the self-described reformist prime minister visited the New York Stock Exchange and raised the specter of Gordon Gekko, the greed-is-good villain of Oliver Stone's 1987 film, *Wall Street.* While the Big Board has been try-ing to weed out insider trading since the 1980s, Abe declared without irony: "Today, I have come to tell you that Japan will once again be a country where there is money to be made, and that just as Gordon Gekko made a comeback in the financial world . . . so, too, can we now say that Japan is back."

Abe's pained simile prompted a rapid, rather awkward clarifica-tion from Japan's government: The prime minister, of course, was refer-ring not to the original *Wall Street* but to Stone's 2010 sequel, subtitled *Money Never Sleeps,* in which Gekko emerges from prison driven by revenge and lust to rehabilitate his reputation. The second awkward moment came when Abe used the heavy-metal band Metallica as a plot device to talk up Japan's prospects and excitement over the 2020 Tokyo Olympics. "Japan is once again in the midst of great elation as we prepare for the Games seven years from now," Abe said. "It is almost as if Metallica's 'Enter Sandman' is resounding throughout Yankee Stadium—you know how this is going to end."

Perhaps Abe missed the fact that Mariano Rivera, the Yankees' closer who enters games to Metallica's 1991 hit, has retired and won't be around anymore to guarantee a winning end. Abe may also want to check out the less-than-optimistic lyrics to "Enter Sandman." It's tempting to look for Freudian angles to these rather strained pop-culture references. One is the level of Abe's delusions of grandeur when he implored the crowd to "buy my Abenomics." Referring to yourself, or a phenomenon you unleash, in the third person is often an ominous sign. When Abe says his nation is "in the midst of great elation," I'm thinking he needs to stop believing his own press and get out more. Confidence in Abenomics is still an overseas phenomenon, not a domestic one. Is Sony using its sudden return to profit to up wages? No. Are Japanese households releasing a couple of decades' worth of pent-up demand? Hardly. Are expansion-minded companies like Honda and Mazda opening new factories in Japan? Try Thailand. Isn't radiation still leaking 135 miles away from Tokyo's own equity bourse?

What looked suspiciously like an Abe victory tour of America is wildly premature. Yes, Abe deserves credit for hiring Kuroda to run the Bank of Japan, where the governor engineered a huge change in international perceptions about a nation that was left for dead just months ago. But almost nothing has been done to better utilize the female workforce, reduce trade barriers, cultivate entrepreneurship, prepare for an aging workforce, internationalize corporate tax rates, find an alternative to nuclear reactors, wrest government power away from a vast, unproductive and sometimes corrupt bureaucracy, and improve relations with Asian neighbors. It's great that Abe is putting these issues on the table for discussion, but it's far too early to be telling Wall Street that Japan is back and better than ever. That day is years off, at best. Stone's Gekko character, remember, was never meant to be a hero, but the personification of the hubris of a particularly delusional moment in time. It's too soon for Abe to be indulging his own delusions so early in a multiyear battle against vested interests that are determined to halt Abenomics in its tracks. Of course, that may be easy compared to mending fences in Asia.

■ ■ ■

In May 2013, Abe was taken aback when a U.S. Congressional Research Service paper characterized him as a "strong nationalist." Abe's rebuttal came before parliament days later, where he expressed dismay that foreigners were misinterpreting his policies. Then again, Abe himself has made impassioned remarks over the years espousing the merits of nationalism. In an October 2, 2006, parliament address, Abe said "nationalism as I think of it is a sense of belonging to the nation, ancestors, family, and the local community where one was born and brought up and with which one has become familiar. This sense of belonging is not something that we are told to have, but is completely natural and spontaneous." He concluded by saying that being called a nationalist is a compliment.

Shintaro Ishihara is an unapologetic nationalist who favors acquiring nuclear weapons and has tossed enough insults at women, foreigners in Tokyo, and gays to fill a small library. He also bears direct responsibility for rapidly deteriorating relations between Japan and China. Ishihara prodded the national government to buy disputed islands that the Japanese call Senkaku and the Chinese call Diaoyu. On September 11, 2012, Tokyo did just that, paying $26 million to take a stand against China. Fourteen months later, Beijing took its own.

During November 9–12, 2013, China's Communist Party leader held a summit that recast Xi as a reformer extraordinaire and produced its first foreign-policy initiative: poking Japan in the eye. That seemed to be the point of China's declaration of a vast "air defense identification zone," in which Beijing has essentially claimed the airspace around disputed islands administered by Japan. The provocation came just two weeks after the party called for a new national security council to coordinate military, domestic, and intelligence operations in China. Political analysts who worried that the body might herald a deepening Asian Cold War weren't being entirely paranoid. There's nothing particularly shocking about establishing such a council, state-run media said. The United States and Russia both have one, after all, and even Japan is talking about creating its own. Besides, as the Xinhua News Agency was kind enough to inform readers in a November 22 explainer piece, "China is a stabilizer for world peace and security, and the new commission is like a performance guarantee for the stabilizer and will in turn bring benefits to the whole world."

Tell that to Itsunori Onodera, Japan's minister of defense, who had to decode what China means when it warns that its military may take "defensive emergency measures" if planes don't identify themselves in the new air defense zone. Or Onodera's Korean counterpart, Kim Kwan-jin: Some of China's zone overlaps with waters off Jeju Island. Or Chuck Hagel, the U.S. defense chief, who got dragged into the controversy and responded, boldly, by flying two unarmed B-52 bombers into the area as a warning to Beijing to back off. China's move belied all the talk of its peaceful, magnanimous rise as a world power. A tiny accident or miscalculation in the skies above the disputed islands could easily spiral out of control, dragging Washington into a clash that would shake the global economy. Instead of being a stabilizer, China is proving to be a provocateur. It's hard not to wonder if political testosterone has gone to Xi's head. He emerged from China's November conclave as the most powerful Chinese leader since Deng Xiaoping. Xi may be especially willing to risk a confrontation with Japan right now in order to distract opponents of his proposed reforms, as well as ordinary Chinese who are growing restless over pollution, income inequality, and official corruption. Nothing brings China's 1.3 billion people together so easily as hating the Japanese.

China doesn't deserve all the blame for the precarious state of northeast Asian affairs, of course. Just like Abe, Korean President Park rarely misses a chance to hammer Japan about the sins of the past, though the points she scores at home come at the expense of a critical bilateral relationship. Yet it's China's actions that most risk sparking conflict. They also contradict the spirit of reform and "opening up" repeatedly hailed at the Communist Party's recent plenum. In addition to Japan and Korea, China's air zone is sure to worry officials in Brunei, Indonesia, Malaysia, the Philippines, and Taiwan, all of which are embroiled in territorial disputes with Beijing. A group of Chinese scholars even want Beijing to claim Okinawa, too.

Much of it really is an argument over China's controversial "nine-dash" map. First published in the late 1940s, the map extends China's territorial claims as much as 800 miles from Hainan Island to the equatorial waters off the coast of Borneo. China says the map proves its "indisputable sovereignty" over more than 100 islands, atolls, and reefs that form the Paracel and Spratly Islands. The rest of Asia disagrees.

However powerful Xi has become, he's not adding to China's store of soft power with such behavior. The country took a big hit abroad for its miserly aid offering to the typhoon-devastated Philippines. Its inflammatory new policy will only further alienate neighbors in a region it's seeking to woo away from the United States. America would be wise to take advantage of this dustup to advance its pivot to Asia that until now has lacked both carrots and sticks. U.S. officials should prod Abe to lead his people toward more enlightened engagement with Asia rather than follow his base's nationalist instincts. They should encourage Park to work with Abe, even if just on trade, the environment, North Korea, and the challenges of governing a fast-aging population. Washington also should push the case for regular three-way summits between the leaders of Japan, China, and Korea no matter what's afoot. Face-to-face meetings can create momentum toward deeper ties. But America's sternest conversation should be with Communist leaders in Beijing. China says its global ambitions are peaceful and war isn't in the national DNA. That's great. It says it believes in mutual respect for other countries' domestic affairs. That's fine. It says it wants to "make Chinese culture go global." It all sounds good. Beijing's recent actions, however, inspire little confidence in its words.

One reason China's efforts to develop its soft power have failed is the utilitarian way Beijing approaches the rest of the world. Instead of using culture, adept diplomacy, and trashy movies to seduce other countries, China hands out cold, hard cash. All the investment poured into railways in Indonesia, tunnels in Brazil, power grids in Cambodia, hydroelectric projects in Laos, bridges in Vietnam, roads in Zambia, factories in Malaysia, airports in Myanmar, and mining rigs in Uzbekistan comes with a high cost. In return, China demands complete docility. That's the message being sent to the Philippines now.

As hundreds of thousands of Filipinos struggled to find food, water, shelter, and the bodies of loved ones in the wake of Typhoon Haiyan, China quickly dipped into its world-leading $3.7 trillion of currency reserves and came up with—all of $100,000. That was Beijing's first miserly offer of aid on November 12, 2013, to the storm-tossed Philippines. Two days later, an international outcry over China's stinginess shamed it into upping its pledge to a modest $1.6 million worth of relief materials such as tents and blankets. But the damage was already done.

"It's very hard to call for de-Americanization and then leave your wallet at home when there's a human disaster the scale of the typhoon in the Philippines," said Ian Bremmer, president of Eurasia Group in New York. "Yes, China is a poor country. Yes, they have troubled relations with the Philippines. But this sits badly with anyone thinking about China's rise in the region." If he were advising President Xi Jinping, Bremmer says, "I'd push for major humanitarian aid to the Philippines." Instead the bulk of that aid is coming from elsewhere: roughly $30 million each from Japan and Australia, $20 million from the United States, $17 million from the European Union, $16 million from the United Kingdom, $10 million from Japan, $5 million from South Korea, $4 million from the Vatican, and $2 million from Indonesia. China was clearly stung by the critical news coverage. Korean figure skater Kim Yu-na herself gave $100,000—about enough to buy nine bottles of a 2006 Romanee-Conti. Even the new Chinese offer is rather paltry. New Zealand's $167 billion economy is a rounding error compared with China's $8.4 trillion one. Yet officials in Wellington have come up with $1.7 million, even more than the People's Republic.

Why the insultingly small sum for a geopolitically vital nation of 106 million people that by many measures is much poorer than China? Manila's close ties with Washington have always worried China. But this is personal. Philippine President Benigno Aquino refuses to bow to China's territorial claims in the South China Sea, and enraged Beijing by daring to challenge its maritime claims before a UN-endorsed tribunal. Aquino also demands that China treat the Philippines, one of Asia's oldest democracies, as an equal, not a subordinate. Nations hold grudges, of course. But China's actions in November 2013 dramatically undercut what had been a very deliberate and strenuous—and supposedly successful—recent charm offensive. After President Obama skipped out on a summit of Asia-Pacific leaders last month, Xi and Premier Li gleefully toured Southeast Asian capitals, handing out investment deals to show how generous China could be with its neighbors, how eager it was for friendly relations. The Philippines crisis offered an opportunity for China to show it had developed into a mature, cooperative nation and to win goodwill across the region. As a matter of fact, Chinese and U.S. troops trained together in November 2013 for the first time in Hawaii, as part of a drill in which the two nations cooperate in a humanitarian relief operation in a third country. Why not agree to jump in and cooperate on enormous international rescue efforts like the one in the Philippines in the future? Instead, officials in Beijing find themselves evading awkward questions about their miserliness toward a nation that had given China $450,000 after the 2008 Sichuan earthquake. Even after China upped its aid offing to the Philippines, it still paled in comparison to what furniture maker Ikea Group donated and the $4.88 million Beijing gave to Pakistan after an earthquake there in September 2013.

To more compliant nations, ones that don't challenge its ambitions, China's diplomatic checkbook is far more open. Arvind Subramanian, author of the 2011 book *Eclipse: Living in the Shadow of China's Economic Dominance*, says China is going to be a "peculiar kind of superpower," one whose attraction is more materialistic than heartfelt. "It won't have the soft power the United States has—people wanting to come, people wanting to live, people wanting to emulate it," he said. "That soft power is lacking, but it will not impede China."

I'm not so sure. If I were Aquino, I might've told China to keep its money; maybe Xi could use it to hire a public relations firm. As badly as the Philippines needs the help, so does China's image.

But Abe's return has tossed its own wild card into Asian geopolitics. Of all the nightmares Xi figured he would have to face, a resurgent Japan Inc. surely wasn't among them. A major slowdown in the Chinese economy? Yes. Social instability? Absolutely. Debilitating pollution? Check. Rampant corruption eating away at the Communist Party's legitimacy? You bet. An economically resurgent Japan emboldened to challenge China for leadership in Asia? Hardly. With an assertive Abe at the helm, though, Japan may be poised to do just that, in ways that could upend the dynamics of Asia's future. The emphasis here is on *may*. For all the excitement over Abenomics, it's still a vague and unimaginative blueprint to end Japan's 20-year funk. Still, let's say the optimists prove right and Abe ends deflation and restores Japan's economic clout in the region. It's doubtful that the steady, "peaceful" rise to dominance envisioned by China includes sharing power with a renascent Japan. The Japanese recovery the world has long sought could well make Asia a much more dangerous place. This is the minefield into which the Obama White House is wandering as America rediscovers it's a Pacific nation. The United States spent the past dozen years forgetting a fact that's obvious from consulting a map or tracking container ships. When George W. Bush's administration bothered with Asia, it was all terrorism all the time. Quite odd, considering how reliant the largest economy became on Asia's money during his tenure. The region, as pointed out earlier, became America's banker. Obama's pivot east meant to end the neglect that allowed China to begin challenging U.S. primacy, and Beijing isn't happy. It's high time for this shift as a crisis-racked Europe turns inward and Asia booms. Yet the United States must engage Asia more wisely, constructively, and sincerely than in recent decades.

China's irritation can be seen in what might be termed a culture war. The Americans and the Soviets had their Cold War; Washington and Beijing are now battling over soft power. First China took on Google Inc.'s search engine. Now the battle is over something bigger and more existential—saving the Chinese soul from Western encroachments. Is this a new Cultural Revolution? Not exactly; but China's trepidation over Washington's renewed interest in Asia was fleshed out in January 2012 by outgoing President Hu Jintao. Writing in *Seeking Truth*, a magazine that serves as a platform for bedrock Communist Party principles, he said: "We must clearly see that international hostile forces are intensifying the strategic plot of Westernizing and dividing China, and ideological and cultural fields are the focal areas of their long-term infiltration."

While partly an effort to shore up support for Hu's government by appealing to sentimental nationalism, the article's timing was no coincidence, coming just six weeks after Obama visited Asia with big plans, including a deployment of troops in northern Australia. China clearly got the memo. Obama's Asian shift was solidified at the November 19–20, 2012, East Asia Summit in Bali. There, maritime security and territorial disputes in the South China Sea and East China Sea were up for discussion in ways that irked China to no end. All the talk of China expanding its soft power is met with skepticism when the topic of claims to the resource-rich waters of the Asian seas comes up.

The issue encapsulates why many leaders in Asia welcome America's return and view China's assumptions, ambitions, and ever-expanding territorial claims with wariness.

China tends to have little time for the sensitivities of governments from Vietnam to the Philippines to Malaysia—and especially Japan. This attitude fuels perceptions of a China convinced that its interpretation of history matters most, be it disputed claims to tiny islands hundreds of miles from its shores, the motivation behind its sizable military buildup, or the fate of 23 million Taiwanese governed by a democratically elected president.

There's little doubt over China's trajectory. Barring a major crisis, China's economy might surpass that of the United States by the end of this decade. Yet there's great debate about the merits of China's belief that world hegemony is its due and that small economies should pay it tribute with undying loyalty and natural resources while an undervalued yuan hurts them economically.

The bottom line is that anyone who thinks the power shift from the United States to China will go smoothly is dreaming. Just look at how the shift from Japan to China is unfolding. Possible flash points are currencies trading, intellectual property rights, climate change, military spending, North Korea, scarce global resources, human rights, control over cyberspace, Beijing's coddling of rogue regimes, and China's vast holdings of U.S. Treasuries. China is also increasing its rhetoric during American elections.

China can learn from Japan's failure to garner more soft power. If China wants to enhance its soft power, then it should use its influence to rein in Kim Jong-un in Pyongyang and Iran's saber rattling over the Strait of Hormuz. President Xi should accelerate the rise in the yuan and play by international rules of commerce, not bending the World Trade Organization to China's benefit at the expense of everyone else.

The United States must do its part, too. It's no longer in a position to lecture Asia the way Bill Clinton's White House did. The 2008 financial crisis and the Iraq war before it did great damage to the American brand and sapped its economic power. The United States must leave the arrogance of the past at the door as it reenters Asia. This return must go beyond appearances and be a genuine partnership.

As China tries to extend its sway in Asia, the United States must realize that its own regional ambitions need some polishing, too.

But really, this is up to Abe, Xi, and Park. What the latter two leaders can learn from Abe and his party is this: A leader should guide his or her people toward more enlightened engagement with neighbors rather than follow his base nationalist instincts. For too many years, and with way too many governments, Japan has been reluctant to get a grip on its isolationists and fully join the Asian community. Here, just like the economy, inertia isn't a viable policy.

Japan, China, and Korea must act to get a grip on these tensions. Sitting back and letting things escalate by the day imperils Asia's outlook. Asia should be signing free-trade agreements; linking stock markets and bond markets; harmonizing immigration, tax, and accounting standards; and discussing what to do with the trillions of dollars of U.S. Treasuries sitting unproductively on government balance sheets. None of that is possible as Asia's past gets in the way of what should be a prosperous and peaceful future.

Things are tense enough in North Asia as China, Japan, and Korea fight over tiny islands, and Kim Jong-un rattles his saber in Pyongyang. The last thing the region needs is another controversy getting in the way of a trade relationship worth hundreds of billions of dollars in such a chaotic global environment. If Abenomics is to guide Japan down a more prosperous path, Abe's team must leave the nationalism at the door.

"Japan as a security partner in the twenty-first century cannot afford to be saddled with the past through the rubric of denial," said Australian National University's Kersten. "Moreover, Japan's neighbors cannot afford to be seen to encourage historical revisionism in Japan. Abe's narrow vision of contemporary patriotism is effectively working against Japan's national interest."

Chapter 7

Will Abenomics Save the World?

Three weeks into his campaign to end deflation, Abe received an unexpected herogram from one of the world's most famous economists: Nobel laureate Paul Krugman. The Princeton University professor carries quite a megaphone in the form of his *New York Times* column. And in a January 13, 2013, piece, Krugman bemoaned the "dismal orthodoxy" of austerity plaguing governments around the globe, a dynamic that he argued was prolonging the global recession. "But now," he wrote, "it seems that one major nation is breaking ranks, and that nation is, of all places, Japan." If successful, Krugman said, "something remarkable may be about to happen: Japan, which pioneered the economics of stagnation, may also end up showing the rest of us the way out."

Krugman's statement was remarkable in itself; few dare hold Japan up as a model for how to run productive fiscal, monetary, or trade policies. Think of his suggestion as Japanization in reverse. Yet, 10 months later, Krugman seemed a bit less enamored with Abe's handiwork. While Krugman said he's "still moderately optimistic" in a November 14, 2013, interview with John Dawson of Bloomberg Television, making policies work is "difficult," especially with sales taxes going up. "I'm really worried about that consumption-tax increase," Krugman said. "They really need a psychological jolt and I'm crossing my fingers that what they're doing is enough."

This gets at a question economists of Krugman's ilk don't seem to be asking: How much has Japan learned from its lost decades? Has it sufficiently internalized what its policy makers did wrong, when they erred, and how to apply those lessons to their own reform process? It's worth exploring before we address whether Abenomics is applicable more widely. The answer is no—Tokyo hasn't learned enough of its own lessons.

For all the buzz about status-quo-shaking reforms, bold ideas, and a revolution in competitiveness, Abenomics sure looks a lot like what Japan has been doing for 20 years now—just on a bigger scale and with a splashier marketing campaign. Since the early 1990s, Abe's Liberal Democratic Party (LDP) has been building bridges, roads, tunnels, dams, and airports to nowhere and forcing the central bank to add ever more liquidity to the banking system, turning the BOJ into the glue holding Japan together. And what did those unimaginative policies leave their people with? The easy answer is the world's highest ratio of debt to GDP. The harder one: Japan has become a nation that can't proceed without the economic equivalent of a walker.

That image takes on a deeper meaning when you consider Japan's awful demographics and the dearth of ideas to cope with them. Take Finance Minister Taro Aso, who in January 2013 actually said elderly people should "hurry up and die" to relieve pressure on the government to pay for health care. Today, 26 percent of Japanese are 65 or over; by 2060, the proportion will swell to 40 percent.

So, is it really plausible that with just one more try of the same old remedies, Abe's team will get the economy to walk on its own and then sprint ahead? Albert Einstein's definition of insanity is repeating the same action over and over again, expecting a different result. One wonders if Japan is doing exactly that with its economy.

No economist could formulate a credible list of every shot of stimulus and every dose of monetary steroids that officials have pumped into the economy since the early 1990s. There have been too many overlapping treatments to document. None of them, not a single one, achieved what investors are betting Abe will do this time: Make a Japanese recovery self-sustaining.

"I think that the fiscal and monetary policy components are repeats of the past," said the Brookings Institution's Barry Bosworth. "The fiscal is not sustainable and will probably be reversed in the near future. There continues to be a lack of evidence in Japan or the United states that monetary QE programs have a major effect on the economy."

On the bright side, Bosworth said, "the sheer magnitude of the Japanese program did have a dramatic effect on the yen that I and others didn't anticipate. It will have a positive impact on exports over the next two years that potentially could lift the growth rate by as much as one percent, but evidence is still out on that measure. But the important long-term component of Abenomics is regulatory reform because it has the potential to reenergize the domestic nontradables industries whose performance has been so weak." Bosworth's bottom line is this: "It's not yet clear if it is more than just rhetoric or if they will really do something. Thus, I think the impact of the program is still unknowable."

Also unknowable is how other economies would do if they veered Japan's way economically. The United States is indeed displaying some Japan-like qualities: massive debt; falling wages; a central bank having trouble getting rates away from zero; monetary policy losing traction; and politicians preoccupied by petty turf battles while the economy burns—Japanization, indeed.

The thing about Japan's funk is its genteel quality. Asset prices plunged, recession became the norm, companies morphed into zombies, banks went insolvent—and yet Japan never unraveled. Crime never surged, homelessness didn't explode, London-like protests never materialized. Households merely adjusted and lived off their savings. Japan muddled along, even after the 2011 earthquake. Could the United States pull off such a feat? No economic growth for 20 years without mass social instability? I doubt it.

For all its troubles, and there are many, Japan has roughly $15 trillion of household savings sitting under tatami mats to cushion its people from a dismal economy. Highly indebted Americans couldn't survive two months without a paycheck. Japan has been able to muddle along without disintegrating. So, is America about to mimic Japan if its economy falls and can't get up? In some ways, it wishes it could.

Some long time observers make a convincing case for the Japan model, among them Irish journalist Eamonn Fingleton. His January 2012, *New York Times* op-ed, headlined "The Myth of Japan's Failure," generated such huge buzz that it prompted rebuttal from Krugman. Okay, so Fingleton's 1995 book, *Blindside: Why Japan Is Still on Track to Overtake the United States by the Year 2000*, didn't quite work out. In the *Times* piece, he made the case that Japan is still pretty close to a model society: incredibly safe, clean, efficient, predictable, and a consistently quirky place for an expatriate to reside. Japan is reasonably egalitarian (certainly compared to America), offers good air quality, enjoys universal literacy, boasts one of the highest standards of living, and has the longest life spans; its cities also feature the best infrastructure anywhere. On a more superficial level, Japanese cuisine arguably blows away all others and has an excess of Michelin stars to prove it.

Japan is really a tale of two nations. On the one hand, it can be an enviable place to live and work. On the other, it continually disappoints investors waiting for a sustainable rebound. Think of Charlie Brown, Lucy, and the football. Charles Schulz's *Peanuts* cartoon has more to do with investors' relationship with Japan than meets the eye. Time and time again, Lucy convinces Charlie she'll hold the ball for him to kick only to yank it away at the last second. Every time, he lands flat on his back, pondering his gullibility. Bullishness on Japan often seems that way. Every few years, or every few prime ministers, investors rush back to Japan sensing that, this time, things really are different. They queue up to kick the ball and make some profits, only to see officials in Tokyo yank it away. Is this pattern playing out anew? Only time will tell. But if Japan disappoints investors once again, it could be a long time before they return.

Abenomics, of course, is the most interesting animal Japan has seen in over a decade—as long as the prime minister makes good on the so-called third arrow. The problem is the quality of Japan's growth. Since its asset bubble burst more than 20 years ago, policy makers have worked frantically to keep the postwar boom alive. For years, pundits fretted about Japan's zombie companies. The real zombie is Japan's economic playbook. The only reason Japan has any growth can be traced to its growing public debt, the world's largest relative to the size of the economy, and the free money provided by the central bank. The economic equivalent of steroids is what holds Japan Inc. together, not its organic vitality.

The aversion to change of any kind remains formidable, and therein lies the nation's Achilles' heel. The Olympus scandal showed how corporate cronyism safeguarded an insular old-boys club. The radiation leaking from the Fukushima Daiichi reactor was a reminder of how dangerously top-down Japan is in a bottom-up economic world. The Japanese media also are part of the problem. Change requires a vibrant and independent press policing leaders. Even before Abe's secrecy law, Japan's press was subject to a not-so-subtle form of control. If reporters get too enterprising and write stories government industries or companies don't like—say, by questioning Tepco's radiation readings—your press-club membership becomes vulnerable and sources dry up and advertising dollars evaporate, making it hard to be effective. So, most play along. But Abe's obsession with controlling information may prove detrimental to Japan's future.

"The key lesson from the lost decades that Abe is ignoring is that the public desires and deserves transparency and accountability because citizens know that officials operating in the dark get up to no good," Temple University's Jeff Kingston said. "Giving bureaucrats the right to unilaterally bury inconvenient paper trails, and hide their misdeeds puts Abe in the position of being the getaway driver. If he doesn't like democracy, and can't respect the media's and citizen's freedoms and rights, he should get out of politics."

Japan probably could keep its head down and its sense of uniqueness intact for a few more years were it not for China. Japan is now an incredibly expensive property in a poor neighborhood. Yes, it will be decades before China matches Japan in per capita income, if it even can. Yet the competitive energy being unleashed by 1.3 billion incredibly industrious people means the status quo in Tokyo is no longer tenable. Deflationary forces are here to stay as developing Asia chips away at high-cost Japan's market share and its prized egalitarianism.

Investors trying to predict the next debt crisis after Europe's tend to look to Washington or Beijing. What about Tokyo? Those betting against Japanese bonds haven't made much on the trade. Yet, consider one inauspicious milestone reached in January 2012 when youngsters celebrated Coming of Age Day, donning kimonos, visiting temples, and partying the night away. Only 1.2 million Japanese turned 20, half as many as in 1970—a reminder that the population is shrinking as the national debt surges.

Boldness would be to set the stage for a reduction in government debt, or at least capping the increase. Admittedly, investors haven't made much money betting against Japanese government bonds. But Takeshi Fujimaki, a former adviser to billionaire George Soros, is bracing for a fiscal crisis sometime before the Tokyo Olympics. That risk drove him recently to run for an upper house of parliament seat, which he won. "I decided to become a politician because I think financial crisis will come sooner or later," Fujimaki said. "This total debt will continue to increase. I don't think Japan can survive until 2020."

Japan's debt is approaching 250 percent of GDP. The nation will spend 22.2 trillion yen servicing its debt in the fiscal year begun in April 2013, accounting for more than half of total tax revenue and occupying about 24 percent of the government's budget. As yields rise, though, debt-servicing costs will skyrocket and spook markets.

"Because the BOJ is buying huge amounts of JGBs, market principles in this country do not work," Fujimaki said. "Monetary easing is creating a JGB bubble. Sooner or later the market will reflect credit risk."

Noriko Hama of Doshisha University harbors similar concerns. "The Bank of Japan is no longer functioning as a proper central bank," Hama said, referring to the BOJ's ever-increasing bond purchases. "The scariest scenario, and the one we should be most wary of, is a bottom-less crash in the yen" as the global financial community loses faith in the currency.

This really is a time when there are no experts. There are no wise old graybeards to turn to for wisdom. Books by Adam Smith and John Maynard Keynes are of little help to governments walking an unprecedented tightrope between too much debt and too many old people. That doesn't mean Japan's experience can't inform Fed Chairman Janet Yellen and Treasury Secretary Jack Lew. One lesson, of course, is not to do any harm. Japan acted too slowly to dispose of bad loans. Politicians complicated things with an ill-timed tax increase in 1997 and didn't begin recapitalizing banks until a year later or writing down bad loans until years after that. Another lesson: Know when to begin dismantling stimulus programs. Of course, in both of these cases Japan hasn't learned the lessons from Japan.

"Japan has never really resolved the overinvestment orgy of the 1980s," said Michael Pettis, a finance professor at Peking University. "Instead of writing down bad debt, it effectively transferred much of it to the government balance sheet, and now this huge debt burden is itself becoming, I think, a constraint on the success of policies designed by Tokyo to spur growth."

The United States must avoid that mistake. Only time will tell if it can find the exit strategy from extreme monetary stimulus that eludes Japan. In fact, anyone worried about the Yellen Fed shaking the world with a series of big interest-rate hikes should spare a thought for Toshihiko Fukui. Bank of Japan governor from 2003 to 2008, Fukui was the last central banker to attempt a tapering process akin to the one Bernanke launched in December 2013. In 2005, Fukui began scaling back on massive bond purchases amid signs growth was perking up, and by March 2006 he scrapped Japan's quantitative-easing program. In July of that year, he raised the benchmark rate above zero for the first time since 2000 and followed that 25 basis-point move with another in February 2007.

Things didn't go well. Japan's deflationary economy quickly worsened anew and short-term rates were back at zero. When Masaaki Shirakawa succeeded Fukui in April 2008, his first act was to resurrect Japan's QE experiment. And, of course, Haruhiko Kuroda has taken things to unprecedented extremes since arriving at BOJ in March 2013. Japan's experience shows why markets may have less to fear from the Fed than many believe. The lesson from Tokyo is that it's a lot easier to slash rates to zero and beyond than returning them to normal.

Japan is now on its sixth central bank governor since its asset bubble burst in 1990, and BOJ governors are still doubling and tripling down on QE. Janet Yellen is likely to fare no better as she inherits the unenviable task of exiting the Fed's ultralow rate regime. Why? As Japan demonstrates, entire economies tend to get hooked on free money. Sure, folks complain publicly about irresponsible policies and currency debasement, but bankers, investors, and politicians alike become reliant on excessive liquidity—especially in nations carrying huge debt loads. So go ahead and brace for a brutal few years of Fed normalization and financial sobriety as Yellen & Co. yank away the punchbowl. More likely, the Fed will be forced to leave the bar open indefinitely.

In economic circles, no slight stings more than being compared to Herbert Hoover. The thirty-first U.S. president, who helped make the Depression of the 1930s great, ranks among history's worst growth killers. Ryutaro Hashimoto, Japan's prime minister from 1996 to 1998, went to his deathbed in 2006 seething over being tagged as Asia's Hoover. Among those doing the labeling was former Sony chairman Norio Ohga. Hashimoto's crime was the same as Hoover's: an ill-timed and ill-advised tax increase that ended Japan's post-bubble recovery. Hashimoto may soon have company in the annals of Hooveresque economics. Japan okayed a doubling of the sales tax in two steps—8 percent from 5 percent starting in April 2014, with a further 2 percent increase in the cards for 2015.

Never mind that deflation is still ingrained, the population is shrinking, and the ranks of the working poor are swelling. The government says higher taxes are needed to pay down the nation's debt. Some politicians are praising Abe for bold leadership, but raising taxes on a population traumatized by two decades of economic drift and 2011's earthquake is taking the easy road. It's a quick fix that's likely to backfire and erase the little dynamism that's left in an economy that has been overtaken by China.

True leadership would be to undertake major reforms. Japan's problem is less the size of the debt than the absence of healthy growth since the early 1990s. If the government were to lead, it would tell farmers—and other narrow special-interest groups stopping Japan from signing job-creating free-trade agreements like the Trans-Pacific Partnership—to go away. It would spend less time coddling Japan's nuclear industry and more championing energy alternatives to the dangerous reactors in the nation's midst. A green revolution would fuel an employment boom. Leadership also would have politicians pushing for increased immigration. Never mind that homogeneous Japan doesn't think it's ready to open its borders; economic reality makes it a necessity, not a choice.

If politicians really wanted to lead Japan's economic revival, they would demand that companies become more shareholder-friendly and accountable and offer incentives for executives to hire more women as full-time staff and senior leadership, ending the neglect of half the country's most valuable resource. Leadership would have lawmakers devising ways for women to manage both a career and a family, including more affordable child care and lower taxes for couples having babies.

Gender is perhaps the clearest example of why Abenomics is more PR than reality. Consider that even what passes for good news for Japanese women is often bad. A November 2013 government survey found that the labor participation rate among women ages 15 to 64 hit a record 63 percent. That was billed as an early victory for Abe's drive to pull women into the workforce. The details of the Internal Affairs and Communications Industry's findings told a darker story: Most of these women are being pushed into part-time and temporary positions that pay less, offer few benefits, and provide no job security. In other words, corporate Japan is still using women as Band-Aids to fix today's staffing needs, rather than harnessing their talents to increase productivity and innovation as recommended by IMF head Christine Lagarde.

This dynamic could worsen Japan's prospects. The wage increases needed to make Abenomics a success aren't materializing, in part because companies are using women to reduce total payroll costs. Abe talks a great deal about deregulating industry and lowering trade barriers but much less about increasing immigration to offset a shrinking labor force. Instead, women end up filling those jobs: Almost 57 percent of working women now hold part-time and temporary positions with salaries heading down rather than up.

It's a trend that gets lost in translation overseas, as United States Vice President Joe Biden can attest. On December 3, Biden and American Ambassador Caroline Kennedy visited DeNA Co., a Japanese Internet company founded by a woman who does a better job than most of taking the female workforce seriously. There, Biden approached five women and asked, "Do your husbands like you work-ing full-time?" The "gaffe" was treated as big news by the *Washington Post* and *Wall Street Journal* and became prime-time fodder for talk radio and CNN. In a *Crossfire* segment, Newt Gingrich accused Biden of offending Japan and waging a "war on women" of the kind usu-ally associated with his Republican Party. "How do you explain Biden's inability to stay in touch with reality?" Gingrich asked.

Sadly, Biden is completely in touch with the reality of half of Japan's population people. The real disgrace, Gingrich's ignorance aside, is how little is changing for Japanese women even under a prime min-ister who has pledged to empower them as never before. Now, there's reason to think institutionalized sexism is undercutting Abe's plan to end deflation. There also are fresh reasons to lament how madden-ingly low the bar is for Japan's women. Consider the supposed female-empowerment model Biden's handlers chose for him to tour with to highlight gender equality. Yes, DeNA was founded by a woman, Tomoko Namba, but it's run by a male chief executive officer (CEO), a male chairman, and male chief financial and technology officers. Namba is the only woman on the board of a company whose work-force is 80 percent male. It's not a place Gloria Steinem would prob-ably celebrate, but in male-dominated Japan, it counts as a trailblazer.

American pundits can giggle all they want at Biden's "awkward question," as the Internet news site BuzzFeed called it. But it's the right one. The graybeards who run Japanese companies—fewer than 1 percent of CEOs here are women—are stuck in a 1970s mind-set that women should work in supporting roles until they find a husband and quit. As many as 70 percent of Japanese women leave the work-force after having a child. Simply talking about tapping Japan's most underutilized resource isn't enough. Abe must redouble his efforts to change not only the structure of the economy but also the antiquated mind-sets that underpin it. Gingrich and his ilk can get away with cheap talking points—Abe can't.

True audacity would mean nationalizing Tepco and commanding all resources to clean up Fukushima and invite international exper-tise. Real leadership would be to set a new national goal to promote English proficiency. Like it or not, English is the lingua franca of the Internet Age, not to mention the global economy. Twenty years ago, foreign executives had to do things Japan's way—translators, ambiguous signals, the reluctance to offer a definitive "yes" or "no" to questions. Today, those executives have choices from Korea to China to Indonesia. Change means urging companies to rethink hiring practices. Students begin seeking lifetime employment in their junior year of college, or even their sophomore year. Fear of missing out on this recruitment process dissuades many from studying abroad or taking time off to travel before joining the ranks of the salarymen. It has created an odd generational quirk: Today's young Japanese are often less international than their parents.

■ ■ ■

Boldness means calling on companies to stop bellyaching about the yen's value and learn to live with it. Japan's currency has been strong for 12 years now—figure it out. Yes, those changes are being mulled right now. More and more companies are seeking cheap production overseas. Recent surveys show that large manufacturers are only modestly more upbeat amid Abe's reform pledges.

Also, audacity would be to admit that Japan's deflation may be more secular than cyclical. As Kuroda tries to spur Japan's inflation rate, he faces a worrying question: What if his BOJ predecessor was right about why he will fail? In June 2011, then-Governor Shirakawa faced extreme pressure to double the monetary base, a step Kuroda took just days after replacing him in March 2013. When Shirakawa, a University of Chicago–trained economist, was asked why he had refused to budge, he offered a surprising excuse: Japan's aging population, whose fixed incomes would be eaten away by rising prices. China, too, was placing downward pressures on costs everywhere, especially Japan. Politicians thought the rationale was a copout and Abe's first act as prime minister was to dump Shirakawa.

Turns out, Shirakawa was on to something. In a September 2013 paper, "Shock from Graying: Is the Demographic Shift Weakening Monetary Policy Effectiveness?," IMF researcher Patrick Imam offered convincing evidence that aging societies in Japan, Germany, and, to some extent, the United States can no longer be manipulated so

easily by central bank policies. Why is this so? Changes in official interest rates are about influencing long-term expectations and short-term
behavior. Cutting rates is meant to make buying a new house, opening a business, splurging on a flat-screen TV, or betting on stocks more
attractive today than next year. But such activity is disproportionately
conducted by the young. That's Japan's problem. Today, Japan's average
life expectancy at birth is 83 years, a figure projected to exceed 90 for
women by 2050.

Even that isn't the whole story. Along with ugly demographics
and China's growing influence, Kuroda faces a Japanese public that has
learned not only to live with deflation but also to enjoy it. Just as there
is good inflation, though, many in Japan have benefited from good
deflation. By 1990, asset prices weren't the only things that had veered
into bubble territory in Japan. Arguably, the entire economy had. As
the 1970s gave way to the heady 1980s, costs surged throughout the
economy: food, transportation, service fees, power, telecommunications,
education, entertainment, apparel, you name it. The story of Japan these
last 20 years, from the government to banks to companies, has involved
keeping consumer prices steady. Deflation has acted like a stealth tax
cut for households and restored some sobriety to costs.

When economist Kosuke Motani made this argument in his
2010 book, *The Real Face of Deflation*, it fell with a mighty thud in
Nagatacho. Motani thinks Japan is experiencing "nonmonetary deflation" on account of a national cost structure that overshot to the
upside decades ago, a graying population that favors falling prices over
rising ones, and a political system that doesn't understand that deflation is a symptom of Japan's malaise, not the cause. The theory among
neoclassical economists that quantitative easing can overcome deflation,
Motani argued, is "just like a religion." He could as easily have said
"cult." In fact, as odd as it sounds, Japan's deflation has been as much a
choice as a punishment. In order to avoid big, destabilizing reforms, the
government has amassed mountains of debt. Deflation, which lowers
nominal bond yields, makes that burden easier to service.

That's the paradox staring Abe and Kuroda directly in the face.
Until now, the focus has been on how bond traders will react as Japan
begins to produce sustained inflation. An equally important question
is how the nation's growing share of elderly will cope. "In Japan, all

players have adapted to a deflationary environment: Households are used to increasing living standards without expecting higher wages, companies live off cost-cutting without fighting for bigger markets, the government needs low interest rates for most of its finance," said Martin Schulz, a former BOJ researcher and now senior economist at Fujitsu Research Institute. "Turning all this around will not be easy."

Odd as it may sound to monetary purists, Japan's deflation was more of a choice than an economic-gloom sentence. Economist Robert Feldman of Morgan Stanley MUFG Securities Co. explored how the decision, be it active or passive, evolved into reality policy in a September 2010 report. Feldman argued, for example, that Japan could have left deflation in the rearview mirror in 2006 but the national psyche intervened to keep consumer prices on the decline. He offered four explanations why.

First was a central bank that was too timid to establish an inflation target until it was too late. The economy was growing at a healthy pace in 2006, enjoying the supply-side policies of Junichiro Koizumi, prime minister from April 2001 to September of that year. It wasn't until 2006 that the BOJ presented an actual definition of the "price stability" it was aiming for. And not until December 2009 did the government offer its own: a GDP deflator growth rate of 1 percent over time. But the Democratic Party of Japan in charge back then was reluctant to declare an explicit inflation target, or to change the BOJ's charter to reflect such a goal.

Second was demographics. Comparisons between Japan and the United States are dicey because the former is aging far more rapidly. Also, Japan's aging masses have far greater political clout than young voters, especially those just starting out in the labor force. That means Japan's entire societal structure, skewed toward savers, is incentivized to favor deflation. As Feldman pointed out, the working-age population (15–64) peaked in 1995 at 87.3 million and had fallen to 81.5 million by September 2010. At the same time, Japan's graying contingent— those 65 and over—has jumped from 18.3 million to 29 million.

Third was an underappreciated generational divide. This dynamic is mostly thought of in terms of a strong yen, which benefits Japan's growing ranks of the elderly at the expense of the young. The ruling Liberal Democratic Party that has led Japan virtually uninterrupted for nearly six decades has long relied on the support of rural—and in recent decades, rapidly aging—voters. LDP leaders have been reluctant to cross their base with a falling yen, especially with prime ministers often changing every 12 months or so.

"The aging of Japan's population has increased this tendency to favor deflation, because a large share of the population lives on fixed incomes," Feldman wrote. "Yes, nominal interest income has fallen sharply with the drop of nominal interest rates. However, complaints about this have largely faded, as pensioners see the benefits of falling prices, relative to their fixed incomes." The bottom line is that a legislative universe overrepresented by older voters is prone to adopt deflationary policies.

Fourth was Japan's obsession with current-account surpluses. This, too, skews incentives toward falling prices because it enables Tokyo to run large, and growing, budget deficits as a means of putting off major upgrades to the domestic economy. Deflation, it's important to note, lowers nominal bond yields and makes large public debt loads easier to service. According to Feldman,

> Thus, the pressure for productivity-enhancing reforms, both in the public sector itself to contain spending and in the private sector to raise growth and tax revenue, was interdicted. So long as the current-account surplus remains, the incentives to exit deflation will be weak, barring wholesale capital flight by domestic investors, which appears very unlikely.

■ ■ ■

One problem facing Abe and Aso is perceptions versus reality. Many Japanese love the idea of defeating deflation because it represents a break with the nation's malaise. It irks the government, too, that *Japanization* is a catchphrase among economists warning about the evils of falling prices and political gridlock. Japanese yearn for a return to the days when they wowed the world with high-tech innovation, bullet trains, avant-garde stadiums, neon-lit skylines, and can-do spirit. But are they ready to see rents, utility bills, school costs, and the prices of taxi rides and bento boxes rise? Perhaps not.

That's why it's so important that Abe implement the third "arrow" of his revitalization program. The first phase—Kuroda's huge liquidity boost—cheered markets. The second, fiscal pump-priming, may get a boost from Tokyo's preparations for the 2020 Olympics. The third and most vital, though, is deregulation to encourage companies to expand and fatten paychecks so consumers can spend more. Only phase three can help the BOJ's largess get real traction on deflation.

"The only easy part is starting to print the money because it does not hurt anyone for the first year," Schulz said.

> But after that, when prices start to go up, it really depends on the view at that time: Will people only see the higher costs, or will they see the brighter future that the government is selling with its money? If they don't, a turn in public opinion will stop the BOJ before expectations have changed enough to get the economy on an inflationary track.

Kuroda could yet prove his predecessor wrong, but he's going to need help from his prime minister—and soon. Abe should work with the BOJ to devise more creative ways to get banks to lend. Wave after wave of central-bank liquidity isn't resulting in the credit creation Japan needs to jump-start growth. Rather than tax consumers, why not tax banks that hoard cash? Why not force bankers to do their jobs and make loans? That might offset the effects of higher taxes. Japan also lacks a vibrant venture-capital industry. How about announcing a government-driven incubation campaign with lower corporate taxes for new companies? Okay, that would be anathema to economists from Adam Smith to Milton Friedman. But there's a reason Japan is losing ground as scrappy startups and social-media offerings level the economic landscape. Japan Inc. still sees nothing wrong with most of its innovations and patents coming from huge companies, as opposed to Mark Zuckerberg types. That arrangement needs to change and if it comes from the government, so be it. The Facebook founder met with Japanese policy makers in Tokyo in late 2012, just as they were debating higher taxes. At that moment, Zuckerberg was on the cusp of his own bit of history: the Internet's biggest initial public offering. The big difference, of course, is that as Zuckerberg is creating wealth, Japan's leaders may be about to destroy it, Herbert Hoover–style.

Japan has seen bursts of entrepreneurial zeal before. One coincided with Silicon Valley's dot-com boom in the late 1990s, when a commercial area in Tokyo's trendy Shibuya district was dubbed "Bit Valley." The euphoria fizzled as America's Nasdaq bubble exploded and Japanese venture capital failed to materialize. Another came in the early 2000s amid excitement about the Koizumi government's free-market policies. Yet it evaporated along with Livedoor Co.'s market capitalization when founder Takafumi Horie was locked up, ostensibly for securities fraud. For many would-be tech magnates, Horie's downfall was a cautionary tale about how Japan Inc. pounces on a scrappy outsider who ignores its rules.

Increased paper wealth, optimists argue, will provide more currency for prominent Japanese tech incubators like Samurai Startup Island or innovation consultants like Quantum Leaps Corp., which was founded by former Sony CEO Nobuyuki Idei. Yet it will take more than excitement to unleash Japan's animal spirits. The government must facilitate the process with tax incentives, financial assistance, and help to encourage more risk taking in a deeply conservative corporate culture. Or will it be the Ronald Reagan moment Japan investors have long fantasized about? Abe's plan to restore Japan's economic might draws heavily upon principles long associated with the former U.S. president: welfare-spending cuts, debt-swelling tax reductions for the wealthy and corporations, deregulation, a lowering of trade barriers, and reforms that make it easier to fire workers. Yet while investors have greeted this supply-side shock therapy with enthusiasm, Japan's people may not find its side effects quite so pleasing. As in the United States, Abe's reforms could well hollow out the middle class and create the kind of gulf between rich and poor that Japan has long tried to avoid. Everyone from officials at the U.S. Treasury to punters in London trading pits to salarymen in Osaka are so ecstatic to see a Japanese leader acting boldly that they've forgotten to study his strategy. It's great that Abe wants to shake Japan Inc. out of two decades of complacency. It's equally important, though, that his fixes are the right ones and are implemented carefully.

Take Abe's plan to cut the 35.6 percent corporate tax rate— the second-highest level among Group of Seven nations—while at the same time doubling consumption taxes. How exactly does Japan hope to encourage households to spend more to boost gross domestic product while raising the cost of consuming? The last time Japan tried something similar, in 1998, tax increases scuttled the recovery from a financial crash eight years earlier. "To raise the consumption tax while cutting corporate taxes will further shift things in the wrong direction," says Richard Katz of the Oriental Economist Report. "That does not make sense for a country where consumer spending is chronically weak due to weak consumer income."

What would make more sense is clamping down on tax-dodging executives. An eye-popping 73 percent of companies in Japan pay no tax, according to Nicholas Smith of CLSA Asia-Pacific Markets. "This breaks into two groups—companies that are uneconomical and companies that are economical with the truth," Smith said. Abe's labor reforms pose risks, too. Japan should indeed scrap the antiquated practices of lifetime employment and seniority-based promotions while reducing the power of uncompromising labor unions. The country ranks 134th out of 144 nations in terms of ease of hiring and firing, according to the World Economic Forum's Global Competitiveness Report. Yet Japan lacks a public safety net to catch the hundreds of thousands of workers who could soon be out of a job.

Since the Koizumi years, Japan has seen a rapid increase in the number of workers being switched to part-time positions with few benefits; "freeters," or low-wage workers going from temporary job to temporary job; "NEETs," or young people not in education, employment, or training; and "parasite singles," twentysomething and thirtysomething unmarried Japanese who live with Mom to save on costs.

Japan eschewed an American-style unemployment-insurance system because companies never laid off workers. The reason Tokyo spent so much time and money propping up banks in the late 1990s and early 2000s was so they could keep zombie companies afloat and unemployment low. Before Abe helps companies to sack 20,000 workers here and 50,000 there, he must create a social-benefits program and fund *extensive* job-retraining programs. Otherwise, Abenomics will only exacerbate Japan's underappreciated working-poor problem. Among OECD members, Japan ranks fifth in the number of working-age persons living on less than half the average national income. The dynamic began in former Prime Minister Koizumi's day and accelerated with what Japanese call the "Lehman shock" in 2008. Government statisticians are only now catching on to the problem.

Between 2001 and 2006, Koizumi dabbled a bit in Reaganomics himself. Japan's preference for consensus over conflict meant he moved more gingerly than Reagan did, or than Margaret Thatcher did as Britain's prime minister in the 1980s. Koizumi's signature achievement was privatizing the sprawling Japan Post, which plans an initial public offering by April 2015. Yet Koizumi also cut pensions and tweaked labor laws to allow companies to hire more workers on a part-time basis at lower pay and without benefits. That slammed incomes in the middle of the wage spectrum and hit women especially hard. It's led to many unexpected consequences, including an epidemic of shoplifting among the elderly. Abe's move to get the Bank of Japan to double the monetary base excites hedge-fund managers but punishes savers who must live on a fixed income. These changes would be less destabilizing if trickle-down economics actually worked. It would help, too, if Japan had a buoyant startup industry creating scores of new jobs to fill the void. It's still the case that Japan's entrepreneurial animal spirits are dormant. Even if Abe complemented Reaganomics with a dash of socialism and financed a venture-capital industry publicly, it would take years to yield results. Many of Abe's policies are exactly what Japan needs. Joining the U.S.-led Trans-Pacific Partnership would pump fresh energy through Japan Inc.'s atrophied veins. So would deregulating sectors from energy to medical services to education to agriculture. Yet reforms that should bear fruit in the long run lack the financial cushions and economic checks and balances needed in the short run. Abe must develop a transition plan to keep his strategy from polarizing Japan's proudly egalitarian society. It's not as if most Americans are happy with that legacy of Reaganomics.

"All Abenomics is, really, is a race to nowhere," says Sean Corrigan, chief investment strategist at Diapason Commodities Management SA in Lausanne, Switzerland.

■ ■ ■

Abe's administration should be mulling radical remedies for the tsunami-ravaged Tohoku region. One idea is to use the games as an excuse to spread the "Bilbao Effect" to the rural northeast. The most influential Olympics have always been those that provide a catalyst at an ideal moment: Think about the 1988 Summer Games in Seoul, which fueled South Korea's transition from autocracy to democracy, and Sydney 2000, which, pre–Group of Twenty, highlighted Australia's place as a global power. The 2020 Games happen to coincide with Abe's push to open up Japan, through both lowering trade barriers and getting the Japanese themselves to engage with the outside world after decades of looking inward.

Tokyo-based author Robert Whiting thinks the games will complement Abe's efforts. "It will further help to globalize Japanese, in line with Abe's goal or vision of making Japanese more international-minded and active," Whiting said. "People will be focusing more on learning English to prepare for the Olympics, and parents will be more oriented toward having their children learn the language as well."

An Olympic boost could also give Abe the political cover he needs to deregulate an economy badly in need of some supply-side shock therapy. Big changes are always easier when optimism is on an upswing. A groundswell of public support would help Abe steamroll the vested interests standing in the way of freer trade, increased immigration, upgrades to corporate governance, and tax tweaks that promote entrepreneurship. It worked for Abe's grandfather Kishi in 1964, when he used the proud inauguration of the bullet train to launch a major infrastructure spending drive. It might just work for Abe ahead of 2020.

Moving some of the sporting events to Tohoku would yield the infrastructure boom most of the region desperately needs and force an acceleration of the Fukushima cleanup. Japan's bureaucratic and indecisive central government has proven ill-equipped for the task of rebuilding the towns and villages wiped out on March 11, 2011. The disaster left almost 19,000 dead or missing and forced cartographers to redraw maps of Japan's northeast coastline. Tohoku could use a big boost. Careful planning would be needed to see that sports facilities will be used after the Olympics, and to ensure transparent efforts clear away the last traces of radiation near the damaged Fukushima nuclear reactors. Why not ask architecture rock star Frank Gehry to rural Japan?

What about a dose of Bangladesh? Abe also could run with an idea proposed by Muhammad Yunus. In August 2012, the Nobel Peace Prize winner choked back tears as he surveyed the wreckage: pulverized buildings, debris strewn for miles along urban waterfronts, giant ships sitting atop roads like discarded toys—macabre memorials to the thousands of dead and missing. Yunus is no stranger to nature's wrath. In his native Bangladesh, earthquakes, floods, cyclones, and mudslides are a tragic way of life. But these scenes were of another magnitude. The devastation surrounding him wasn't testing the mettle of a poor nation, but prosperous Japan.

That visit to the devastated northeast Tohoku region was on the one-year anniversary of the nation's worst earthquake and tsunami on record. Like many, Yunus came away haunted by an economic question: How can the Tohoku region not only rebuild, but reinvent itself and thrive in a time of austerity?

Yunus came back with an unlikely suggestion, one that created its own tremors in Nagatacho, Tokyo's Capitol Hill: Japan needs a microfinance industry. The Nobel prize was for Yunus's role in promoting lending to the poor, a group typically ignored by bankers. Tiny amounts—$20, $50, or $100 so a family can buy a cow to start a dairy farm, or a mobile phone to open a communications business, or chickens to launch an egg company. In 1976, he founded Grameen Bank, which brought microfinance global.

What does any of this have to do with Japan? It is near the top of national per-capita income tables, has one of the highest savings rates, and Tokyo and Osaka are routinely in the running for world's most expensive city. Japan gives impoverished Bangladesh billions of dollars in aid each year.

"It's needed everywhere—it doesn't matter where you are," Yunus said in Tokyo on July 26, 2012. "When you come to a disaster area like Tohoku, it's all the more important. You have to rebuild everything all over again. There's no house, there's nothing."

By "there's nothing," Yunus also means the general lack of economic life in a region that was dying even before the disaster. Take Rikuzentakata, which like many cities on Japan's rugged northeast coast was suffering from economic decline and a shrinking population. When the tsunami hit, it killed 1,700 of its 24,000 inhabitants and destroyed most of its downtown buildings. There was the expectation, however farfetched, that the disaster would be the kind of event that would topple the status quo and complacency that has held Japan frozen in place for two decades.

That hope has since been dashed by paralysis in Tokyo and a return to the petty infighting that passes for political leadership. That is prompting local officials to take matters into their own hands. Rikuzentakata is working to create a small, self-sufficient city that creates new jobs in renewable energy to replace those lost to the decline of agriculture and fisheries. That is a long-term project, though. It is being hindered by the central government's failure to channel more money into Tohoku communities, and by its reluctance to delegate spending decisions to regional leaders. It is here where microfinance might pay sizable dividends. Locals can pool their savings and lend them out to would-be entrepreneurs—$10,000 here, $100,000 there.

It could be a boon for households that lost everything, with an added benefit: Microfinance tends to extend more credit to women than other lenders. Many Tohoku residents lost their collateral and might be considered poor credit risks, and women have limited access to credit. Tohoku is a relatively poor region in Japan and enjoys strong social cohesion, something that would be useful in monitoring how loans are used and repaid.

Microfinance-like currents are already stirring in Japan. Tokyo-based Music Securities Inc. has set up small-lot lending programs that helped sake brewers, coffee shops, musicians, fish retailers, and soy-sauce makers gain access to financing. Yet we need to think bigger in an economy faced with a surplus of liquidity and a dearth of credit. Microfinance on a grander scale might enable the northeast's community leaders to steer around the paralysis in Tokyo, where bureaucrats are impervious to their demands and clueless about their needs. It would help local credit systems gain traction in ways the BOJ's zero-rate policies can't. Japanese need alternatives to banks, which aren't lending or offering creative financial products. Micro-lending could help businesses and households steer around the credit logjam.

Japan's government could provide some startup cash to supplement local savings. Given the huge sums of money it doles out for infrastructure projects in Hokkaido and Kyushu in the far north and south of the country, respectively, the cost of setting up a kind of Grameen Japan would be minuscule and the risks limited. Is that likely to happen? The odds aren't great given how averse Tokyo's bureaucrats are to anything that smacks of originality or setting a precedent. Yet Yunus showed it was possible for poor people in Bangladesh to get the credit they deserve. There's no good reason to think the same can't happen in Japan.

■ ■ ■

The Tohoku region also could use a dose of China. If you want to silence a room filled with Japanese politicians, suggest they should learn from the Communist Party. The conventional wisdom favors the flipside of this dynamic: China should be studying Japan's playbook. Japan, after all, is an example of both what China needs to do (create a vibrant domestic economy and high living standards) and what it mustn't (slide into bad-loan crises and deflation). Yet here's one word for Japanese policy makers who dismiss the idea they should heed China's example: Shenzhen. For two decades now, economists have been urging Tokyo to create a special-enterprise zone or two. The idea is to have a laboratory where officials could try drastic alternatives to Japan's rigid, bureaucratic, and change-resistant model—a controlled environment in which the nationwide laws and norms that thwart economic energy could be repealed. Abe has talked about such an experiment, but as currently envisioned it would more like Shenzhen-lite. Southern China features such a place. In 1980, Deng Xiaoping started China's first special-economic zone in a coastal village that was nothing to look at. Today, Shenzhen is a teeming collage of huge skyscrapers, thriving industrial parks, 10 million people, one of the world's busiest ports, and some of the biggest manufacturing and outsourcing industries anywhere. It's the center of Chinese experimentation. There, officials can test what works and what doesn't: which corporate tax rates offer the best balance of attracting foreign investment while filling government coffers in Beijing, which labor standards make the most sense, which corporate-governance standards are most advantageous, which immigration procedures are optimal, which regulations stay or go. Chinese authorities are now experimenting anew with a Shanghai free-trade zone. China's experience inspired nations as disparate as

Angola, Bangladesh, Brazil, Iran, Kazakhstan, the Philippines, Poland, Russia, and even North Korea to erect special economic regions, and India, too.

You can argue that India's software industry is such an entity—one immune enough from New Delhi's dysfunction to create the growth and jobs India so badly needs. Why not Japan? Koizumi broached the issue in the early 2000s, but his vision was never effectively implemented. Of all the growth-revitalizing strategies employed by Tokyo, the most favored ones are debt and concrete—debt to finance white-elephant public-works projects, and concrete to build them. Japan is too much about saving unproductive jobs, not creating innovative new ones. What Japan never tried is a dose of well-calibrated supply-side economics. Japan shouldn't embrace of the ideologies of Ayn Rand and Ronald Reagan. But it has gotten as far it can with financial socialism. Even after more than two decades of start-and-stop growth, Japan's focus is on preserving its way of life, not adjusting to the demands of globalization and Chinese competition. The big debates in Tokyo are over raising taxes and joining free-trade deals. Some fresh thinking is in order, and Japan's March 11 earthquake and tsunami provided a perfect opportunity. There are many cities the government could declare as economic-policy labs: Fukuoka, Kobe, Nagasaki, Sapporo, and Yokohama. The devastated northeastern Tohoku region is a better choice. Tohoku can be to Japan what Shenzhen was to China: Allow large-scale deregulation, cut red tape that frustrates businesses, offer 10-year tax holidays for new investments and incentives for employers generating full-time jobs, apply a corporate tax rate in the neighborhood of 11 percent, suspend gasoline taxes, subsidize electricity, eliminate sales taxes, and structure a variety of enticements to attract capital into renewable-energy research and production.

Martin Schulz, of the Fujitsu Research Institute, would take things a step further and simply make Tohoku corporate-tax free. That, he argues, would get young people and families into a region that was dying demographically even before the earth shook and the waters rose. China has much to learn from Japan. From the ashes of World War II, it created a safe, prosperous, universally literate, environmentally stable, and reasonably egalitarian nation. Yet Japan has long since lost the vibrancy and policy innovation that propelled it to today's heights.

Abe should create a Japanese Shenzhen. It would be a much-needed recognition that if Japan can't beat China, it can at least learn a thing or two from Asia's economic upstart.

The western city of Fukuoka also is a worthy candidate for free-trade zone status. This city of 1.5 million aims to become Japan's Silicon Valley. As technology-crazed as Japanese are, the government has never encouraged universities, companies, and investors to join hands to help the economy. The result is less innovation in a nation that should be awash in it. People such as Masaharu Okada of Kyushu University are working to change that. If they succeed, Japan's economic future will brighten. If they don't, expect the decades-long slide in living standards—and markets—to accelerate. Okada is the first to admit he's an odd character on campus. A lawyer by training, he spent many years working for technology firms in Boston, New York, Seattle, and Tokyo, including Nippon Telegraph & Telephone Corp. and Access Co. Now he's back in his hometown to light a fire under his students. "Japan has always been about big companies and lifetime employment," Okada says. "What's missing are startup companies like the ones in the United States that come out of nowhere, create many good-paying jobs, and change the world. We need to support this kind of thinking, and that is why I returned to Fukuoka and decided to work with students."

Okada works closely with the University–Industry International Collaboration Center, and his specialty is intellectual-property strategies. It's all about encouraging students with an idea and a dream to execute it and locate the financing needed to create profitable companies from scratch. Why Fukuoka? Japan has long been too Tokyo-centric. Many executives aim to succeed in the nation's business and political center before looking overseas. Fukuoka has a number of things going for it. One is its proximity to China and South Korea. Another is an international mind-set that can seem more prevalent than in Tokyo or Osaka. And, well, it's a terrific place. In 2012, *Monocle* magazine named Fukuoka the twelfth-most-livable city in the world. The criteria included urban planning, transportation links, crime rates, educational facilities, and environmental initiatives. The quality of life Fukuokans enjoy is the envy of many Japanese. It's also about fiscal reality. The global crisis means areas far outside Tokyo, like Kyushu, increasingly need to generate their own economic output. There's simply less public spending to go around. The tax system favors giants over startups, which exacerbates the concentration of new ideas in a handful of corporate boardrooms. It's time to change that, and Fukuoka is worth a look at ground central for Japan's startup boom. A growing hunger for green technologies around the globe is fueling Fukuoka's optimism. Around the city, small companies are producing more efficient hydrogen and solar energy, meeting global demand for recycling technologies, and making diesel fuel out of discarded edible oils. The city's entrepreneurial spirit prompted former Sony CEO Idei to hold his annual Asia Innovation Initiative in Fukuoka. In the end, it doesn't matter where Japan sets up its Silicon Valley, just so long as it does. As China, India, and Southeast Asia raise the competitive pressure, Japan's ability to maintain a profitable export business for its large manufacturers is getting squeezed. The challenge is to create postindustrial export industries that are more about ideas and services.

America's Silicon Valley didn't come about overnight. It was the result of a venture-capital system; robust private and public universities; brainpower from abroad; flexible labor markets; large research and development budgets, including those of the U.S. government; and loads of contrarian thinking. The importance of strong antitrust laws and openness to foreign investment also can't be understated. Considering all these ingredients, Japan faces an uphill climb. Getting over a deeply rooted resistance to immigration will be difficult enough, never mind cultivating a risk-taking dynamic in an aging workforce more accustomed to working at big companies than hanging out a shingle. All this would make Japan more about job creation from the ground up than job protection from the top down.

Two numbers colored Shinzo Abe's 2013 and offered hints about Japan's prospects this year: 57 and 49. The first, of course, is how much in percentage terms the Nikkei 225 stock average surged in 2013. The prime minister even dropped by the Tokyo Stock Exchange on December 30, 2013, to celebrate with floor traders, declaring, "Next year will go well. With this thought, I want to do my best. Next year too, Abenomics is a buy." The second number—49—makes that unlikely. It corresponds to Abe's public approval rate as of December 24, 2013. History shows that Japanese leaders with sub-50 percent support rates get little done and don't tend to last very long. And Abe's could actually be far worse. That *Mainichi* poll was done two days before he angered the world with his provocative visit to the Yasukuni Shrine, an action most didn't support.

That's ominous news for Abe's so-called third arrow. The first two arrows—monetary and fiscal pump priming—hit the target well enough, as evidenced by the largest surge in the Nikkei since 1972. But the rally is predicated on the third phase of Abenomics, the structural reform part that failed to materialize at all in 2013.

The hope remains that in 2014, Abe will boldly trample over the vested interests standing in the way of lower trade barriers, less regulation, and a greater embrace of free-market principles. In the Chinese zodiac, the 12 months of the horse are an opportunity for revitalization and improvement. Clearly, foreign investors had this ethos in mind, at least indirectly, when they drove up shares. The year 2014 is Abe's to gallop toward epochal change. Here are four reasons they are likely to be disappointed.

One, Abe's window is closing. The time to force through controversial changes was in the second half of 2013, when the Bank of Japan's monetary bonanza was exciting business leaders and driving Abe's approval ratings toward the 80s. Back then, Abe could practically do no wrong. He could have taken the floor of parliament and said something like, "Japan is back, and the investors of the world are responding with great enthusiasm. To sustain this high, we must act quickly and decisively. And so, each month I will unveil a deregulatory step that lawmakers of the past lacked the courage to take to make Japan more vibrant. First, corporate tax reform. Next month, legislation to empower women in the workforce. The month after that, moves to loosen the labor market. After that, cutting trade tariffs, encouraging startups, attracting more foreign workers, and initiating a new energy policy to make Japan a global power in renewables. And by the start of 2014, my third arrow will be flying toward our ultimate goal: less deflation and greater dynamism."

Two, looking for growth in the wrong places. Instead, of the above, Abe spent political capital restarting nuclear power plants against public opinion, traveling the world to sell reactors for Hitachi Ltd. and other companies, pushing through a sales-tax increase that will dent consumption, passing a controversial secrets bill that undermine press freedom, and irking two of Japan's biggest customers with his December 26, 2013, shrine visit. The only way Abenomics works is if companies benefiting from a weaker yen return the favor and boost wages.

Three, the nationalist fix seems to be in. The longer I cover Abe, the more I think of historian Thomas Frank. His 2004 book, *What's the Matter with Kansas?*, was about America and how conservatives there essentially win the hearts of the middle class with a bait-and-switch strategy. They get households to vote against their economic interests by distracting them with social issues like abortion and gay marriage, giving them a free hand to enrich the 1 percent without a backlash. Abe does that in reverse: distracting Japan with talk of growth and prosperity so that he can carry out his rightward agency. His visit to Yasukuni, which honors 14 class A war criminals from World War II, suggests that he is more interested in catering to nationalists than Chinese and South Korean consumers. And Abe's push to revise school textbooks to whitewash Japan's military aggression during World War II means his eye is now on the real prize: imposing the deeply revisionist take of history he inherited from his grandfather. Former Prime Minister Nobusuke Kishi was himself jailed for war crimes before eventually returning to politics. As Abe carries out this bit of family business, his true mandate from voters, economic reforms, will get short shrift.

Four, the Trans-Pacific Partnership (TPP) may unravel. When optimists toast Abe for making bold decisions, his move to join the U.S. trade deal is exhibit A. But Japan's entry could also be the undoing of the 12-nation pact. The reason: the number of exceptions Tokyo is demanding for entry, including agriculture and automobiles. A watered-down version of TPP was never the idea—this deal is supposed to touch every sector of every economy. So, expect other signatory nations to expect the Japan treatment: Malaysia can say its affirmative-action policies are off the table; Vietnam can protect its state-owned enterprises; New Zealand can designate its dairy industry as no-go zone, and so on. Abe supporters see TPP as an economic Trojan horse that once inside Japan Inc.'s walls will beat back vested interests. Thanks to Abe's timidity, not so much.

Japan has no time to waste. Prime Minister Abe must break with the half measures of the past and focus all his energy on creating a whole new generation of innovators. That wouldn't just pay huge dividends for faster economic growth, higher living standards, and getting Japan off Galapagos. It would morph Japan into a global role model once again, with all the soft power and self-confidence that accompany that status. For centuries, Japan has shown it can do just that. It's time for Abe to prove that "Japan is back" isn't just a slogan but a blueprint for renewal from which the world can learn.

Bibliography

Abe, S. (2006). *Towards a Beautiful Country*. Tokyo: Vertical.

Abe, S. (2013, September 25). *Address by H.E. Mr. Shinzo Abe, Prime Minister of Japan, at the New York Stock Exchange*. Retrieved from http://www.kantei.go.jp/foreign/96_abe/statement/201309/25nyse_e.html.

Adelstein, J. (2010). *Tokyo Vice: An American Reporter on the Police Beat in Japan*. Tokyo: Vintage.

Adelstein, J. (2011, September 23). "Yakuza Goes Hollywood." *Daily Beast*.

Adelstein, J. (2013, November 30). "Japan: The New Uzbekistan of Press Freedom in Asia." *Japan Times*.

Akerlof, G., and R. Shiller (2009). *Animal Spirits*. Princeton, NJ: Princeton University Press.

Alexander, E. (2013, May 28). "Prada vs. the UN." *Vogue*.

Associated Press. (2003, July 6). "Japan's Quietly Accepted Discrimination Surfaces." *Taipei Times*.

Automotive News. (2002, February 7). "U.S. Automakers Seek White House Action on Weak Yen."

Bank of Japan Media Center. (2010, October 10). "Economic Policy Challenges Lying Ahead." Transcript.

Bartlett, B. (2012, May 29). "Economix: Republican Keynesians." *New York Times*.

Benedict, R. (1946). *The Chrysanthemum and the Sword*. Boston: Houghton Mifflin.

Blustein, P. (2001). *The Chastening*. Cambridge: Perseus Books Group.

Bremmer, I. (2012). *Every Nation for Itself: Winners and Losers in a G-Zero World*. New York: Portfolio Hardcover.

Brooke, J. (2002, January 30). "Japan's Foreign Minister Is Fired after Months of Feuding." *New York Times*.

Byron, C. (1981, March 30). "The World's Toughest Competitor: How Japan Does It." *Time*.

Chambers, A. (2010, August 3). "Japan: Ending the Culture of the 'Honourable' Suicide." *Guardian*.

Chan, S. (2010, July 29). "Within the Fed, Worries of Deflation." *New York Times*.

Chancellor, E. (2013, March 31). "The Ghost of Takahashi Haunts Abenomics." *Financial Times*.

Choyleva, D., and B. Reading (2013). *China's Chance to Avoid Japan's Mistakes*. London: Lombard Street Research.

Clenfield, J. (2011, March 11). "Japan Nuclear Disaster Caps Decades of Faked Reports, Accidents." Bloomberg News.

Clifford, M. (2011). *Reimagining Japan: The Quest for a Future That Works*. San Francisco: VIZ Media.

Cooper, R. (2013, June 28). "Poor English Saved Japan's Banks from Crisis." *Telegraph*.

Coxon, M., and I. Reynolds (2013, May 27). "Japan's Hashimoto Says Use of Wartime Sex Slaves Was Inexcusable." Bloomberg News.

Crichton, M. (1992). *Rising Sun*. New York: Alfred A. Knopf.

Cunningham, L. (2013, September 13). "Will the Bedroom or Boardroom Save Japan?" *Washington Post*.

Dawson, J. (2013, November 14). "Paul Krugman Says ECB Can in Principle Do More Easing." Bloomberg Television.

Demetriou, D. (2009, October 4). "Meet the New, Young and Female Faces Causing a Stir in Japanese Politics." *Telegraph*.

Dower, J. (1999). *Embracing Defeat*. New York: W. W. Norton.

Dujarric, R., and S. W. Woon (2013). *Japan's Deglobalization*. Tokyo: Temple University.

Duncan, R. (2012). *The New Depression: The Breakdown of the Paper Money Economy*. Hoboken, NJ: Wiley.

Ehrbar, A. (2013, February 3). "Great Bond Market Massacre of 1994." *Fortune*.

Fackler, M. (1997, November 26). "Yamaichi Collapse Raises Specter of Hidden Losses Elsewhere." Bloomberg News.

Fackler, M. (2013, October 2). "Former Prime Minister Declares Opposition to Nuclear Power in Japan." *New York Times.*

Fackler, M., and S.-H. Choe (2013, November 24). "A Growing Chill Between South Korea and Japan Creates Problems for the U.S." *New York Times.*

Feldman, R. (2010). *Deflation: Will America and Europe Follow Japan?* Tokyo: Morgan Stanley.

Fingleton, E. (2012, January 6). "The Myth of Japan's Failure." *New York Times.*

Flitton, D. (2010, December 6). "Rudd the Butt of WikiLeaks Exposé." *Sydney Morning Herald.*

Fox, M. (2013, January 1). "Beate Gordon, Long-Unsung Heroine of Japanese Women's Rights, Dies at 89." *New York Times.*

Friedman, M. (1962). *Capitalism and Freedom.* Chicago: University of Chicago Press.

Golden, A. (1997). *Memoirs of a Geisha.* New York: Alfred A. Knopf.

Haworth, A. (2013, October 20). "Why Have Young People in Japan Stopped Having Sex?" *Observer.*

Hewlett, S. A. (2013, September 27). "What's Holding Japanese Women Back?" *Time.*

Howard, C. (2013, May 22). "The World's Most Powerful Women, 2013." *Forbes.*

Hu, C. (2013, August 6). "China's Surging Debt Pressures Xi-Li to Avert Lost Decade." Bloomberg News.

Hudson, V. (2012). *Sex and World Peace.* New York: Columbia University Press.

Imam, P. (2013, September). "Shock from Graying: Is the Demographic Shift Weakening Monetary Policy Effectiveness?" IMF working paper.

Ishikawa, M. (2013, September 27). "Soros Adviser Turned Lawmaker Sees Crisis by 2020: Japan Credit." Bloomberg News.

Ito, T. (2013, November 26). "BOJ Beat: Minutes Show Split Among Policy Board." *Wall Street Journal.*

Jiang, S. (2013, July 19). "Japan PM Abe Looks to Put Economy Back on Track with Deng-Style SEZs." *South China Morning Post.*

Kassenaar, L. (1997, June 24). "Hashimoto Threatens to Sell U.S. Treasuries, Buy Gold." Bloomberg News.

Kattoulas, V. (2002, January 17). "The Yakuza Recession." *Far Eastern Economic Review.*

Kennedy, S. (2012, October 11). "Europe Misdiagnoses Fiscal Pneumonia as Diabetes in Koo Warning." Bloomberg News.

Kerr, A. (2001). *Dogs and Demons*. New York: Hill & Wang.

Kim, S. (2013, May 15). "Abe's Pose Resurrects Horrors of Unit 731." *Korea Joongang Daily*.

Kingston, J. (2011). *Contemporary Japan*. Oxford: Wiley-Blackwell.

Koo, R. (2009). *The Holy Grail of Macroeconomics: Lessons from Japan's Great Recession*. Hoboken, NJ: Wiley.

Korea Joongang Daily (2013, November 7). "Tokyo's Insensitive Application."

Krugman, P. (2013, January 13). "Japan Steps Out." *New York Times*.

Kuebler-Ross, E. (1969). *On Death and Dying*. New York: Scribner.

Kun, J. (2013, May 22). "Washington Alienated by Tokyo Rightists." *Global Times*.

Kwan, C. (2002). *Economics of Engrish*. Tokyo: Japan's Research Institute of Economy, Trade and Industry.

Lagarde, C. (2012, October 12)." Annual Meeting Speech: The Road Ahead—A Changing Global Economy, a Changing IMF." Retrieved from http://www.imf.org/external/np/speeches/2012/101212.htm.

Langeland, T., and T. Hyuga (2013, October 23). "Yakuza Mobsters Losing AmEx Cards Whacked by Regulators' Tactics." Bloomberg News.

Lee, H. (2013, October 14). "South Korea to Scale Back Nuclear Reliance After Safety Scandal." Bloomberg News.

Li, S. (2011, March 30). "Gladwell Says 'Overconfidence' Fueled Financial Crisis." Video (M. Gladwell, Interviewer).

Manabe, H. (2013, September 17). "Interview/Carol Gluck: Change in Japan Is a Long-Distance Run." *Wall Street Journal*.

Martin, B. (2006). *Under the Loving Care of the Fatherly Leader: North Korea and the Kim Dynasty*. New York: St. Martin's Griffin.

Matsutani, M. (2012, October 27). "Axed Manager's Sexual Harassment Lawsuit Against Prada Japan Fails." *Japan Times*.

McCormick, L. C., and D. Kruger (2013, May 7). "Bond Buyers See No 1994 as Bernanke Clarity Tops Greenspan." Bloomberg News.

McCurry, J. (2013, October 15). "Plummeting Morale at Fukushima Daiichi as Nuclear Cleanup Takes Its Toll." *Guardian*.

McGray, D. (2002, May 1). "Japan's Gross National Cool." *Foreign Policy*.

NAIIC. (2012). *National Diet of Japan Fukushima Nuclear Accident Investigation Commission*. Tokyo: National Diet of Japan Fukushima Nuclear Accident Investigation Commission.

National Institute of Population and Social Security Research. (2011). Annual Population and Social Security Surveys. http://www.ipss.go.jp/pr-ad/e/eng/06.html.

Nikkei. (2013, November 25). "Japan Inc. Snubs Staff in Spending Plans." *Nikkei Asian Review.*

Ocheltree, J. (2012, August). "Is Microfinance the Answer for Tohoku?" *Metropolis.*

Oi, M. (2012, October 24). *Japan's Women: Can They Save the Country's Economy?* Retrieved from http://www.bbc.co.uk/news/business-20053254.

Otsuma, M. (2012, August 9). "Japan's Debt Exceeds 1 Quadrillion Yen as Abe Mulls Tax Rise." Bloomberg News.

Park, S., and L. Heesu (2013, August 9). "False Reports After Fukushima Bolster Anti-Nuclear Korea." Bloomberg News.

Reading, B. (1992). *Japan: The Coming Collapse.* New York: HarperCollins.

Reporters Without Borders. (2013, November 27). "Prime Minister Shinzo Abe Urged to Abandon State Secrecy Bill."

Rohwer, T. (2008, October 2). "Grassley Suggests a Japanese-Style Approach to Corporate Governance." *Daily Nonpareil.*

Russolillo, S. (2013, December 5). "Irrational Exuberance, 17 Years Later." *Wall Street Journal.*

Samuels, R. (2013). *3.11: Disaster and Change in Japan.* Ithaca, NY: Cornell University Press.

Sandberg, S. (2013). *Lean In: Women, Work, and the Will to Lead.* New York: Knopf.

Scully, V. (1997, December 1). "Australia Bans Japanese Banks from Debt Swaps." Bloomberg News.

Siegel, J., L. Pyun, and B. Cheon (2010). *Market Discrimination, and the Capture of Competitive Advantage by Exploiting the Social Divide.* Cambridge, MA: Harvard Business School.

Smith, L. (1990, February 26). "Fear and Loathing of Japan." *Fortune.*

Snow, N. (2013, November). "Uncool Japan: Japan's Gross National Propaganda." *Metropolis.*

Soble, J. (2013, February 22). "Abe Lays Out Vision of Japan Power in Asia." *Financial Times.*

Suessmuth-Dyckerhoff, C., J. Wang, and J. Chen (2012). *Women Matter: An Asian Perspective.* McKinsey.

Tabuchi, H. (2013, May 10). "Sony Posts Annual Profit for First Time in 5 Years." *New York Times.*

Transparency International. (2013). *Corruption Perceptions Index.* Berlin: Transparency International.

United Nations. (2012). "Progress of the World's Women, Fact Sheet."

Vivoda, V. (2013). *After Fukushima: The Future of Nuclear Power in Asia.* South Bank, AU: East Asia Forum.

Vogel, E. (1979). *Japan as Number One.* Cambridge: Harvard University Press.

Walsh, B. (2007, February 5). "In Japan, a Revolution Over Childbearing." *Time*.

World Economic Forum. (2013, November). *The Global Gender Gap Report 2013*. Retrieved from http://www.weforum.org/reports/global-gender-gap-report-2013.

World Economic Forum. (2013–2014). *The Global Competitiveness Report 2013–2014*. Geneva: World Economic Forum.

Whiting, R. (1999). *Tokyo Underworld*. New York: Random House.

Willitts, W. (1997, November 25). "Hashimoto Says Japan Still Studying Bank Bailout." Bloomberg News.

Wilson, I. (2013, March 11). "David Suzuki Says Japan Squandering Fukushima Crisis Opportunity." Bloomberg News.

Wolf, M. (2013, November 19). "Why the Future Looks Sluggish." *Financial Times*.

Wong, E. (2012, January 3). "China's President Lashes Out at Western Culture." *New York Times*.

Woodford, M. (2012). *Exposure*. London: Portfolio Hardcover.

Xinhua News Agency. (2013, November 22). "China's New Security Commission Conducive to World Peace."

Yonhap News Agency. (2013, October 18). "China Summons Japanese Ambassador Over Minister's Visit to War Shrine."

About the Author

William Pesek is the Asia-Pacific columnist for Bloomberg View, based in Tokyo, providing opinions and commentary on economics, business, markets, and politics throughout the region.

Pesek's columns routinely appear in the *International Herald Tribune*, *Sydney Morning Herald*, *New York Post*, the *Straits Times*, the *Japan Times*, and many other publications around the globe. He writes a monthly column for *Bloomberg Markets* magazine and is a regular on Bloomberg Television. He is a winner of the Society of American Business Editors and Writers' 2010 award for commentary.

He worked previously as a columnist for *Barron's*, the Dow Jones weekly magazine, in Washington, DC, writing about global economics, politics, markets, the Federal Reserve, the U.S. Treasury Department, the International Monetary Fund, and the World Bank. Before that, Pesek worked at Dow Jones Newswires in New York City, covering economics, companies, and markets. In the mid-1990s, he wrote the daily credit markets column for the *Wall Street Journal*. Prior to that, he was a reporter at the *American Banker* and *Bond Buyers* newspapers in New York City.

Pesek has a bachelor's degree in business journalism from Bernard M. Baruch College.

His work can be found at www.bloomberg.com/view/bios/william-pesek/.

He can be followed on Twitter at @williampesek.

Index

221

CPSIA information can be obtained
at www.ICGtesting.com
Printed in the USA
BVHW081057250619
551594BV00008B/8/P